ABORIGINAL STUDENT ENGAGEMENT AND ACHIEVEMENT

ABORIGINAL STUDENT ENGAGEMENT AND ACHIEVEMENT
EDUCATIONAL PRACTICES AND CULTURAL SUSTAINABILITY

Lorenzo Cherubini

Foreword by Lyn Trudeau

UBCPress · Vancouver · Toronto

© UBC Press 2014

All rights reserved. No part of this publication may be reproduced, stored in a retrieval system, or transmitted, in any form or by any means, without prior written permission of the publisher, or, in Canada, in the case of photocopying or other reprographic copying, a licence from Access Copyright, www.accesscopyright.ca.

22 21 20 19 18 17 16 15 14   5 4 3 2 1

Printed in Canada on FSC-certified ancient-forest-free paper
(100% post-consumer recycled) that is processed chlorine- and acid-free.

Library and Archives Canada Cataloguing in Publication

Cherubini, Lorenzo, author
    Aboriginal student engagement and achievement : educational practices and cultural sustainability / Lorenzo Cherubini ; foreword by Lyn Trudeau.

Includes bibliographical references and index.
Issued in print and electronic formats.
ISBN 978-0-7748-2655-6 (bound). – 978-0-7748-2656-3 (pbk.) –
ISBN 978-0-7748-2657-0 (pdf). – ISBN 978-0-7748-2658-7 (epub)

    1. Native peoples – Education – Ontario. 2. Native students – Ontario. 3. Academic achievement – Ontario. 4. Public schools – Ontario. I. Title.

E96.65.O58C54 2014	371.829'970713	C2014-905324-X
		C2014-905325-8

Canadä

UBC Press gratefully acknowledges the financial support for our publishing program of the Government of Canada (through the Canada Book Fund), the Canada Council for the Arts, and the British Columbia Arts Council.

The author would like to acknowledge the Social Sciences and Humanities Research Council of Canada (SSHRC) for its generous support of this and other projects.

UBC Press
The University of British Columbia
2029 West Mall
Vancouver, BC V6T 1Z2
www.ubcpress.ca

*To Michelle, Joshua, and Anthony ... for always being there.
May all your dreams come true!*

*A mia madre,
Per il tuo esempio, affetto e sacrufi.*

*A mio padre,
Non posso credere alla tya scomparsa.
Non puoi immaginare quanto mi manchi.*

To Lyn Trudeau ... for your kind spirit and thoughtful wisdom.

*To all those who have contributed to the journey ...
what a journey it has been.*

Contents

Foreword / ix
LYN TRUDEAU

Introduction / 3

Part 1 Background

   1 Evoking the Past, Framing the Future / 9

   2 Setting the Story / 23

Part 2 From Theory to Practice

   3 The Conversations / 35

   4 Subplots / 97

   5 Climax: Learning from the Stories / 119

Appendices / 165

Works Cited / 177

Index / 187

Foreword

It is late summer as I write this foreword. Before long, the tell-tale signs of autumn will be upon us. A cool breeze touches my skin, telling of change; new energy will soon be ushered in with the coming of a new season. I sit as Wind rustles softly ... It is a good time to give voice to this work.

In many ways, this work displays a beautiful growth of Spirit. This growth stems from our Aboriginal communities reaching out to collaborate with Western educational authorities in order to make old dreams new realities: our students, at least in the program and school featured in this book, are now receiving instruction that is culturally rooted and that nurtures a true sense of our identity, of who we inherently are. This book also speaks to holistic education by providing a thought-provoking analysis that takes a fresh look at what *is* working for Aboriginal youth as opposed to the all too often negative focus on what is not working.

Lorenzo Cherubini gets to the heart of what Aboriginal education seeks to be. He offers a holistic approach and takes into consideration all the concerns that the Aboriginal learner needs to see addressed. He shows an understanding of, and a reverence for, our traditional ways, and it is due to a mutual respect that his works are able to move forward and be rewarding for all those involved. Dr. Cherubini has taken the time to be mindful of our practices and to forge good relationships with all the communities that played a role in this research endeavour. It has been a pleasure working alongside someone who welcomes our ways of knowing and encourages the harmonious inclusion of all knowledges. Work that not only involves but also revolves around our teachings is always worth pursuing.

This work displays:

> Strength of Courage ...
> Strength of Weakness ...
> Strength of Good Medicine ...

Many peoples, Aboriginal and non-Aboriginal, gave selflessly of their time to develop and initiate positive stratagems to implement in the learning environment, thereby affording our Aboriginal youth a safe place to receive instruction and to learn. Only when we can identify and reflect on our weaknesses and areas of concern can we move forward with wisdom and insight. It is from this place that new strength and power is drawn. Good Medicine in Aboriginal culture is meant to speak to sources of healing and overall goodness and wellness. Medicines are received, given, and enacted.

This book speaks to educators, parents, community members, and policy makers alike and shows what can happen when we listen to one another and work together to create better learning environments and communities for all our children: engaging the Spirit engages the mind.

Wind has come to visit today, and for this I am thankful. Wind is a powerful spirit that echoes across all lands carrying the voice of our ancient ones, prayers to the open skies, and even carrying the power of change. Today Wind carries this Good Medicine towards a transformative season for Aboriginal youth in the realm of education.

All my relations,
Lyn Trudeau,
Ojibway, Eagle Clan

ABORIGINAL STUDENT ENGAGEMENT AND ACHIEVEMENT

Introduction

Canadian public education is experiencing decreases in enrolments and increases in school closures. School-aged Aboriginal children are one of the few growing demographics within education, with one in five children being Aboriginal and 70 percent of the Canadian population now living in urban centres. Combined with the recent call for greater transparency, ministries of education across Canada are being asked to account for the dismal levels of completion rates, specifically among the Aboriginal student population. This has contributed to various federal and provincial initiatives, and yet the increase in graduation rates across the country has been less than impressive. This book is a partial response to these inconsistencies.

One wonders to what degree colonialism still exists in provincially funded education in Ontario. A central theme of *Aboriginal Student Engagement and Achievement* concerns the fact that the schooling experiences of Aboriginal students are affected by colonialist factors that continue to marginalize them within public school culture. As Kanu (2011) suggests, formal education and Eurocentric scholarly practices promote and validate the knowledge paradigms of dominant groups. Despite various educational reforms intent on changing these experiences for Aboriginal students, public school classrooms often continue to typify Eurocentric educational principles, which fail to recognize the legitimacy of Aboriginal epistemologies or to adequately incorporate them into curricula. As Tharp et al. (1999, 15) suggest, there have been "waves of well-intentioned but misguided reform fads that have failed precisely because they are disconnected from the educational needs" of Indigenous students and so have resulted in "new rounds of discouragement." For the most part, educational systems have not accounted for Aboriginal students' learning styles and preferences, nor have they defined students' academic progress according to meaningful and culturally appropriate benchmarks (Garcia 2008). Moreover, institutions responsible for teacher education in Canada and the United States have generally not paid adequate attention to the crisis of publicly funded education as it relates to Aboriginal and American Indian/Alaska Native children. Prospective teachers do not have the same awareness of the needs of Aboriginal students as they do of the needs of mainstream students, and, for this reason, they are unable to create culturally relevant learning environments for the former (Allington 2002; Reyhner and Hurtado 2008). Apart from Manitoba, no province or territory in Canada requires coursework in Aboriginal education for credentialing its teachers. Against this background, *Aboriginal Student Engagement and Achievement* tells a poignant story of how one school created a holistic and integrated educational space for Aboriginal students – a space that enabled the creation of a critical consciousness very much grounded in Aboriginal spiritual, emotional, intellectual, and physical realities.

It should be noted that the word "Aboriginal" includes First Nations, Inuit, and Métis as the three main groups of peoples in Canada as per the Constitution Act, 1982. Although I refer to Aboriginal students, learners, communities, and worldviews throughout this book, this is not meant to negate the fact that each group is separate and unique in its traditions, cultures, and histories (see Kanu 2011). Equally significant is the fact that the word "Aboriginal" is used in the *Ontario First Nation, Métis, and Inuit Education Policy Framework* (Ontario Ministry of Education 2007, 36), which defines Aboriginal peoples as "[t]he descendents of the original inhabitants of North America. Section 35(2) of the Constitution Act, 1982, states: 'In this Act, "Aboriginal peoples of Canada" includes the Indian, Inuit, and Métis peoples of Canada.' These separate groups have unique heritages, languages, cultural practices, and spiritual beliefs. Their common link is their indigenous ancestry."

This book considers the current literature related to Aboriginal public education in Canada, the United States, and elsewhere and – through a detailed discussion of recent governmental policy and social and cultural trends related to Aboriginal education in Ontario and Canada – presents a story of change. The book shares a number of stories related to an inner-city

Aboriginal community that conceptualized and implemented a comprehensive response to the educational needs of Aboriginal learners, and it includes a number of key perspectives related to the Aboriginal Student Program (ASP) that can be helpful to other Aboriginal communities, boards of education, school administrators, educators, and policy makers as they envision their responses both to provincial policies and to the needs of Aboriginal students. What follows in the stories within the story of the ASP at Soaring Heights Secondary School (SHSS) is an exploration of multiple perspectives on Aboriginal education within a mainstream secondary school. They include observations on program reports and surveys as well as the narrative experiences of female and male Aboriginal students attending SHSS, school and program administrators, youth counsellors, parents, various non-Aboriginal faculty members working in the ASP, and the elder involved in the program. The respective narratives are framed in the voices of the participants themselves so that their stories can speak to the truths both of the ASP and of their experiences in it.

The stories of the various participants help us to understand how Aboriginal students internalize a sense of where they fit in the mainstream school culture in light of their own traditions, culture, and epistemologies. *Aboriginal Student Engagement and Achievement,* in many respects, addresses Briggs's (2005, 20) recommendation that scholarly evidence must resonate with policy makers and practitioners alike by addressing "what has worked and what will work." The intention is not to discredit the valiant efforts of educators, nor is it to suggest that educational and school policy is intentionally inattentive to epistemic diversity; rather, it is to contribute to evidence-based reform in educational circles within and beyond the Province of Ontario as a way of Indigenizing public school curricula. I concur with Slavin (2007), who concludes that educators and policy makers will more readily consult with educational research before making significant decisions about programs and practices when that research is evidence-based. This book, which in many ways is a narrative, invites you to consider the evidence provided by the socio-cultural location of Aboriginal students in the ASP at SHSS – evidence that indicates how they broadened their spiritual, traditional, and epistemic horizons. Ultimately, the discussions bring to light exemplary educational practices for Aboriginal peoples and indicate how teachers, school administrators, school communities, and educational policy makers can participate in sustaining these across schools and communities.

PART 1

BACKGROUND

1
Evoking the Past, Framing the Future

This chapter provides a historical perspective on the colonialist suppression of Aboriginal languages and traditional knowledge and discusses the contemporary implications for Aboriginal students and communities. I focus on the seminal Ontario Ministry of Education policy document titled *Ontario First Nation, Métis, and Inuit Education Policy Framework* (2007) because it not only recognizes the distinct learning preferences and worldviews of Aboriginal students but also commissions teachers and schools to incorporate these into provincial classrooms in order to improve Aboriginal student achievement. In discussing the conceptual framework within which the research is situated, I shed light on provincial educational policy as it relates to (1) Aboriginal education, (2) school culture and Aboriginal student identity, (3) Aboriginal learners, and (4) teacher education. I also present some related literature that will be useful for educators and policy makers who are working in public education. This literature attests to the significance of public school cultures and classrooms that respect Aboriginal epistemologies and thus contribute to the attainment of a positive Aboriginal student identity and academic proficiency. Finally, in order to familiarize the reader with the subject at hand, I discuss Soaring Heights Secondary School and its Aboriginal Student Program.

The Backdrop
It must be understood that the experiences of Aboriginal students in public schools across Canada have been influenced by a complex combination of

socio-historical and socio-cultural realities. Aboriginal students have often endured an array of adverse experiences that have negatively affected their education. Traditionally, Aboriginal epistemologies, considered to be distinct from Western epistemologies, have not been represented in public schools across Ontario (Castellano, Davis, and Lahache 2000; Frideres and Gadacz 2005; Haig-Brown 1988; Hill 2000; Womack 1999). According to Mikmaq educator Marie Battiste (2002), the well-chronicled assimilationist practices imposed upon Aboriginal children in residential schools and afterwards were intended to force them to comply with Eurocentric concepts of teaching and learning. These oppressive practices have not only cast out Aboriginal epistemic traditions but also, in the process, dismissed Aboriginal students' unique learning preferences (Dei et al. 2000; Duggan 2003).

Consider that, as recently as 2004, the auditor general of Canada stated that, in provincial schools, Aboriginal students were twenty-eight years away from achieving the same academic standards as non-Aboriginal students (Battiste and McLean 2005). In many instances, despite various educational reforms, Aboriginal students continue to be affected by the same experiences that have always marginalized them within public school cultures. Many public school classrooms continue to reflect Eurocentric educational principles – principles that relegate Aboriginal epistemologies to a lesser status (Cajete 2008; Villegas, Rak Neugebauer, and Venegas 2008).

Aboriginal peoples in Canada continue to struggle to fulfill a vision of an educational system that reflects their socio-linguistic and socio-cultural values. The preservation of Aboriginal societies depends, to a large extent, upon providing Aboriginal students with a culturally sensitive education. This involves Paulo Freire's theory of conscientization, which emphasizes how important it is for teachers, principals, and educators to acquire a critical understanding of the intricate relationship between power, myth, and oppression and how it reflects political, social, and economic inequalities. For the most part, the literature on public education in Canada overwhelmingly confirms that, in publicly funded schools, the Aboriginal student's experience is one of cultural and epistemic discontinuity (Huffman 2001; Piquemal 2005). Aboriginal peoples demand and deserve educational practices and school programs that are culturally sustainable and that lend themselves to Aboriginal student success (Castellano 2000; Cherubini and Hodson 2008).

Consider, too, that over the past thirty years public schools in Canada have endorsed multiculturalism as the prevailing model for student identity formation. Canada is seen as a mosaic, while the United States is seen as a melting pot (Bruno-Jofre and Henley 2000). Although Canada is presented as being founded on three ethnically diverse national groups – English, French, and Aboriginal – Aboriginal peoples are not formally recognized as a founding nation (Kymlicka 1996). This lack of formal recognition is mirrored in the fact that, typically, Aboriginal student identity has not been represented in Ontario schools, curricula, or classrooms. In fact, critiques of colonialism and contemporary colonialist influences are often not a component of what is presented as a multicultural education curriculum. Not surprisingly, the educational experiences of Aboriginal students were not significant considerations during Canada's constitutional crisis or, indeed, throughout the 1970s and 1980s. Colonialism has had a profoundly adverse effect upon Aboriginal peoples and, among other things, has resulted in a far greater likelihood that Aboriginal, as opposed to non-Aboriginal, students will drop out of school (Cooper and Stacey-Moore 2009; Darotich 1991; Halloran 2006). Malott and Pruyn's (2006) work on critical multicultural social studies underscores the importance of recognizing cultural diversity in the classroom. Such work places students and communities at the centre of a pedagogical approach that focuses on social justice issues as they arise within social and historical studies.

The disconnect between Aboriginal peoples' cultural traditions and mainstream educational experiences has been well documented (Cherubini 2009a, 2009b; Moyle 2005; Neegan 2005). The statistics are clear: more than fifty thousand Aboriginal students are currently enrolled in Ontario public schools (Ontario Ministry of Education 2007), more than 12 percent of Aboriginal people in Canada renounce their formal education after elementary school, and almost 50 percent of the Aboriginal population between eighteen and twenty-four years of age do not have secondary school diplomas (Robertson 2003). The manner in which Aboriginal people teach their children is, obviously, informed by Aboriginal worldviews. Although these should not be thought of as being uniform (indeed, they are multifaceted), typically Aboriginal children are actively involved in tasks, learn by demonstration and repetition, and are allowed to show their learning when they are prepared to do so (see Aikenhead and Michell 2011; MacIvor 1995; Rowland and Adkins 2003).

These distinctions deserve further elaboration. According to *The State of Aboriginal Learning in Canada*, "learning from – and about – culture, language and tradition is critical to the well-being of Aboriginal people" (Canadian Council on Learning 2009, 5). Implicit in this paradigm of learning, and hence in various Aboriginal epistemologies, is the emphasis on the social process of learning, which fosters relationships both in the immediate family and across the community. Aboriginal epistemologies consist of distinct socio-cultural traditions and worldviews and, as a result, learning is perceived as a lifestyle that accounts for all of the knowledge one gains from childhood to adulthood. Equally significant are the relationships established throughout life's journey as they contribute to the transmission of beliefs and traditions and to the development of individual identity. Consequently, Aboriginal epistemologies view learning as a holistic process that engages each student in mind, body, and spirit. The holistic view of learning contributes to a whole and vibrant person (Archibald 2008). Learning is considered to be a lifelong journey that is influenced by knowledge and tradition. It is perceived as experiential and is often practised in traditional ceremonies, storytelling, and observations.

The learning of authentic Aboriginal content is enhanced by hands-on activities that require students to be active learners. The teaching of oral traditions and the practice of drumming and dancing contribute to the learner's ability to create genuine knowledge (St. Denis 2010). Learning is connected to language and to a community's linguistic traditions. Aboriginal epistemologies consider the learning of both traditional and contemporary knowledge to be the responsibility of the community (Canadian Council on Learning 2009). Archibald (2008) suggests that Aboriginal epistemologies include an understanding of the various academic, social, political, and cultural contexts of modern-day society as well as of traditional knowledge. They resonate with cultural values that focus upon cooperation among students in both formal and informal learning environments, learning that is based on the interconnectedness of humans and nature, and a firm belief in the role of elders as parent figures, teachers, and leaders (Cokley and Williams 2005; Garrett et al. 2003).

It should be noted that, in Canada, education comes under provincial jurisdiction (with the exception of First Nations schools, which are the responsibility of the federal government). Aboriginal peoples have sought educational experiences for their children that will enable them to recognize and to celebrate their unique traditions and, in so doing, to enhance their sense of self-identity (Norris 2006). Aboriginal epistemologies foster in students an awareness of Aboriginal values, which are related directly to traditional knowledge. Obviously, Aboriginal worldviews reflect Aboriginal linguistic and cultural values (Cohen 2001; Kavanaugh 2005; Norris and

MacCon 2003). Research suggests that Aboriginal worldviews are appreciated in public school classrooms when students are given the time to explore and to reflect upon the interconnectedness of all living things, when they are able to communicate their newly discovered knowledge through small-group activities. Central to such a pedagogical approach, according to Aikenhead and Michell (2011), is the teacher's ability to understand learner-centred instruction in an Aboriginal context – one in which Aboriginal students value the community over the individual.

The reality is that Aboriginal students in Ontario often remain in the margins. Despite the various educational reforms in this province, particularly over the past thirty years, Aboriginal students' epistemic practices are not embedded in the standardized curriculum, their learning strengths and styles are not reflected in standardized tests, and their learning needs are frequently not being met by the well-intentioned and predominantly mainstream teachers in public school classrooms (Cherubini and Hodson 2008; Sears and Hughes 1996). In many respects, the educational reforms that are intended to standardize curriculum, assessment, evaluation, and pedagogy (often in the guise of public accountability and transparency) have "silenced the dissident voices" of Aboriginal students (Bigelow 2003, 232). Independent scholar Curry Malott (2008) cites the work of Freire, Macedo, Kincheloe and other scholars to suggest that the waves of educational reform that have swept the continent over the past several decades are manifestations of privileged mainstream power – a power that legitimizes certain types of knowledge and worldviews at the expense of others (see also Kincheloe 2005). Consider, too, that, as public school students enter the higher grades, educators contend with heightened external pressures pertaining to public accountability and generally rely on more traditional pedagogical and assessment strategies (e.g., lectures, memorization of facts, formal testing practices, to name a few) that are characteristic of school hierarchy and student compliance (Gilbert 2009; Wee et al. 2007).

For Aboriginal students, public education in Ontario often involves experiencing cultural and epistemic discontinuity (see, for example, Huffman 2001; Piquemal 2005). In fact, the Ontario Ministry of Education (OME) has drawn attention to the "achievement gap" between Aboriginal and non-Aboriginal students (Ontario Ministry of Education 2007). This gap seems to quantify, and thus lend credence to, educational realities in public schools – realities that have been intimately and painfully familiar to Aboriginal children, youth, and their parents for several generations.

Across North America, Aboriginal students rank consistently lower in terms of achievement than do non-Aboriginal students. The predominantly Western-based ideological curriculum, along with its standardized expectations, delivered, for the most part, by traditionally trained teachers, is notably ineffective when it comes to engaging Aboriginal students (White, Maxim, and Spence 2004).

Research suggests that including Aboriginal epistemic and socio-cultural traditions in the mainstream curriculum can positively enhance Aboriginal students' self-esteem and sense of identity. Yet there is little evidence that mainstream public school classrooms are doing this (Paquette and Fallon 2010). Despite their best intentions, teachers appear to remain largely unaware of Aboriginal socio-historical and socio-cultural realities. Thus, Aboriginal learning needs are not being adequately addressed. Far too many Aboriginal students feel disconnected from the institutional practices and classroom realities of publicly funded schools (Cherubini 2009c; Cherubini et al. 2010). Furthermore, Western ways of knowing put students who favour oral discourse styles at a disadvantage, while privileging those who favour the written discourse styles reflective of Eurocentric schooling practices. Examples of pedagogies that honour discussion and storytelling in mainstream classrooms and that afford students time to co-create knowledge are few and far between (Malott, Waukau, and Waukau-Villagomez 2009).

The nature of my research, therefore, is best explained as a commitment to conceptualizing "re-search" processes and perspectives. It is a holistic approach to research that honours the words of the participants and aims to understand their experiences as embedded within their particular socio-cultural contexts.

Indigenous methodologies comprise multiple worldviews and perspectives (Moreton-Robinson 2000; Smith 1999). One of the aims of Aboriginal research is to decolonialize the oppressive epistemic practices that, historically, have marginalized Aboriginal scholars and communities (Bishop and Glynn 2003; Howitt and Stevens 2005; Shaw, Herman, and Dobbs, 2006). Students and teachers today live with the consequences of a system that has undermined Aboriginal knowledge and that continues to adversely affect traditional teachings, spirituality, and spiritual leaders across Aboriginal communities (Absolon and Willett 2004).

Aboriginal Student Engagement and Achievement examines the multiple perspectives of the key stakeholders involved in an Aboriginal student program in a publicly funded secondary school in Ontario. It shares the testimonies of Aboriginal students, youth counsellors, a program leader, parents/caregivers, and an elder. The members of the project team approached everyone with whom they collaborated with the clear intent of honouring that person's experiences (see Berg et al. 2007) and, in so doing, acknowledged that Indigenous methodologies are rooted in Aboriginal people themselves (Bishop 1997; Mihesuah 1998; Smith 1999; Battiste 2000; Battiste and Youngblood Henderson 2000). The research team was sensitive to the fact that these methodologies are fluid and that they are highly relational to the people/places from whom/which they arise (Kovach 2005).

The Research Team

It is important to share what brought the research team to this story. It was an intercultural team that consisted of a cross-section of Aboriginal and non-Aboriginal researchers and graduate students. Many of the team members had been involved in previous research projects related to Aboriginal education and public policy. One esteemed elder was not directly involved in this research project; however, some members of the research team had benefited from his wisdom and guidance in previous endeavours. The collective expertise of the research team was strengthened by the key partnership with the Aboriginal leadership from the Tecumseh Centre for Aboriginal Research and Education (Brock University, Faculty of Education), which served to link the educational communities and provided the cultural leadership for the research.

I am grateful for the contributions of each team member. The eclectic voices and experiences of the research team brought to light both diverse and complementary perspectives. By bringing together and acknowledging their respective abilities, the team members were stronger together than they were individually. The team was compelled to prompt dialogues that enabled the voice of each participant to emerge. In this context, the team reaffirmed for me the significance of honouring participants' voices and experiences (see Chapter 2).

I am a first-generation Canadian of Italian descent. My roots are in a picturesque mountain region in Abruzzo, Italy, where my family lived off the land and had an intimate connection to it. I am honoured, in my capacity as a professor, to work with Aboriginal educators, scholars, and community members. The learning involved has been invaluable to my professional and personal growth. My research specialty concentrates on policy analysis and teacher development. My interest in new teacher-induction policy introduced me to my Aboriginal colleagues at the Tecumseh Centre for Aboriginal Research and Education at Brock University, and that is where the conversation began. Since then, I have developed an appreciation for the complexity of learning as it relates to different epistemic paradigms. I am grateful for the exciting (and terrifying) experiences known to many professors whose research takes them beyond the fine edges of academia.

The Framework

The research that informs this particular story addresses the perceptions and experiences of Aboriginal students, educators, youth counsellors, community leaders, parents/caregivers, and an elder as they participated in the Aboriginal Student Program at Soaring Heights Secondary School, a mainstream public secondary school in Ontario. The Ontario Ministry of Education's policy related to Aboriginal education is significant to this program.

Ontario Ministry of Education Policy Related to Aboriginal Education

The Ontario Ministry of Education (2007) document titled *Ontario First Nation, Métis, and Inuit Education Policy Framework* (hereafter the Framework) needs to be understood in the context of Aboriginal socio-cultural and epistemic realities. In the introduction to the Framework, the Ontario Ministry of Education states its commitment to providing an exemplary education for all students. Cited in the introduction is a previous publication of the provincial government, *Ontario's New Approach to Aboriginal Affairs* (2005), which sought to establish vibrant Aboriginal communities. Education is posited as a means of improving sustainable future opportunities for Aboriginal students; the OME, hence, identifies 2016 as the date for meeting its two challenges: (1) improving the academic achievement of Aboriginal students in Ontario schools and (2) closing the gap between Aboriginal and non-Aboriginal students as measured by literacy and numeracy scores, student retention, graduation, and admission to postsecondary education. The Framework is the OME's strategic policy, and it crosses into ministry, school board, and school contexts. Moreover, it sheds light on the key relationships between the provincial government, senior school board administrators, and schools in what is described as a collaborative and concerted effort to improve the academic achievement of Aboriginal students.

The Framework recognizes the unique learning needs of Aboriginal students, the community-centred nature of their socio-cultural traditions, and the critical need for public school teachers to authentically reflect these needs and traditions in their pedagogy. It states:

> The strategies outlined in this framework are based on a holistic and integrated approach to improving Aboriginal student outcomes. The overriding issues affecting Aboriginal student achievement are a lack of awareness among teachers of the particular learning styles of Aboriginal students, and a lack of understanding within schools and school boards of First Nation, Métis, and Inuit cultures, histories, and perspectives. Factors that contribute to student success include teaching strategies that are appropriate to Aboriginal learner needs, curriculum that reflects First Nation, Métis, and Inuit cultures and perspectives, effective counseling and outreach, and a school environment that encourages Aboriginal student and parent engagement. It is also important for educators to understand Aboriginal perspectives on the school system, which has been strongly affected by residential school experiences and has resulted in intergenerational mistrust of the education system. It is essential that First Nation, Métis, and Inuit students are engaged and feel welcome in school, and that they see themselves and their cultures in the curriculum and the school community. (OME 2007, 6)

The OME's policy statement with respect to this document articulates its commitment to Aboriginal student success and to developing strategies to

- Increase the capacity of the education system to respond to the learning and cultural needs of First Nation, Métis, and Inuit students;
- Provide quality programs, services, and resources to help create learning opportunities for First Nation, Métis, and Inuit students that support improved academic achievement and identity building;
- Provide a curriculum that facilitates learning about contemporary and traditional First Nation, Métis, and Inuit cultures, histories, and perspectives among all students, and that also contributes to the education of school board staff, teachers, and elected trustees; and
- Develop and implement strategies that facilitate increased participation by First Nation, Métis, and Inuit parents, students, communities, and organizations in working to support academic success. (7)

The four core principles of the Framework are (1) excellence and accountability; (2) equity and respect for diversity; (3) inclusiveness, cooperation, and shared responsibility; and (4) respect for constitutional and treaty rights. These principles focus on delivering quality education to Aboriginal students in order to build sustainable communities. They attest to the importance of school and learning environments that contribute to the positive development of Aboriginal student identity and that honour the rich diversity of Aboriginal cultures, histories, and traditions. Equally important is the need for governments, governing bodies, schools, and faculties of education to cooperate and to be responsible for meeting the unique needs of Aboriginal students.

As part of the Framework, the OME identifies seven specific strategies:

1. "Build capacity for effective teaching, assessment, and evaluation practices" (11).
2. "Promote system effectiveness, transparency, and responsiveness" (13).
3. "Enhance support to improve literacy and numeracy skills" (14).
4. "Provide additional support in a variety of areas to reduce gaps in student outcomes" (15).
5. "Build educational leadership capacity and coordination" (17).
6. "Build capacity to support identity building, including the appreciation of Aboriginal perspectives, values, and cultures by all students, school board staff, and elected trustees" (18).
7. "Foster supportive and engaged families and communities" (19).

Each strategy identifies a subset of goals for the key educational stakeholders and their constituents, which include the OME as well as provincial school boards and their associated schools. Schools, for example, are to "develop ... awareness among teachers of the learning styles" of Aboriginal students (12). Teachers will employ instructional strategies "designed to enhance" Aboriginal students' learning, implement meaningful Aboriginal "perspectives and activities when planning instruction," and identify learning strategies "for effective oral communication and mastery of reading and writing" (12 and 18). The Framework categorizes effective teacher practice as involving a constructive style of knowledge generation that is relevant to the socio-cultural realities of Aboriginal learners.

The Framework is meant to improve the educational experiences of Aboriginal students across the province as well as to heighten teacher awareness of the unique needs of Aboriginal learners. The lack of achievement on the part of Aboriginal students is a consequence of colonialism

– of the discontinuity between Aboriginal students' upbringing and what they face inside and outside educational institutions (see, for example, Ndura 2004; Parsons, Travis, and Simpson 2005). And their continued vulnerability is indicative of the continuation of colonialist practices. Institutional practices of cultural discontinuity, understood "as a school-based behavioral process where the cultural value-based learning preferences and practices of many ethnic minority students ... are discontinued," increase Aboriginal students' vulnerability in a social and political setting within which they are already marginalized (Tyler et al. 2008, 281).

Clearly, the OME Framework is central to this study. Its vision and policy statements served as the platform for our conversations with stakeholders, and its specific strategies informed the discussions in which people were invited to participate. These strategies provided the impetus for the inquiry. Participants, depending upon their roles as students, teachers, administrators, or parents, had the opportunity to share their perceptions and experiences of the OME's, the school board's, and/or the school's responses to the strategies outlined in the Framework.

Origins of the Aboriginal Student Program
Numerous boards of education, schools, and Aboriginal communities across Ontario have recognized the significance of implementing the OME's *First Nation, Métis, and Inuit Education Policy Framework*. Yet there seem to be various inconsistencies in the nature and extent of these implementations. This may be due in part to the relatively few examples of successful Aboriginal student engagement in public schools and classrooms. Such pragmatic and culturally sensitive examples must be provided in order for boards of education and Aboriginal communities to make public schooling more meaningful for Aboriginal students. Soaring Heights Secondary School, along with the Aboriginal community in southern Ontario, may be considered an example of a school, and a community, that has implemented a comprehensive response to the needs of Aboriginal students. This book tells its story and reflects upon it from a number of perspectives – those of an Aboriginal elder, youth counsellors, students, parents, community leaders, non-Aboriginal teachers, and school administrators. In doing this, I hope to reveal the practical approaches that can inform other Aboriginal communities, boards of education, school administrators, educators, and policy makers interested in developing their own responses to educational change.

It is important to state that the decision to provide pseudonyms for this school and its student program was intentional. It is based on the fact that SHSS is a typical example of public secondary schools across Ontario. Although perhaps a bit more culturally diverse than some of the other schools, its student, faculty, and catchment area (as measured by the number of K-to-8 elementary schools that reside within the boundaries of the regional secondary school) are generally similar. Furthermore, in presenting SHSS as a typical secondary school in southern Ontario, it is possible to generalize the research findings across the province, country, and beyond. In this way, they may be of benefit to other publicly funded mainstream schools.

The ASP has been in operation since 2003. It began when an anonymous donor expressed an interest in funding an Aboriginal-specific project to assist in keeping Aboriginal youth in school. With this background in mind, the local school board put forward a vision of the ASP as a program designed to provide a support system based on Aboriginal culture as well as on mainstream academic culture – a system that would allow Aboriginal students to flourish within a mainstream secondary school environment. Critical to the success of the ASP is the fact that it cultivates the relationship between the culture of Aboriginal youth and the culture of mainstream education.

The story of the ASP at SHSS is complex. Prior to the inception of the program there was a disproportionately high Aboriginal student dropout rate within the school district, largely attributable to poor health, lack of academic achievement, and poor socio-economic circumstances. The Aboriginal youth who were consulted during the investigative process in advance of the implementation of the program indicated that their disengagement from formal schooling was the result of a lack of culturally sensitive support within the school environment as well as an absence of culturally relevant pedagogy. One might suspect that Aboriginal youth across the country would provide similar reasons for giving up on their education.

This book explores what the OME accurately depicts as the gap between Aboriginal and non-Aboriginal student cohorts with regard to educational participation and achievement. It suggests that this enduring gap represents the relative ineffectiveness of both Eurocentric curricula and the dominant approaches to teacher education, along with the lack of support services for Aboriginal students in public education. Hence, non-Aboriginal peoples are challenged "to open up a space for Aboriginal initiatives ... so that Indigenous ways of knowing can flourish and intercultural sharing can be practiced in a spirit of coexistence and mutual respect" (Castellano 2000, 23). The stories shared in *Aboriginal Student Engagement and Achievement* will encourage teachers, school board administrators, community members, and policy makers to juxtapose the successes of the ASP with the successes/challenges of their own classrooms, schools, and governing bodies.

Educators can take the testimonies of Aboriginal students and communities as evidence that culturally relevant classroom experiences and learning have a far more enduring impact on students than do Eurocentric pedagogical approaches involving memorization, exploration, and test-taking (see also Aikenhead 2006; Hutchison and Hammer 2010). Research shows that cultural participation in public school classrooms improves Aboriginal student learning. Such cultural-historical pedagogical approaches include storytelling, learning scaffolds, learning by doing, communal learning endeavours, and authentic relationships with teachers characterized by clear and open communication (Kanu 2011). The voices of the students, elder, caregivers, counsellors, and administrators that you hear in this book speak directly to the positive effects that including Aboriginal cultural perspectives in public schools, classrooms, and communities can have on student learning, school attendance, and retention (Agbo 2004; Apthorp et al. 2002; Miller-Lachman and Taylor 1995).

It is my hope that the stories shared in this book will be useful not only to district leaders, policy makers, school board personnel, school administrators, and teachers working with Aboriginal students but also to the Aboriginal educational community at large. In some respects, this book serves as an example of just how important it is for public schools to honour "a two-way approach to teaching – Indigenous and Eurocentric" (Battiste 2000, 202) – that draws upon the strengths and wisdom of two knowledge systems (see Hatcher, Bartlett, and Marchall 2009; Marshall 2007).

The stories are meant to encourage readers to think critically about Aboriginal student learning, achievement, and being, and to do so from their own perspectives, whether as teachers, school board administrators, community members, or policy makers. Perhaps the stories will encourage readers to interrogate the assumptions and biases that inform their own worldviews. As readers attempt to integrate different worldviews and practices into mainstream schooling, they may experience what Richardson (2008) identifies as cultural dislocation, and this may serve as the impetus for further self-reflection (see also Friesen and Friesen 2002). The hope is that all stakeholders in public education will be compelled, first, to acknowledge the accomplishments and challenges of the ASP and, then, to ask how the various interventions of this culturally sensitive program can be brought into their own classrooms, schools, boards of education, and communities.

As you read about safe and inviting educational spaces, Aboriginal community involvement, and the testimonies of Aboriginal students themselves, you are encouraged to consider how these constitute a major step in accomplishing and enacting fundamental changes to public education processes and protocols. In addition, these stories contribute to the much larger issue of Indigenizing curriculum and knowledge in public school hallways and classrooms. The stories within the story of the ASP at SHSS enable readers to further consider how Aboriginal knowledge can exist and thrive in school curricula – understood as programs whose focus is on what ought to happen in public education (Ellis 2004; Tanner and Tanner 1995). The larger debate focuses on how, meaningfully and comprehensively, to include in public schools the socio-linguistic and socio-cultural worldviews that inform the cross-generational teachings of Aboriginal traditional knowledge (Elijah 2002; Kavanaugh 2005). This book offers readers various possibilities in this regard. The story it shares can inform the varied educational roles that readers bring to the text, enabling them to learn about what might work for their specific contexts. Indeed, the reader may very well see images and shadows of her or his own predicament reflected in this story.

2
Setting the Story

The point of conducting discussions with key individuals at Soaring Heights Secondary School was to reflect as accurately as possible their perceptions and experiences of the Aboriginal Student Program. A case study (or what I prefer to call a "case story") approach was ideal since it ensured the necessary flexibility to hear, document, and discuss the distinct issues that these individuals identified (Creswell et al. 2003; Stake 2000). SHSS was the setting of this case story.

In order to arrive at a complete picture of the ASP, it was necessary to gather information from multiple sources. To this end, representatives of the research team met with six male and five female Aboriginal students (ranging from Grades 9 to 12); three Aboriginal youth counsellors working at SHSS; two mainstream teachers whose teaching assignments include Native studies courses (as they are identified by OME curriculum documents); the principal and vice-principal of the school; an elder who is regularly present at SHSS; the Aboriginal community leader and partner responsible for the coordination of the ASP; and ten Aboriginal members of the Aboriginal community, most of whom are parents or caregivers of youth attending SHSS. Since it was all but impossible to speak with all faculty, a survey was administered in order for their voices to be heard. Various documents dealing with ASP reports, student surveys, and student records that chronicled the program's evolution were also considered.

Soaring Heights Secondary School
The school is located in a city in southern Ontario and has a multicultural population of approximately eleven hundred students who, according to the school administrators, speak sixty different languages. Ontario contains 21 percent of Canada's Aboriginal population, and 43 percent of these people are twenty-four years of age and younger (Rice 2008). In fact, Aboriginal peoples are the youngest and fastest-growing segment of the national population (Ontario Native Affairs Secretariat 2005). The school is close to two large First Nations communities and a significant Métis population. Educational authorities in the region identified SHSS as an innovative school, and it boasts a staff of 115 individuals, including both teachers and support workers.

The ASP began at SHSS in 2003 and is directed at Aboriginal students. Before the inception of the program, research (conducted internally by school personnel) revealed that a disproportionate number of Aboriginal students across the district were dropping out of school. The reasons for Aboriginal students' choosing to leave school included poor health, lack of academic achievement, and poor socio-economic circumstances (which interfered with daily attendance). Aboriginal youth who were consulted during this research also indicated that their disinterest in formal schooling was often the result of (1) a lack of culturally sensitive support within the school and (2) a curriculum that had very little cultural relevance to them. I would speculate that such a disconnect between one's culture and one's school is not uncommon for Aboriginal students across Canada. This being the case, the ASP is designed to establish a support system founded upon Aboriginal culture and to foster Aboriginal success within a public secondary school.

The ASP at SHSS provides educational and cultural support within a dedicated space – the Native Room. It should be noted that the students themselves identify this space as "the Native Room." Students have access to this space and to the ASP's Aboriginal youth counsellors, who are available to assist them with class assignments, to provide cultural support and guidance, to resolve peer or teacher conflicts, and to meet their nutritional needs throughout the course of the school day. The program explicitly states that culture is an integral component of its services and that its purpose is to instill in Aboriginal students a sense of identity and cultural awareness. Peer leadership, traditional teachings, and culturally specific extracurricular activities are central components of the ASP.

The Aboriginal Students

The Aboriginal youth counsellors told all ninety-five of the male and female Aboriginal students who were actively participating in the ASP of the invitation to speak with us in informal research conversations. The counsellors informed the research team that the students were cautious about participating in a project that asked them to speak of their personal educational experiences. The team was grateful that a number of students accepted the invitation. One Grade 9, three Grade 11, and two Grade 12 male students attended the research conversation (almost 15 percent of the male student Aboriginal population in the ASP). Of the six students, three had lived on a reserve prior to enrolling at SHSS, while three had attended a public elementary school in the same urban district. The youth counsellors also told all fifty-three of the female students in Grades 9 to 12 enrolled in the ASP of the opportunity to participate in a research conversation. One Grade 9, one Grade 10, one Grade 11, and two Grade 12 students attended (nearly 10 percent of all female Aboriginal students). Three of these students had lived on a reserve before migrating to the urban centre, while the other two had attended public elementary school in the urban district.

The three Aboriginal youth counsellors at SHSS were generous in taking time to speak with some members of the research team. The first counsellor, Jordan, had three years' experience in the ASP at SHSS. Jordan is between twenty-five and thirty-five and earned an undergraduate degree from an Ontario university. He is fluent in his traditional language and very well versed in traditional teachings. The second counsellor, Mark, had three years experience in the ASP and is also between twenty-five and thirty-five years' of age. Like Jordan, Mark too has a postsecondary education, including an Ontario college diploma. Mark is also very fluent in his traditional language and is knowledgeable about traditional teachings. The last of the all-male Aboriginal youth counsellors at SHSS is Brian. Brian, at the time of the research conversation, was in his first official year of employment in the ASP; however, prior to this, he had been involved at the school as a community representative of various drumming groups. Brian is between thirty-five and forty-five. He is fluent in his traditional language. Like Jordan and Mark, Brian is also quite learned in traditional teachings. The three counsellors are each descended from a different Aboriginal group.

Bob and Paula, two non-Aboriginal teachers at SHSS who taught Aboriginal-specific courses, were invited to speak with the team as well. Bob had four years of experience and had been teaching at SHSS for two years, while Paula had twenty-three years of experience and had been teaching at SHSS for fifteen years. Their teaching assignments included at least one section of Aboriginal-specific courses in both semesters of the academic year. Bob, the less experienced teacher, claimed to have had limited knowledge of Aboriginal worldviews prior to his experience at SHSS, while Paula claimed to have been relatively well versed in Aboriginal traditions.

It was important to learn about the experiences of those in formal leadership positions within the school and the greater school community. Their experiences could be a source of profound learning for school board administrators, community leaders, and school principals, all of whom have a vested interest in Aboriginal education. The principal of the school was a seasoned educator with over twenty-five years of experience and was a driving force behind bringing the ASP to fruition and sustaining its development. The vice-principal was in his first year at SHSS and had been an educator for approximately ten years. The elder associated with the ASP was part of the school community. The community leader, also of Aboriginal descent, had had various experiences throughout her career facilitating various interventions for Aboriginal students of all ages within mainstream communities. She was involved in the ASP from its inception.

The reader is reminded that the Framework (Ontario Ministry of Education 2007) clearly identifies the need to foster the participation of Aboriginal parents and Aboriginal communities in working to support educators in their attempts to improve student achievement. Hence, various community members and parents/caregivers of Aboriginal students attending SHSS were invited to visit with representatives of the research team. The invitation was extended at a community feast, at which approximately seventy individuals were present. The team was grateful to the ten individuals who shared their experiences. Collectively, they represented students in each of the grades from 9 to 12. Two of the female community representatives (Katie and Sarah) were graduates of the ASP, as was James (the sole male participant). Katie had a child of her own, while Sarah considered herself a voice in the community. Katie, Melissa, Sarah, and James were between twenty-one and thirty years old. Mary (who was caring for her niece and nephew) and Linda were in their fifties and were secondary school graduates. Jane and Andrea were in their forties, and both had postsecondary school education. Andrea was not of Aboriginal descent but was married to an Aboriginal man and advocated for Aboriginal education on her children's behalf. Cherry was a well-spoken middle-aged woman who considered herself to be in touch with her culture. Susan was middle-aged and spoke readily of her experiences as an Aboriginal student in public school, comparing them to what she perceived to be her children's experiences.

Making Sense of the Voices
It is beyond the scope of this book to discuss the technical details of the social research design. Instead, I make a modest attempt to inform the reader about the principles and the methodology used to ensure a structured, consistent, and evidence-based exploration that would allow the voices of the various stakeholders to emerge. The methodology ensured that all of the multinational demographics of those who sat with the research team in Circle during the research conversations were honoured (see Kanu 2011; Kompf and Hodson 2000). The team was sensitive to establishing a rapport with the students and staff, thus ensuring that they felt at relative ease with the process. Some members of the research team spent considerable time with the students and counsellors at the school well in advance of the research conversations.

Since the research conversations were recorded digitally, those team members present were free to participate in the discussion and to direct their full attention to the words of each individual. The methodology employed in this study was conducive to this endeavour because it established a welcoming and sacred environment based on various Aboriginal spiritual traditions. As an example, participants met and conversed in a Circle for each of the research conversations. Each Circle began with a ceremony and engaged all participants in their respective discussions. The research conversations were conducted in a Circle to represent holism, inclusivity, and respect for all peoples and their opinions.

Although there were a few pre-scripted questions for the guests in each Circle, the questions themselves were subject to revision (Fultz and Herzog 1996). The following are some of the general promptings and questions that provided the parameters for the Circle discussions with the Aboriginal students: (1) Tell us about where you are from and about some of your experiences in public school before you began attending SHSS; (2) Describe the influence that the ASP has had on you as an Aboriginal person and student; and (3) What are some of your experiences of being a student in this school who attends the ASP?

Using a culturally respectful social constructivist qualitative analysis, the initial findings from the transcripts were encoded in the respondents' own words, collapsed into categories, and converted into a narrative explanation of what had been recorded (see Eaves 2001; Glaser and Strauss 1967; Glaser 1978). The validity of the observations was confirmed through member checks and triangulation.

Enrolment and Attendance Documents

The school administration conducted various internal studies prior to this investigation to document the number of Aboriginal students who enrolled in the program, attended classes, and withdrew from the program. The student enrolment, attendance, and withdrawal records dated from September 2003 (the inception of the ASP) to October 2008 were also considered to be significant (see Appendix 2).

School Records

From 2006 to 2008, six interventions – volunteer, parental, educational, health, social support, and cultural – were tracked by the school's Aboriginal youth counsellors. Volunteer interventions involved the number of times volunteer activities were introduced into the ASP by individuals from the Aboriginal community who assisted in classrooms, taught culturally appropriate arts, were involved with fundraising, and demonstrated how to prepare traditional foods. Parental interventions involved specific occasions when parents were consulted about their children's progress and attended feasts or potlucks and other celebrations hosted by the ASP at the secondary school. Educational interventions involved study periods, study-skills workshops, career information nights, and preparation activities for external provincial assessments that the ASP extended to Aboriginal students. Health interventions involved the provision of breakfast and snacks

FIGURE 1 Surveys

Respondents	Method(s)	Instruments
48 Aboriginal students enrolled in the ASP	Quantitative	7 statements
41 teachers, department chairs, and counsellors	Qualitative and quantitative	8 Likert-scale responses and 3 open-ended questions

throughout the day in the Native Room, drum-making workshops, and workshops on nutritional foods. Social support interventions involved the number of times students attended Aboriginal healing and outreach programs, Aboriginal health centres, and Remembrance Day ceremonies. Last, cultural interventions involved youth drumming and dancing, regalia making, moccasin-making workshops, and participating in various regional powwows (see Appendix 3).

Program Reports

Between 2006 and 2009 the youth counsellors authored eleven program reports. Included in these reports were anecdotal notes that highlighted both the ASP's significant accomplishments and its challenges. These reports served as the basis for various consultations between school administrators, Aboriginal youth counsellors, the district school board, and the supporting community agencies.

Aboriginal Student Survey

In June 2006, the school administration offered all eighty Aboriginal students enrolled in the ASP the opportunity to complete a survey. Forty-eight students did so, representing a 60 percent response rate. Forty percent of the students were eighteen years of age, representing the largest number of respondents. Thirty percent of the students were seventeen years old, 20 percent were sixteen, while 10 percent were fifteen (representing those who had participated in the ASP for the shortest period of time – one academic year) (see Figure 1). Fifteen students were male (representing 31 percent of all students) and thirty-three were female (representing 69 percent of all students). The survey consisted of seven Likert-scale questions that asked participants to choose one of the following three responses: *always, sometimes,* and *never* (see Appendix 1).

In order to gain as complete a picture as possible of the ASP, we administered a survey to each teacher, subject/department chairperson, and guidance counsellor working at SHSS in the late spring of 2009 (see Appendix 5). The survey collected additional responses from a larger number of stakeholders, including those faculty who did not participate in the research conversations (Taber 2000). The objective of the survey was twofold: first, to understand the faculty's perception of the effectiveness of their pre- and in-service teacher education in preparing them to address Aboriginal student learning (as it is described in the Framework) and, second, to provide insight into how teachers and counsellors address the key aspects of Aboriginal students' experiences in the context of the ASP.

Forty-one faculty members participated, including thirty-two classroom teachers, four counsellors, and five department chairpersons. The teachers represented 45 percent of the total sample, while the counsellors and department chairpersons represented 67 percent and 56 percent, respectively. Two percent of the survey responses were discarded during data analysis due to response prevarication. The survey afforded faculty the opportunity to anonymously offer more detailed open-ended responses to the more direct Likert-scale items (Creswell et al. 2003) (see Appendix 1).

The Analysis

The responses from the student surveys were tallied and recorded according to the percentage of students who chose either *always, sometimes,* or *never* as a response to each of the seven statements. The quantitative data from the faculty survey were analyzed for means and frequencies. Further, a post hoc Bonferroni repeated-measures (at an alpha of 0.05) for significant differences was examined across the following comparisons: (1) teacher and department chairpersons, (2) teachers and counsellors, and (3) department chairpersons and counsellors.

The qualitative responses from the faculty surveys were selectively coded and constantly compared. The open coding process distinguished discrete concepts and the properties associated with each (Strauss and Corbin 1990). Phrases that were considered key were captured in the participants' own words and used in the line-by-line examination of their responses. Through a constant comparison of concepts and themes, the main topics that emerged in participants' responses were identified.

It is imperative to allow oneself to authentically engage in this sort of conceptual conversion without manipulating an individual's words to fit with predetermined assumptions. In this way, researchers must exercise the patience to "enable that which enables" and, hence, allow the voices of the participants to materialize (see Charmaz 2000; Priest, Roberts, and Woods 2002). The "re-search" utilized a holistic approach that honoured the words of the research participants and that was committed to understanding their experiences as embedded in their socio-cultural contexts. As a result, participants' stories were not fragmented for the sake of a predetermined research agenda. The story of the individuals invited to the research conversation circles remained at the centre of all discussions.

It was important, too, that the research be conducted in "a good way"; thus, it began with ceremonies. These ceremonies evoked the spirits of the ancestors, the land, and the human and animal worlds in order to direct our inquiry. In this way, the research honoured the spiritual realm (Trudeau and Cherubini 2010).

PART 2
FROM THEORY TO PRACTICE

3
The Conversations

This chapter offers observations from participants and includes key excerpts to honour their voices (pseudonyms used throughout). It captures the stories of the female and male Aboriginal students, the Aboriginal counsellors, and associated educators who shared their reflections on the Aboriginal Student Program. These reflections permeate the stories told and attest to the sensitivity located at the intersection of student identities, relationships, and mainstream educational practices. These individuals gave freely of their time and shared their perceptions of the ASP and of the Aboriginal students it serves. Their stories are multilayered and offer many lenses through which to perceive the story presented in this book.

Aboriginal Female Students
The team was honoured by the presence of the five female students who participated in the research conversation (one from Grade 9, one from Grade 10, one from Grade 11, and two from Grade 12). When the discussion concluded, three topics emerged: (1) impact upon school culture, (2) issues of identity, and (3) power relations.

Impact upon School Culture
According to the Grade 9 and 10 female students, the ASP provides a secure space for them in the existing school culture. Because of the ASP, these

students were able to discuss how their values and beliefs as Aboriginal people were reflected in the culture of the school and how this affected their sense of academic engagement. Before the ASP, as one of the Grade 10 girls stated, they tended to "sit there ... and just stare at" the classroom assignment. As the Grade 9 student admitted, "I used to skip classes a lot." The ASP, however, affords them the opportunity to use the Native Room and to complete their assignments in a welcoming environment. Both students made numerous references to the impact of the cultural interventions offered by the Aboriginal youth counsellors in the Native Room: "Everybody is there and they will explain just what you have to do to get your work done" (Grade 10 student). The female students admitted that, prior to the ASP, they felt marginalized within the mainstream school culture and disengaged from their academic commitments. The ASP offers them culturally relevant learning environments, and as the Grade 9 student candidly stated, "[the ASP] really makes a difference [because] it is really good to learn."

Being immersed in a school environment that honours Aboriginal values and beliefs translates into purposeful learning. These students spoke at length about how mainstream teachers who effectively incorporated their epistemic realities into their pedagogy and celebrated Aboriginal traditions influenced the entire school culture. The Grade 10 student explained: "She [the classroom teacher] does not talk at you. She gives you a project and she will teach you. Other teachers will talk at you forever until the end of the period then give you your work and be, like, here you go and do it. Ms [referring specifically to Paula] will help you." The students extended their observations to suggest that the supportive teachers and the availability of the Native Room encourage an inclusive learning environment, with the result that Aboriginal and non-Aboriginal students "kind of all hang out together and stuff" (Grade 9 student). This contributes to a respectful school culture that is supportive of Aboriginal students' social, spiritual, and epistemic uniqueness but does not ghettoize them within the broader school culture. As the Grade 10 student suggested: "We have lots of friends that are not a part of the program [ASP]. We become friends with everyone. It's a good environment." These students attest to the significance of a culturally receptive learning environment, of interventions and supports that engage them in their studies, and of the impact of the program upon some mainstream teachers who practise culturally inclusive pedagogy. The Grade 10 student succinctly stated that the program's success, in terms of affecting the entire school culture, is largely attributable to "the counsellors, teachers, ... and people like that ... [being] there."

The Grade 11 and Grade 12 female students also spoke to the ASP's impact on school culture. One Grade 11 female was especially grateful for the opportunity to go to the Native Room when she was struggling in her mainstream classrooms: "I will just go down there if I don't feel comfortable in my classroom. I just go to the Native Room [and] I have never had any problems with any of my teachers." The Native Room and the ASP are accepted components of the school culture; they are culturally respectful spaces that honour Aboriginal students' epistemic and socio-cultural realities. The older female students, like the younger students, hold the Aboriginal youth counsellors in high regard. In fact, they see their counsellors as having the same status as their teachers as they regularly observed the two interacting as part of the professional school culture. One Grade 11 participant described the counsellors' influence as instrumental in her re-engagement with public school:

> They [i.e., mainstream teachers] send you to class, and I used to skip a lot. Being in there [i.e., the Native Room], the counsellors tell you to go to class and they will talk to you about why you should go to class, and why it is important to go to class ... I never used to have this ... The way they [i.e., counsellors] talk to you, it makes you realize why you should go to class.

Clearly, the Aboriginal counsellors are important to these Aboriginal students. They offer fluid interventions that are not only authentic but also pragmatic with regard to reconnecting them to the broader school culture. As a Grade 12 student suggested, the ASP seems to embody "someone who cares [– someone who] ... is watching and knowing what is going on" in students' lives and in the rest of the school community. The other female students agreed with this assessment. They feel affirmed by the ASP and are enriched by a sense of belonging to the larger school culture, which they now feel they can influence. And they are proud of the fact that their non-Aboriginal friends "can be a part of it [i.e., the Native Room]" (Grade 11 student) and that their own contributions to school-wide events are recognized by the school community: "We do the opening of the talent show, and everyone sees our traditions" (Grade 12 student).

It is interesting that all five of the female students cited the impact of the mainstream teachers who brought the ASP into their classroom culture. The Grade 12 student stated: "We all skipped to go to her class"; a Grade 11 student added: "My teacher knows that I go there [i.e., a culturally responsive classroom]." The students are clearly aware that the learning environment is different in classroom cultures in which Aboriginal epistemic preferences are as valued as mainstream ones. The Grade 12 student continued:

> Mostly everyone knows we go there, even my first period teacher. There are three other Native kids in my class, but two of them really like to go drumming, so lots of times they will just go and ask the teacher if they can go and drum ... instead of being in his class, and lots of times he lets us ... He is really understanding about it.

Even some of the more traditionally minded teachers allow the Aboriginal students to attend other classes – a practice that, quite conceivably, would not occur in school cultures that do not embrace a program such as the ASP. The female students indicated how mainstream teachers practise and interact differently in culturally respectful mainstream classrooms. In these learning environments, students perceive the value of teachers who "know most of the students ... and [with whom] everyone is comfortable" (Grade 12 student). The ASP affords these female students opportunities to explore their epistemic preferences in culturally rich learning environments that, so far from being perceived as distinct cultures, allow the strengths of Aboriginal students to flourish within a broader, culturally respectful school community.

Issues of Identity

The ASP was instrumental in furthering Aboriginal female students' sense of identity. The Grade 9 and Grade 10 students credited the program with connecting them to Aboriginal traditions, values, and beliefs that illuminated their identity as Aboriginal persons. These students agreed with the Grade 10 student, who said: "Before I came here [SHSS] I did not know anything about it ... my culture ... I learned a lot more. Now I know how to sing some songs and drum. We made some drums and everything, so that was good." On a number of occasions, they referred to the positive influence of their cultural awareness and its impact on their identity as Aboriginal people. According to the Grade 9 student, she was able to "learn[] more when [she] came here"; according to the Grade 10 student, "There is not really much that I experienced until I came to [SHSS]." The ASP not only re-engaged these students academically but also enhanced their perception of the traditions and values unique to them as Aboriginal people. For these girls, still in the formative stages of their lives, it became clear that "it is nice to know about [our] background and the history behind everything. It is interesting too and good to learn about" (Grade 10 student).

The ASP was also instrumental in rekindling familial connections through traditions and feasts that celebrated their identities. The Grade 9 student commented on how it was "interesting to bring [her] family" to the feast housed at the school and coordinated by the ASP and the Aboriginal community. The Grade 10 student continued: "I have a six-year-old brother who does not really know anything yet, so it is good to bring him to that." Students felt engaged by the possibility of furthering their awareness of their Aboriginal identity and extending this awareness to parents and siblings. Just as community members attend feasts and learn about ceremonies, so the female students shared with us how this engagement enabled them to discover a greater sense of identity. They appreciated the value of listening to the elders' traditional teachings and stories and observing their actions at ceremonies. Typically, the Grade 10 student observed: "It makes you think: 'Wow, there are people that live like that!' I think it is good to learn about it even though we are living the way we are and things were the way they were back then. It makes you think in a positive way."

The Grades 11 and 12 female students also spoke of how the ASP positively influenced their sense of identity. The Grade 11 student discussed her preference for SHSS, where she is better able to identify with members of her own community: "I did not like it [i.e., the previous school] because I was the only Native person at the school and I just did not feel comfortable." In comparison, "being with [one's] own people" is much more conducive to identifying with one's cultural values and beliefs. The opportunity to better identify with other students of Aboriginal descent led the female students in Grade 12 to conclude that one's identity grows stronger in an environment in which "everyone has something in common." Like the younger students, these students considered the presence of the elders and other community leaders to be a critical component of the ASP. The students "try to learn as much as they can" (Grade 12 student). The stories and traditional teachings offered by the voices of the community "tell us things about ourselves. It's like having a grandma around. It's really comfortable and awesome" (Grade 11 student).

Students also readily associated their sense of identity with learning about their language. They shared examples of their experiences (e.g., giving opening addresses in their own language) and indicated how they discovered that "language is important to [them and that they] want to speak it fluently. [They] want to understand more" (Grade 11 student). The combination of learning about their heritage and their socio-linguistic traditions led each of them to conclude that they are "better student[s] than before" their enrolment in the ASP and that "[they] think that [they] have changed" (ibid.). Students attributed the various components of the program to their heightened identity and to the fact that they felt proud to be Aboriginal students in a mainstream public school: "Without the program, I would not know a lot about my own nation. I would not know what I know now. I think that it really helps with identity" (Grade 12 student). The young women also spoke on behalf of some other Aboriginal students who, through the ASP, discovered a greater sense of their identity and have taken great comfort in sharing their experiences with their own people. The research team heard descriptions of students who had felt alienated in other schools who "now just love" (Grade 11 student) SHSS and take full advantage of the drumming and cultural activities associated with their identities.

Power Relations
The female students often acknowledged their gratitude for being able to remove themselves from their mainstream classrooms during uneasy circumstances. Students, using their own discretion and with the permission of the teacher, have the opportunity to decide if the Native Room is better suited to their learning needs than the regular classroom: "The program makes it easier for me because I struggled with my classes in math, and with the room you can get one-to-one help or whatever if you need it. Or if you have trouble working in the classroom with other students you can go down there, and there is [someone] if you need to talk" (Grade 10 student). The school administration made it clear to faculty that the Native Room provides Aboriginal students with a respite from the challenges and tensions of mainstream classroom practices. Aboriginal students are empowered to request access to the Native Room for cultural support, and they are trusted to leave the mainstream classroom and tend to their school work in a more culturally suitable environment. Students know they "can go to them [i.e., the Aboriginal counsellors], not like a normal teacher" (Grade 9 student).

It was clear that students perceived the counsellors to be their advocates. The counsellors are the voice, both symbolic and literal, for Aboriginal students who experience a conflict with teachers, administrators, or outside community agencies: "You can go to them, and they will stand up for you if you are in trouble. They will help you in any way ... I feel more comfortable with them than I would a normal teacher" (Grade 9 student). Students believe that their counsellors have the power to advocate for them both inside and outside of school. They did not always see their mainstream teachers in a similar light. While there is no indication that Aboriginal students do not respect their mainstream teachers, there is every indication that they see their counsellors' authority as unequivocal. The fact that the counsellors "are there" (Grade 10 student) and accessible provides Aboriginal students with a voice and a sense of power in mainstream school culture.

The Grade 11 and Grade 12 students also discussed opportunities to be dismissed from classes in order to seek support from the counsellors. The Grade 12 student compared her experience in the ASP with her experience in a similar program at another school and concluded that the success of the SHSS program is largely attributable to those teachers who "accept the program." This student's perception of her previous experiences was founded upon circumstances in which mainstream teachers were generally reluctant to relinquish a degree of authority and to allow students access to a different classroom during their instructional periods. The senior students, like their junior counterparts, considered their youth counsellors to be advocates in terms of mediating conflicts with teachers: "If I have a problem with my teachers and they are not treating me fairly, or if they did something I did not like, I could tell them. I could tell [the counsellors], and they will talk to the teacher for me and settle any problems that we have" (Grade 12 student). Because the ASP recognizes that Aboriginal students typically withdraw from conflict, it ensures the availability of counsellors to serve as mediators between students and teachers. Students feel that the counsellors make the teachers aware of their concerns, thus enabling the teachers to keep them engaged.

At SHSS there is an implicit understanding of shared power relations between student and teacher, student and counsellor, and counsellor and teacher that cannot exist in a non-supportive school culture. Even at SHSS there are instances when mainstream teachers consider student requests to go to the Native Room as excuses to visit "the party room": "They [i.e., some of the teachers] just think that people do not do any work there" (Grade 11 student). In those instances when "teachers give you the biggest problem" over requests for access to cultural interventions, the students feel compelled "to get the principal to talk to them" (Grade 12 student). The Grade 11 student attributed teachers' resistance to "just see[ing] what they see" and not understanding the epistemic conflict that is often inherent in mainstream learning environments.

The research conversation with the female students was very enlightening. They spoke to the success of the program and told of their sense of belonging in an inclusive and culturally respectful school culture. They credited the ASP not only with re-engaging them academically but also with fostering a greater sense of self-identity. They also acknowledged the opportunities the program afforded them to exercise their own discretion in terms of using ASP youth counsellors as powerful advocates.

Aboriginal Male Students

The research conversation with the male Aboriginal students consisted of one Grade 9, three Grade 11, and two Grade 12 students. These students identified three main topics: (1) the Native Room as an inviting space, (2) learning preferences and student engagement, and (3) establishing relationships.

The Native Room as an Inviting Space

In various ways, all of the male students referenced the positive influence of the Native Room as an inviting space. In a number of instances, they suggested that the Native Room was distinctive in that it was a place within the school where their culture, art, and traditions were especially celebrated. In each case, the boys expressed their appreciation of the fact that neither the ASP coordinators nor the Aboriginal youth counsellors coerced students into participating in the program; rather, students understood that assistance and support were available "when [they] ask[ed]" (Grade 9 student). The supports that are available through the Native Room follow from the ASP's philosophy, which is to offer opportunities to Aboriginal students but not to determine the degree to which they take advantage of them. According to the male students, the success of the Native Room is based on the opportunities it provides for Aboriginal students. As one Grade 11 student commented, "I came here, and it [i.e., the Native Room and its services] helped me out a lot because you can go down there and work during class and stuff ... I think it is easier to work in the Native Room than it is in class." The Native Room represents an inclusive and culturally reflective space that is uniquely attentive to the distinct learning, physical, emotional, and spiritual needs of Aboriginal persons and students. It is an alternative site within the school that invites students to work, study, and learn according to more traditionally aligned perspectives than are available in the mainstream classrooms. Typically, a Grade 12 student offered the following reflection: "I find that it is extremely nice that they serve food most of the time and that there is a place to go if you need any help with anything. It is really good." For these students, the Native Room offers sustenance and support in a different form than is traditionally found in mainstream schools. For students struggling to discover something meaningful in their studies, the Native Room offers an alternative to skipping classes and becoming involved in high-risk behaviours. The boys readily distinguished it as a positive influence on their experiences as SHSS students.

Just as the students were acutely aware of the Native Room's benefits, so they were also aware that some teachers questioned its validity as a viable means of providing academic support. They sensed the cynicism of some teachers when they requested permission to leave the classroom to go and work in the Native Room. All of the Grade 11 students declared their resentment of any teacher's reluctance to allow them to fully participate in the ASP. One student stated: "A couple of teachers will not let me go." Another offered this explanation: "Well, when they walk by [the Native Room], sometimes they see people fooling around and they think we are just going there to fool around, and it is just the odd time that they walk by ... So when we ask to go down there they think we are fooling around." Students believe that these teachers have made up their minds regarding the usefulness of the room based solely on a chance observation. In their eyes, this misperception undermines the integrity of the ASP. They resent the fact that teachers "walk by ... usually at lunch time" (Grade 11 student) and "think that [students] are going there to fool around, lie down, and get juice" (Grade 12 student).

According to the oldest student in the Circle, teachers who do not perceive the utility of the Native Room do not understand that it provides culturally appropriate academic support that is not available in mainstream classrooms. Students do not blame the teachers for not providing a more culturally inclusive pedagogy in their classrooms; rather, they describe the Native Room as a resource that complements their learning. "I have a hard time," the oldest student confessed, "sitting in a classroom with a bunch of people because they always talk. So, I go down to [the Native Room] and I get my work done. I have computer access; I have books and dictionaries. I have everything I need right there to do a project, a collage, or anything." A Grade 11 student concurred with these thoughts, adding: "I like how I can go down there and get out of class and work. It is easier." For these students, the Native Room is an inclusive place that is tailored to their needs and is welcoming of all students. The Native Room is considered to be "for everybody ... not just Natives" (Grade 11 student). In many respects, the room enhances cross-cultural student relationships as it stands as an example to all students that culturally respectful schooling practices – practices that honour Aboriginal students' needs and capacities – can exist within the larger school culture.

Learning Preferences and Student Engagement

All of the male students recognized how the ASP contributed to their academic achievement and to their commitment to graduate and pursue postsecondary aspirations. In comparison to their elementary school experience (and for three of the six students who attended other high schools), the young men unanimously agreed with a Grade 12 student's observation: "This has got to be one of the most helpful programs that I have ever been in." The students commented on how the ASP aligned their cultural practices and beliefs with culturally sensitive epistemic practices. One of the more profound observations emanating from the research conversation concerned the fact that these Aboriginal youth were able to define their learning preferences and to develop an appreciation for their learning strengths. In many cases, this awareness was brought to light by their experiences in mainstream classrooms. Mainstream classroom practices, according to one Grade 11 student, "[lead to students] not doing anything. They sit in the class and do work in the textbooks and talk about things. So, I find it better here [i.e., the Native Room] because when I work hands-on I learn a lot more." Students admitted that traditional teacher-directed pedagogical practice is not their preferred means of learning and that, in fact, it leads to their uninterest in education. In the Native Room, however, students engage in a collaborative and intimate learning environment that is sensitive to their worldviews. They shared their experiences of being put off by the top-down models of instruction in traditional classrooms, whereby knowledge is generally transmitted from teacher to student. At one point, one Grade 11 youth abruptly stated: "You have to do it instead of them reading something and saying, 'Okay, do it.' I sit there, and I do not know what to do." In the eyes of these students, the indirect instruction that fosters oral communication between students and teachers creates a much preferred learning environment.

The students also identified their preferences for cultural interventions that are responsive to their epistemic traditions. They described experiences with the Aboriginal counsellors, who provided clear instructions for their assignments: "I would rather be told [the instructions on a particular classroom task] straight up rather than later on when you could have been doing it right throughout that time period" (Grade 11 student). At times, students felt out of place in mainstream classrooms, and they certainly preferred a more culturally sensitive learning environment. They were confident that the learning environment created in the Native Room was more suited to their learning styles and less threatening than what they encountered in mainstream classrooms. One Grade 12 student spoke of those "hard times sitting in a classroom with a bunch of people" whose epistemic traditions were generally unsupportive of Aboriginal ones. With regard to the Native studies courses and teachers at SHSS, students indicated that they extended the philosophy of the Native Room into the classroom. In these courses, students confirmed that their preferred learning styles were facilitated by the inclusion in the curriculum of culturally relevant material. The Native studies courses employed collaborative, indirect, and active learning strategies to teach students about various Aboriginal linguistic and cultural traditions: "They actually taught us how to build our own drum, the rules, and what we can and cannot do around it" (Grade 12 student).

The students freely discussed how the ASP engaged them in their learning. Whereas in their previous schools they admitted to being "isolated" (Grade 12 student), in the ASP they were provided with the opportunity to learn with other Aboriginal students who shared similar learning preferences. According to the students, among the more influential characteristics of the ASP is the fact that it is a part of the school: "I am honestly happy that this program is in a real school. That is a definite plus" (Grade 12 student). Obviously, these youths do not want to be marginalized or relocated to another building in order to benefit from culturally sensitive interventions and epistemic practices such as those offered by the ASP. Students felt connected to SHSS and engaged in their studies. Particularly intriguing were the experiences of one Grade 11 and two Grade 12 students, all of whom admitted to struggling with staying in school (one student had temporarily dropped out of a previous school). In each case, these students credited the ASP with re-engaging them in their schooling. The oldest of the boys stated: "I am doing good. I dropped out ... then I came back because they have the program here. Ever since then I've been getting good grades and I'm ... [graduating] this year." Students felt that the program was in large part responsible for putting them "on the right track again" (Grade 11 student). It was clear that they understood how they are best able to learn and that they appreciated the ASP for re-engaging them in their schooling.

Establishing Relationships
Related to students' perceptions of the Native Room as a welcoming space and to their awareness of learning styles and the benefit of being engaged in

school is establishing trusting relationships. One of the boys in Grade 11 described the benefits of the ASP's cultural interventions as follows: "You get extra help there from people that you know and trust." It was observed that associating with counsellors who have an intimate understanding of Aboriginal epistemic, historical, and cultural realities is critical if students are to establish nurturing and trusting relationships. Students often described the trust they had in their counsellors and peers in the ASP as being at the centre of their academic success. These professional relationships fostered their sense of belonging in a mainstream secondary school culture. They referred not only to the support offered by the Aboriginal counsellors but also to the fact that these individuals took a genuine interest in their personal welfare and academic outcomes. The counsellors earned students' trust, thus enabling the students to establish a strong relationship with them: "You just have to get to know them and what kind of people they are" (Grade 11 student). Three of the students (two in Grade 12 and one in Grade 11) had previously attended an alternative off-site school that offered Aboriginal programming for youth, yet they were all critical of this program because, as one Grade 12 student stated "[The staff] pretty much just sit around and they cannot really help because they are not teachers." Another student added: "The work was not difficult, but actually having your paper officially handed in was difficult ... It was kind of messed [up]." The youth counsellors at ASP are not certified teachers, yet, due to the trusting, professional, and supportive relationships they were able to establish with them, their impact on students was strikingly different from that of the staff in the alternative Aboriginal program.

The students with previous experience in a different Aboriginal program cited its intent to be culturally supportive but observed that its staff was unable to establish trusting relationships with them to further their epistemic and cultural traditions. This speaks to the significant role of the ASP's counsellors as trustworthy advocates of student welfare. Quite interestingly, just like the female students, the males indicated that they perceived the Aboriginal youth counsellors differently than they did their teachers mainly because of the heightened trust they had in them. While the students respected their teachers' authority, they considered the youth counsellors to be the most helpful adult figures in the school. The counsellors are perceived as neither formal "counsellors [n]or teachers" (Grade 12 student); rather, they are seen to occupy a role that is not traditionally identifiable in educational institutions. The counsellors are generally perceived as being "there to help us" (Grade 11 student) in a way that classroom teachers and administrators are not. They are distinguished by their genuine care for students' well-being and for their respectful cultural interventions: "A teacher would just help you, but [counsellors' names are mentioned] would actually come and see us on the weekend if we asked them to help. They are more of a friend than a teacher or a counsellor" (Grade 12 student). Clearly, the youth counsellors offer students support and professional services that are not offered by mainstream teachers.

Students were very aware of the value of the relationships they established with their peers in the ASP. One felt comforted by knowing the character of the students with whom he associated in the Native Room: "There are people that I know in there. It is just because [in] the class ... there are always dumb kids there" (Grade 11 student). One Grade 11 student indicated that non-Aboriginal students who do not understand Aboriginal students' epistemic and socio-cultural practices "piss[ed him] right off." The environment of the mainstream classroom is not necessarily conducive to Aboriginal students' establishing relationships with their mainstream peers. For its part, however, the Native Room, with its cultural celebrations, ceremonies, feasts, and youth counsellors, contributes to the students' willingness to establish relationships. In the eyes of these adolescents, the ASP offers them the opportunity to see themselves reflected in various events and ceremonies. Being together in the Native Room enables students to receive "respect" from the school community, which, in turn, "gives [them] power" (Grade 11 student). They described this power as a sense of belonging and an interconnectedness with other Aboriginal students and the youth counsellors (who serve as role models). Some students suggested that the school environment was conducive to establishing relationships because "the aggression within this school is extremely low compared with most of the schools that I have been to" (Grade 12 student).

Students spoke freely about their perceptions of inviting and non-inviting school spaces, conducive and non-conducive learning environments, and the importance of establishing trusting relationships with Aboriginal youth counsellors. The voices of the students also attest to how their prior life experiences and knowledge bases contributed to their critical reflections and subsequent personal and social behaviours.

The students learned about how they learn best. They discovered the skills, attitudes, and values that are unique to them and their communities. Their awareness of their epistemic preferences and values led to an abstract understanding of their self-identities, and they expressed their pride in accepting their uniqueness as Aboriginal peoples and learners. The words of the adolescents underscore the significance of culturally respectful and appropriate interventions in sustaining a viable relationship with the school.

Youth Counsellors

The research conversation Circle with the Aboriginal youth counsellors offered some of the most telling stories. For over two hours, the youth counsellors spoke eloquently of the significance of three particular topics: (1) negotiating epistemic conflicts, (2) establishing cross- and intercultural relationships within a spirit of community, and (3) encouraging a sense of self.

Negotiating Epistemic Conflicts

According to the Aboriginal youth counsellors, epistemic conflicts are multifaceted. Clearly, when it came to measuring the ASP's success, there was a conflict between the institutional demands of the school board and the first-hand perceptions of the youth counsellors. Jordan, for example, made it clear that it is critical to the success of the program that they "put the word out [to school board officials and to the broader mainstream community] because it is good what we are doing, and we want to show ... that." Jordan also expressed his frustration with the epistemic conflict pertaining to measures of accountability. Both Jordan and Mark cited specific examples of how the Eurocentric mainstream school board assessment of the ASP's success did not always mesh with that of the counsellors. According to Jordan:

> The board always wants to see numbers. They always want to see if student X is getting four credits a semester, if their attendance is getting better, or if they are getting suspended too much. Those are the three things that I have to watch and it [i.e., the ASP] is more than that. It is a lot more than that.

Jordan and Mark spoke freely of their experiences in the ASP and, on numerous occasions, noted that, while they wanted the positive outcomes of the program to be known to a broader audience, the epistemic conflict between the two ways of measuring accountability often hindered this. Jordan, Mark, and Brian suggested that mainstream educators, particularly senior and school board administrators, demanded quantifiable evidence to justify the success of the ASP. Both Jordan and Mark appreciated the viability of this way of measuring accountability within the mainstream-driven educational system, but they suggested that it does not always provide an accurate indication of the ASP's success.

In order to justify their position, the counsellors cited the historical and contemporary cultural realities that challenge Aboriginal students, particularly those living in urban communities. Jordan and Mark explicitly held that numbers of credits, attendance statistics, and suspension records are not the sole measures of the ASP's success because, quite simply, these are not indicators of Aboriginal practices. All of the counsellors understood the importance of measuring the success of the program from a Eurocentric perspective, given that these measures of accountability are strictly aligned to taxpayer dollars. However, they were also adamant that these indicators should not be the only way of justifying monetary investment in the ASP.

For these Aboriginal youth counsellors, the impact of the program and the success or failure of their work are experienced on the ground. As both Jordan and Mark suggested, the success of the program is often best measured on a case-by-case basis. For the counsellors, the unique circumstances of each student who benefits from the ASP is precisely where the program's success may be found. Perhaps Jordan said it best: "It is them [i.e., the Aboriginal students] coming to you with problems and you being able to help them with their problems. Or them getting three credits even though they have 120 absences. They are getting through high school." Mark agreed with this and added that the success of the ASP is seen in its "helping somebody work through something." The epistemic conflict that exists between qualitative and quantitative measures of success threatens to undermine the nature and quality of the relationships that are established between the counsellors and the Aboriginal students. For Jordan and the other counsellors, the success of the program is evident "through our actions and the positive things that we are doing. This kind of combats the numbers. The numbers are good too, there is a significant improvement in the numbers ... You cannot judge it only on numbers. You cannot judge it on those things. You have to judge it on what we are doing, and the [school] board can see that. They can see what we are doing." According to the Aboriginal youth counsellors, the success of the ASP is showcased through the actions and successes of each Aboriginal student.

The counsellors distinguished another facet of the ASP that contributes to its success – namely, their ability to deliver the program in what they all referred to as "their own way." Time and again the counsellors suggested that the program is delivered in a culturally sensitive and culturally appropriate manner and that, as a result, Aboriginal students are drawn to it. It should be noted that Jordan is the lead Aboriginal youth counsellor at SHSS and, given his responsibilities and the institutional memory concomitant with his affiliation with the program, speaks with more authority than the other counsellors regarding the tensions that have existed and that continue to emerge in the ASP. In his various reflections, Jordan reiterated that the measures of accountability required by the school board do not necessarily accurately reflect the program's success. He stated that the various community engagements in which the Aboriginal students are involved, including community breakfasts at which an Aboriginal student shares a Thanksgiving address in her Native Mohawk language or drum groups offer a performance, essentially "combat the numbers" (i.e., the quantifiable records) expected by school board officials.

Jordan often used "combat" as a metaphor to describe the epistemic conflict at SHSS. As Jordan, Mark, and Brian described their experiences in the program, it became strikingly clear that they were strategically "combatting" the quantification of the ASP's success. In the many stories they shared, it became evident that the drumming ceremonies and the activities related to Native languages attracted Aboriginal students and subsequently led to their re-engagement with their education. According to Jordan, "You know, we went to Kingston with the drum group and engaged in all of those things [i.e., various cultural performances], and we can show through our actions the positive stuff that we are doing, and that is what combats the numbers."

Jordan continued to stress that it is imperative that the Aboriginal youth counsellors and the other facilitators of the ASP communicate to senior board administrators that the success of the program cannot be based solely on statistics. According to him: "They can see the stronger people that we are creating, and I think for now that is good enough." Mark complemented this by suggesting that some of the most difficult students, and arguably those most disengaged from formal education, have in fact experienced a profound re-engagement as a result of the ASP. Mark spoke in particular about one student who

> did not have any goals for postsecondary [education], and now he wants to do this and he wants to do that. Being at this school and getting an education has helped him come a long way with wanting to experience what else there is out there. I do honestly think that if he was not as

involved with the program he would not be with us here today. He would be either in jail or in Toronto living on the streets. Now he has goals to go to university and to learn about Aboriginal aspects of life.

Just as, at times, there is an epistemic conflict over qualitative and quantitative methods of measuring the success of the ASP, so, too, there is conflict between Aboriginal and non-Aboriginal cultures within SHSS. According to the Aboriginal youth counsellors, the premise of the program is that the school faculty, staff, student body, and school community should have open minds and be respectful of the traditions and needs of others. As Brian stated:

> I asked them [i.e., the Aboriginal students] to try and have an open mind and I share the teachings that I have learned over the past fifteen years. Those are my teachings. Those are the ways that I have been taught. Everyone has different teachings, so I make them aware of that and of the importance of having an open mind and being respectful of not just my teachings but everybody else's cultures as well.

According to the youth counsellors, the epistemic conflict between cultures is not exclusive to that between the varying Aboriginal cultures that exist in the school. In fact, it is a far more complex conflict. Jordan suggests that it is imperative for Aboriginal youth counsellors, school administrators, and teachers to understand the nature of the conflicts that challenge Aboriginal students in mainstream schools. According to Jordan, Aboriginal students are forced to balance their existence in two very separate and distinct worlds: "You [i.e., the mainstream] belong on your path, and we belong on ours, and we will never cross. I said to our kids that we have crossed, and we cannot untangle that. So you know you have to have one foot in both." It is clear that students are challenged by two different realities – the Aboriginal and the non-Aboriginal. According to Jordan and Mark, if Aboriginal students are going to be successful, they must understand how to learn and to live in both worlds. In fact, Mark suggested that if the students do not learn to live and function in both worlds they will fail in both. These observations underscore the critical role that the Aboriginal youth counsellors play in the ASP. They are the conduits between the Aboriginal and the non-Aboriginal, and they have a clear understanding of their roles. They perceive themselves as guiding Aboriginal students in both worlds in a culturally sensitive and culturally respectful manner. Jordan shared his belief that Aboriginal students "will never be alone" in facing the challenges that confront them in the schools, the classrooms, the hallways, and the offices. He confidently stated: "We are going to build this person [i.e., Aboriginal student] up." Here, he is referring to the fact that the ASP is devoted to the Aboriginal student's entire being. For these counsellors, one of the ASP's primary mandates is to address the stifling isolation that Aboriginal students often experience when attempting to learn and live among the mainstream population.

It is clear that the counsellors have a sound understanding of Aboriginal student realities. They comprehend and appreciate how Aboriginal students have often been adversely situated within mainstream society. As a result, they are committed to assisting Aboriginal students in negotiating what Jordan referred to as "the cultural shift" from living on a reserve to living in an urban core – particularly a large, mainstream, publicly funded secondary school. Aboriginal youth counsellors professed their dedication to helping Aboriginal students make the transition from the reserve to the diversity of SHSS. According to Jordan:

> We are having a lot more kids come into urban cores from the reserves, whether it is for employment, to live with a relative, or whatever. It is a cultural shift for them too from growing up on a reserve to starting to live in a city and even to come to a school like this. We are the most multicultural school around. There are sixty languages spoken here, and it is quite a bit of a shift [for Aboriginal students] to come to a school like this.

The counsellors noted how the trend across Ontario is for Aboriginal students to leave the reserve schools to attend multicultural public institutions such as SHSS.

Related to the tension experienced by Aboriginal students forced to live and learn in both worlds is the fact that their learning needs are considerably different from those of non-Aboriginal students, something that often contributes to epistemic conflict in mainstream classrooms. While in all instances the Aboriginal youth counsellors credited the mainstream teachers with being well intentioned and dedicated to their profession, they did cite various circumstances in which Aboriginal students experienced tremendous frustration due to the tension between them and their teachers. According to the counsellors, some teachers may not understand or appreciate the cultural, domestic, and epistemic realities of Aboriginal students. Mark recounted one example of an Aboriginal student who was having a bad day and wanted to get out of class. The teacher did not allow her to. So the student takes off and comes down to the [Native] Room, and I go upstairs and speak with the teacher. I ask the teacher if it is possible to get the work for the student. The student is not having a good day. Is it all right if the student comes down and works in our room? They are not seeing eye to eye, and the teacher may not understand what is going on because there is probably something going on at home, and the student does not feel comfortable going to class and speaking to the teacher about it.

Jordan suggested that the root of such tension is multifaceted: "There has to be a shift within the school boards to recognize the way that Aboriginal students learn. That is an important step in the way that this or any school board for that matter can help an Aboriginal student to first learn about the way they learn and [also] where they are coming from." The counsellors identified a significant impediment to Aboriginal student learning and suggested that it was basically an epistemic issue. These observations are especially significant because the counsellors are the individuals working most closely with the students and their communities, their teachers, and, in some instances, the various social services. They have first-hand knowledge of the issues, problems, and challenges that confront Aboriginal students on a daily basis. On various occasions, Jordan and Mark, in particular, stressed: "You have to understand where these kids are coming from."

As far as the Aboriginal youth counsellors are concerned, the process of understanding and situating the reality of Aboriginal students is a precondition for engaging their intellects. They suggested, based on their experiences, that if mainstream teachers attempt to engage only the intellects of the Aboriginal students, then they will not commit to formal education: "You have to really, really know what these kids are coming from and the experiences they had" (Jordan). Mark and the other counsellors suggested that teachers need to be open to accepting the varying realities that Aboriginal students bring to their classrooms and to realize that these realities may affect their pedagogical approach as well as their assumptions and biases. "You cannot assume anything with these kids," Jordan suggested, alluding to the danger of teachers' assumptions and biases serving as impediments to engaging Aboriginal students. The counsellors emphasized the fact that mainstream teachers have to take Aboriginal student realities into account: "Aboriginal people are living in poverty. Whether it is in the government's ghetto of a reserve or it is the ghetto they live in within an urban core. They are placed there and are there because they are

Aboriginal" (Jordan). The counsellors stated that Aboriginal students' realities affect all facets of their existence. As they explained it:

> School plays a lesser role when you don't have food in your fridge or you do not have a way to get to and from school. Just the embarrassment of it. Not having clean clothes or hygiene or all of those things is embarrassing. Those are all the barriers that prevent our kids from coming to school. We try our best to combat those things. Are they still living in these areas? Yes they are, but hopefully with our program they can see what is out there. They can see that they do not have to just settle and just exist. They can do more. They can come out of that poverty.

Interestingly, all three counsellors held that their own experiences as children and youths enabled them to better relate to the Aboriginal students in their care. For some of them, life on the reserve had been difficult, filled with poverty and despair. According to one counsellor (name intentionally withheld),

> I just wanted to succeed because of where I grew up and, you know, I would say probably out of a group of twenty of us maybe two of us had a high school diploma ... I thought if I can do it then I can help others and show them that it is possible, that anything is possible. If I can do it from a little remote community up north, then anything is possible, and I just thought that I am younger so I would be able to really help them out in certain areas.

The other counsellors shared the frustration they had experienced living in urban cores and attending mainstream schools. They discussed the irony of having been "successfully assimilated" and, later in their lives, of having been reawakened to the cultural teachings and spiritual traditions of their Aboriginal heritage. They spoke of the significant learning they had experienced as a result of the trying circumstances of their lives, and they were adamant about the positive influences that role models had had on their adolescent development and on their desire to work with youth.

Establishing Cross- and Intercultural Relationships within a Spirit of Community

Throughout the research conversations, the Aboriginal youth counsellors alluded to the significance of establishing positive and professional cross-

and intercultural relationships within a spirit of community. Jordan candidly stated:

> A lot of people do not understand Aboriginal people and the way that they learn, especially in an urban core. That is what we deal with. We deal with Aboriginal people in an urban core, and just through making relationships in the board ... making partnerships with so and so, and talking about this and that. We do presentations about the Aboriginal learner to the board of education.

Yet the counsellors clarified that these relationships with school board officials are not necessarily always of primary significance; rather, it is their professional relationships with Aboriginal students that take precedence. Jordan stated that all of the traditional teachings that are shared with Aboriginal students,

> whether they are Haudenosaunee or Annishinabe, include the importance of "a healthy mind, body, and spirit." Those are a lot of the core teachings, and I do not care what kind of teachings you are talking about, those teachings are coming out of those ones. It does not matter if we are sitting around the big drum or we have a water drum or we have a Haudenosaunee come and talk about Longhouse ... those are the core values. Respect being one of the big ones, and that is rampant through any Aboriginal culture, and it does not matter what it is. That is what we are trying to bring out.

The counsellors, who perceive their role as welcoming and inclusive, emphasize the universality of traditional Aboriginal teachings. What is particularly interesting is how their comments about the universality of traditional teachings reflect the diversity of Aboriginal students who attend SHSS from all across the province. The Aboriginal counsellors are aware of the potential for cultural conflict between Aboriginal students within SHSS. As a result, they include multiple traditions that intersect the core values that unite Aboriginal student cultures. According to the counsellors, one of their key responsibilities is to mitigate potential cultural conflicts within the larger Aboriginal community. To do so, they espouse a broad understanding of Aboriginal culture and seek to build relationships among students and between students and themselves.

Just as the counsellors serve to facilitate positive and professional relationships among Aboriginal students, so, too, they advocate for positive relationships between Aboriginal students, school staff, and the Aboriginal community. They are aware of the Aboriginal community's distrust of formal educational institutions – a distrust born largely as a result of residential schools. This awareness is instrumental in their discussions with an Aboriginal student's parent(s) or caregiver(s). Mark commented that, on many occasions, he "advocate[d] for the student even at home," where he explained to the parents "what actually happened" at the school. The counsellors indicated that they have earned the trust and respect of not only the Aboriginal students who seek their advice but also their parents and caregivers. Mark offered yet another story:

> A mother has been coming in pretty well daily because her daughter seems to get lost from the time she leaves home until the time she gets to school and she is not making it to school until 11:00. I have been speaking with the mother and finding out what has been going on at home. What can we do to prevent this from happening in the future? We actually came up with a plan of action that will hopefully help her out from now ... till the end of school.

What is particularly noteworthy in Mark's story is not only how the parents sought the support of the Aboriginal counsellors but also how the counsellors' interventions on their behalf are culturally sensitive. According to Jordan: "We know the parents by first name, and they know us by first name, and they can call us up any time they want. We are often at their houses picking up their children and going to events because that's the only way they will get there is if we go to their house and pick them up." Jordan's comments attest to the counsellors' willingness to establish a trusting, professional, healthy relationship with Aboriginal students and their families. Jordan suggested that the Aboriginal community's immediate recourse with regard to communicating with school personnel is not to contact the child's teacher but, rather, the Aboriginal counsellors: "Often they will just call to talk to one of us rather than Mr. So and So, there is that kind of relationship that we have with parents and students ... It is a different kind of relationship because we are getting involved and we are advocating for them a lot in the school system." The counsellors point to the fact that it is because of their positive relationship with Aboriginal students that Aboriginal parents often prefer to communicate with them instead of with the teachers. It is, as Jordan made clear, a very distinct professional relationship.

The nature of the relationship between the Aboriginal counsellors, the students, and the Aboriginal community is, in large part, possible because of the relationship between the counsellors and the school administration. According to the counsellors, it is critical for school staff to recognize Aboriginal students' needs and to be able to situate them historically. According to Jordan,

> We are trying to shift the thinking in the school so that we have the support of all staff. I always fear the day that [the principal] leaves here, but we always have his support no matter what. [The principal] gives myself, [Mark, and Brian] carte blanche to do pretty much whatever we want to do. We can walk in the office and pull student timetables, go down to the guidance office and change their classes, whereas another student would need an appointment and have to go back in a week to make changes to their schedule ... [The principal] understands that and he says just do what you need to do. A lot of things will prevent students from getting their timetable, and I will just walk in[to] the guidance office and go get a big stack of timetables and I will just pull them. The office staff gets mad at me, and I will say I am just doing my job. I will tell them if they have a problem they can go and talk to the principal because he is allowing me to do it and that there are reasons behind it. I am not just favouring these kids. I am doing my job ... We are trying to change the way that people are thinking.

Jordan, Mark, and Brian mentioned the need to gain the support of the school administration in order to ensure the success of the ASP. Note how Jordan and the other counsellors have been given licence to act on behalf of Aboriginal students even if it contravenes school protocol. The counsellors recognize that the principal understands that Aboriginal student realities differ from those of non-Aboriginal students and is appreciative of the fact that, at times, the needs of Aboriginal students take precedence over school protocols. For the counsellors, the positive professional relationships they have established with the school administration allow them to relate to the Aboriginal students on multiple levels. In no way do they blame mainstream teachers for embracing the paradigms of mainstream Eurocentric education; rather, they attempt to function as cultural conduits between Aboriginal and non-Aboriginal ways of perceiving learning.

The counsellors provided numerous examples of just how challenging it was for them to attempt to facilitate the relationships between the school administration, the teachers, the students, and the Aboriginal community.

Particularly challenging were the many roles they assumed in nurturing these relationships in order to maintain a strong level of trust and respect between them and the students. As Jordan described it: "It is hard because some days we are their fathers, some days we are their best friend, some days we are their big brother, and some days we are their disciplinarian." In assuming these multiple identities, the Aboriginal counsellors managed to negotiate their roles while being sensitive to the unique nature of each Aboriginal student's needs.

According to the Aboriginal counsellors, it is the notion of identity that often impedes Aboriginal students' relationships with their classroom teachers. Speaking on behalf of Mark and Brian, Jordan explained:

> You cannot assume that these kids have a mother and a father. You cannot assume that they have a computer. You cannot assume that they have a caring person in their life. You cannot assume that they have a phone or any of the things that you assume people have that are basic conveniences. You have to assume nothing. You have to go back to bare, bare essentials ... These kids live under the poverty level. They are usually from a single-parent family, live way below the poverty line, and usually have little to no income as they scrape by at the assistance level. That is what I think a lot of the teachers here do not understand. They come from a different upbringing; they come from a different ... just the fact that they [i.e., teachers] have been to university and they have had the chance to go to university and teachers' college makes them ... alien to these kids. Just the fact that they wear a suit and tie or dress really nice ... That is why we wear jeans and running shoes, because an Aboriginal kid is not going to identify with a person wearing dress pants and a dress shirt and a tie. They are not going to identify with that because that has been CAS [Catholic Aid Society]. Those have been the bad people in their lives, and they are not going to associate with those people. That is a part of life that they want to forget.

Jordan and the other counsellors spoke of the difficulty mainstream teachers sometimes have relating to Aboriginal student realities. They appreciate how difficult it is for mainstream teachers to establish a genuine connection with Aboriginal students due to their very different personal and professional backgrounds. Intriguingly, the counsellors noted how attire sustains middle-class Eurocentric values to which Aboriginal kids simply cannot (and do not wish to) relate. For the counsellors, the concepts of truth and respect strike at the heart of their successful relationships with students. As Jordan commented:

> Show them the respect and the beauty that their culture deserves. Show them that you care about them and their culture ... You have to earn these kids' respect because there are kids that have been here for three years and they are just starting to talk to me now because they finally trust me. Because they never had anyone to trust in their lives before, and once you break that trust you are screwed.

In all instances the Aboriginal counsellors stated that among the strengths of the ASP are the relationships they have established with students and, in turn, the relationships students have established with teachers and administrators. Jordan assured the students: "We are going to get through this together, and that is where the relationships come." Jordan and Mark shared stories of students' reactions to their interventions with teachers and the vice-principal: "Wow, he [i.e., the counsellor] cares about me. He took the time to go and talk with the teacher, to go and talk with the vice-principal, to get a solution. That is where that trust comes from."

Encouraging a Sense of Self
With regard to the ASP, the Aboriginal counsellors recognized the significance not only of conflicts and of relationships but also of encouraging a sense of self and, hence, of self-determination. According to Jordan, Mark, and Brian, one of the program's mandates is to engage Aboriginal students by building their awareness of relevant cultural knowledge. As Mark suggested, it is of paramount importance to reconnect Aboriginal students to their traditions, values, and beliefs: "I think it is the youths' thirst for knowledge right now that drives them. They do not care where it comes from, they just want to learn about it ... As long as they are learning about Aboriginal culture and traditions and ceremonies, it just does not matter." The counsellors emphasized the significance not only of reconnecting Aboriginal youth to their traditions, values, and beliefs but also of literally reconnecting them to themselves. The exposure to traditional knowledge and traditional practices illuminates, for Aboriginal students, the significance of who they are and why their ceremonies are spiritually relevant. Inherent within the testimonies of the Aboriginal counsellors is the notion that Aboriginal students are often motivated to learn about traditional

teachings in order to further their sense of self. According to Mark: "They are always willing to learn ... They are always attentive, and they want to learn."

There were many testimonials regarding the multiple ways in which Aboriginal students perceive themselves both in terms of their education and in terms of the ASP. Counsellors spoke of how they attempted to engage students culturally by fostering the notion of themselves as complete persons. Their work led to Aboriginal students' being able to see themselves both in the present world of the school and in the future. According to the youth counsellors, the fact that the Aboriginal students are able to attain a sense of self within the social, cultural, and epistemic fabric of the mainstream school enables them to believe that they have a productive future. The Aboriginal students participating in the ASP benefit from the productive relationships they have with the counsellors, each other, their teachers, and (often) their families. According to Jordan:

> We are trying to create a different generation. We are trying to create a different generation of people who will break the cycle that a lot of Aboriginal people have fallen into, and we are doing that by creating stronger people. We are creating people that will speak up for themselves, people that will want to go on to postsecondary [education] and do those things we are seeing.

The counsellors stated that the ASP's mandate was to build Aboriginal students' self-confidence and to empower them to be self-determined individuals. In many respects, this describes the fundamental vision of what the Aboriginal counsellors are trying to encourage – namely, a sense of self and, hence, of self-determination. After reflecting upon Jordan's and Mark's statements, Brian added: "I think about having that balance. Having culture there and having an education there. I think it gives them balance ... It is good for the students to have that." Culture is the means by which the Aboriginal counsellors attempt to enable Aboriginal students to gain a sense of self, to see it reflected in their public education. According to Jordan:

> We are trying to make them see what is out there, and I have always told you a lot of these kids have not left the east end, and they do not know what is out there. They do not know what their lives could entail. Since I have started here we are getting kids to ... do something with their lives.

The idea of encouraging a sense of self, whereby Aboriginal students can see themselves and their epistemic practices being enacted in public school, lends itself to the possibility of self-determination and, in turn, to a sense of hope for the future.

In addition, the work of the counsellors, combined with the interventions of the ASP (including drumming and singing groups), speak to a vision that re-engages Aboriginal students with their cultural traditions. Brian referred to the importance of Aboriginal students developing a sense of their own "self-identity": "Filling that cultural gap [i.e., the unknown] is really important ... Elders going into schools ... When I was going to school, I did not have people like myself going into the schools. If there was, I think you would reach out to those children, those students who you could bring awareness to." For Brian and the other counsellors, the notion of sustaining knowledge cross-generationally is of paramount importance. They understand the role of knowledge in enabling self-determination and equipping students to continue to share traditional teachings with the next generation. The counsellors understand their place not only as role models for Aboriginal students but also as fulfilling communal responsibility to the students in the program. They realize that learning about one's culture is not enough. On a number of occasions, they noted that their self-professed mandate is to continue to teach culture to the younger generations so that these people can become self-determined Aboriginal peoples and students.

However, the counsellors identified a significant impediment to the ability of Aboriginal students to realize this vision of self-determination. At different times all of the counsellors spoke to the absence of an ASP in elementary schools. According to Jordan: "For a lot of these kids once they get to high school it feels like we are just throwing them a life preserver and saying, 'Stay afloat and maybe you will get through high school.'" The counsellors recognized the importance of grassroots interventions with regard to getting better results for Aboriginal children in elementary school. They took a proactive rather than a reactive approach to schooling, insisting that issues need to be addressed earlier rather than later if Aboriginal youth are to achieve their full potential. Jordan continued:

> By the time they get to high school, they would not need as much assistance [as] they do now, and we would just be kind of guiding them through and showing them the way through high school and on to postsecondary. There is a gap right now. There is a gap between the time they start school

in kindergarten and the time they get to high school. We do not have that representation at the elementary level, so in a nutshell we need money, we need resources, and we need people. That is my vision. That has always been my vision since I started at [SHSS].

For the counsellors, the lack of an ASP at the elementary school level is a serious problem, one that contributes to the systemic challenges that confront Aboriginal youth. They believe that the support offered at the secondary level is too late for some Aboriginal youth and forces them to resign themselves to helping adolescents achieve less than their potential. All the Aboriginal counsellors shared stories of the difficulties and benefits of endeavouring to help students achieve a sense of self-determination and success. In many respects, the counsellors see themselves reflected in the stories and experiences of the Aboriginal youth in their care. Even though they know that they serve as role models with regard to the benefits of getting an education, the counsellors see themselves more as role models with regard to the benefits of being people who have found their culture. It is apparent that the Aboriginal counsellors emphasize the significance of discovering their identity, and it this self-awareness that enables them to focus their energies on Aboriginal youth.

School and Program Administrators
The school and program leaders shed light on the administrative side of the ASP. Their observations may be useful for educational leaders who are in similar roles. The principal of SHSS served in this role for eight years (but has more than twenty-five years' experience as a teacher) and has been involved in the ASP since the program's inception in 2003. The principal was largely responsible for marshalling the resources, both human and financial, to enable the ASP to operate at SHSS. He was also the catalyst for moving the program forward as it grew and developed. The vice-principal of the school (also male) has been a teacher for approximately ten years and, at the time of the study, was in his first year as a school administrator at SHSS. The community program leader is female and, unlike the two school administrators, who are both mainstream Canadian, she is Aboriginal and has self-proclaimed roots in a local Aboriginal community in Ontario. As part of her portfolio, she is responsible for overseeing the ASP's cultural interventions and ensuring that the resources are such that program facilitators are able to deliver a successful program.

Three topics emerged from the discussions with these leaders: (1) success and the establishing of relationships, (2) community and school engagement, and (3) strategic recommendations.

Success and the Establishment of Relationships

As the principals of the school and the community program leader explained, the impetus behind the ASP was a recommendation from the local Aboriginal Advisory Council. The community program leader added that, once SHSS had been identified as a potential location for the ASP, the school administrator as well as senior school board administrators provided immediate support in order to bring the program to fruition. She stated that, upon receiving various donations and other fiscal support as well as the endorsement of the local Aboriginal Advisory Council, "we started to build relationships with our champions, and [named superintendent of the board of education] is a champion." The community program leader recognized that, without the support of the senior board administration, the ASP would never have become a reality. She also explained at some length the critical influence of the school principal. She credited him with having the vision and the willingness to invest his energy in ensuring that the ASP would be a critical part of the SHSS's culture: "It was just one thing after another, and it was amazing how everything just really genuinely seemed to work together ... and [the principal] used his influence and expertise to make it come together when we needed to pass a motion or get around a policy." Interestingly, both the community program leader and the school principals credited the Aboriginal youth counsellors for a large part of the ASP's success. In fact, they suggested that, from the beginning of the ASP, defining the role of the youth counsellors had been a top priority. As the program leader explained:

> The hiring of the youth advisor was really important to us because we decided that almost 100 percent of the funds would go into the role of the youth worker. We felt that was really important. Everybody backed up this [role] to see if it would get off the ground, and we had a very strong human resource pool. We had people with qualifications as a lawyer, business backgrounds, teaching backgrounds, and everything in between. It was amazing the résumés that we had to sort through, and then we conducted interviews.

The community program leader, as is evident in the preceding quotation, clearly envisioned the potential influence of the Aboriginal youth counsellor role. In many respects, both the community program leader and the school administration were well aware of the monumental responsibility that the Aboriginal youth counsellor would have in sustaining the program and overseeing its efficacy.

As the three administrators discussed the origins of the ASP and the details of funding, resources, and initial struggles, time and time again they attributed the success of the program to the relationships that were established right from its onset. According to the principal, during the first week of the program, "we had four students, a hot plate, and a microwave." To which the community program leader quickly added: "And a lot of passion, including a very enthusiastic youth worker." Equally interesting were the observations the school principal made with regard to the Aboriginal youth counsellor in the early days of the program:

> [The youth counsellor] started circulating around the school and talking to the staff and identifying students. We already had about four students identified in our database as Native status, so he made contact with them and started talking with them and building a relationship. It just sort of snowballed from there. They said, "Well, my cousin goes to this school and he is Aboriginal, and that person there is related to so and so who is so and so's mother who is also Aboriginal." It just grew and snowballed within two years from about four or five kids to almost fifty or sixty, and then after two years things started ... We got sort of a system reputation so kids from all these systems [began attending] and now its going to be a Program of Choice so kids can come from anywhere in the school board.

The principal referred to the fact that boundary restrictions are no longer enforced on students who choose to attend SHSS and live outside the school's catchment area. As he described it, the ASP's success has resulted in its becoming what the school board identifies as a Program of Choice. This means that students from all over the district are free to attend SHSS and participate in the ASP. The principal suggested that the success of the ASP is largely attributable to the relationships that were established between the Aboriginal youth counsellor and the Aboriginal students. All of the administrators noted the energy and dedication of the Aboriginal youth counsellors, whose diligence and sincerity fostered their successful relationships with the students. The community program leader described how, during the first year of the ASP, the influence of the Aboriginal counsellor essentially laid the foundation for the program's success:

> We needed a system to let students [who were experiencing difficulty in mainstream classrooms] out of class and go see the youth worker who could then start exploring why. What triggered them [i.e., the Aboriginal students]? What are the real issues here? Was there an incident at home in the morning? Was it something from the night before that triggered this behaviour in class? We wanted to start looking at that and responding to the root systemic needs of Aboriginal kids, and then we could start building a home for them. We realized that these kids did not identify school as somewhere that they belonged, and, for me, I wanted to create a home where these kids did not have one ... Why could it not be at school? Why could it not be in a school system where their peers are here? Okay, so what do you need at home? You need someone that cares that you showed up at the house. You need family members, you need food, you need clothing, and you need some life skills and some guidance there and someone who believes in you. Everybody has to create that. It cannot be just one person. Each person just took a different approach to making sure that everyone ... worked together.

Once again we see that the program leader alludes to the significant role of the Aboriginal youth counsellors. She is explicit about how imperative it is for the youth counsellors and others involved in the ASP to understand Aboriginal students' personal issues and lived realities. Only by having a genuine appreciation of Aboriginal students' lives can Aboriginal counsellors build authentic relationships in what the administrators describe as a culturally responsive learning and social environment.

It was also interesting to learn how each of the leaders described the significance of establishing a program in a culturally responsive manner. According to the principal and to the community program leader, relationships between the Aboriginal students in the ASP and those who facilitated the program had to be culturally appropriate. This was not possible, however, if student realities were not taken into account. The principal shared the following:

> And the other thing that made this a place that was so accepting was because of the school's socio-economic status. Unfortunately, a lot of our Aboriginal kids come from very impoverished backgrounds, so we have

those supports in place aside from the ASP. We have the Walk-In Closet [for the distribution of free clothes and other material necessities] and we have nutrition programs. So it was just another stream of refugees, but they [i.e., Aboriginal students] are not. They are our First Peoples, so that is why it worked.

The principal, given the intercultural and socio-economic realities of SHSS, shared his understanding of the importance of positioning the ASP within the existing school culture. As for the community program leader, she believed that it was imperative that it be made clear to everyone, including the Aboriginal community, that "this program is culturally based and meant to build intercultural relationships." In many respects, she reinforced the fact that the ASP both stresses and is a part of Aboriginal ways of doing things.

According to the administrators, offering an Aboriginal student program in a culturally sensitive manner involves not only understanding and appreciating student realities but also ensuring that Aboriginal youth counsellors assume an active role in making a difference in Aboriginal students' lives. As the program leader explained: "The youth counsellor was always there to mentor [Aboriginal students] and they had something in common. And then they [i.e., the counsellors] introduced the drum, and that was huge." The youth counsellors are also instrumental in facilitating positive relationships between Aboriginal students and mainstream teachers. All the administrators recognized the profound challenges that faced the Aboriginal counsellor who originally serviced the ASP students, and they each spoke of his success in establishing channels of communication between Aboriginal students and the rest of the school. The community program leader identified the willingness of teachers, administrators, and community members to "sit down and plan together to allow equitable opportunities for our students. With the support of all those people that you would normally see as putting up barriers, actually supporting and having teachers come up to us and say, 'Thank you, you have made my life better because now I am actually helping students, not policing them.'" This is not to suggest that the ASP evolved without challenges. The school principal identified some of the friction with some staff who perceived the ASP as being inequitable given SHSS's multicultural population. As the principal stated: "Yes, there have been some issues, but they have been smoothed over." Again, the importance of establishing positive relationships between all parties was critical to the success of the program. Quite often the community program leader recognized the efforts of the school principal to ensure that the program remained sustainable despite its unanticipated growth. She described instances in which the positive relationships established between herself and the school administration made it easier for the ASP to negotiate various challenges. She also spoke of how developing her relationships with the mainstream school and school board administrators was critical to the program's growth. She identified these relationships as "supportive pathways" that would serve the ASP well on "the road ahead." She also described how, despite having lost a key school board administrator who fully supported the program,

> we still had strong support ... My champions traditionally have moved on, but I think they have twisted some arms, and they will believe in us and see that the program works. But I am also practical. That means getting back to working and continuing to develop new relationships that do not have the history that we have, that do not necessarily have the passion that we have.

The program leader, like the school administrators, acknowledged the support of the mainstream teachers in facilitating the program, particularly in its first year. Yet this did not prevent her from identifying the conflicts that emerged as the relationships between Aboriginal partners and mainstream educators evolved:

> As much as you can say that the teachers were on board, they were on board to learn, but they did not know, the community did not know, the education community did not understand, they just knew the results. They knew what was at the end of the river. They knew about the bodies washing up on shore, and throwing out life preservers was not working either. But you have to teach and educate, and that is why you do it, because everybody would like to help. By the time you stop and teach them, that takes years.

According to these leaders, Aboriginal people understand their realities whereas the mainstream population does not. As far as the school administration and the community program leader are concerned, relationships are fostered through knowledge-sharing. As the community program leader explained, mainstream individuals should be commended for their willingness to assist, but they do not necessarily know how best to assist because they do not always understand the nature of Aboriginal students' realities. A critical component of knowledge-sharing rests with the Aboriginal youth counsellors. Throughout the discussion, the administrators explained how, as well as functioning as advocates for Aboriginal students, the counsellors are responsible for communicating with mainstream teachers, community services, and both Aboriginal and non-Aboriginal parents. The principal explained that, as advocates,

> individual counsellors talk with the teacher about the student and then talk about a different teacher with a student. They talk about an administrator with a student. One of the things that I did put in place was that I never wanted an Aboriginal student to be speaking with the vice-principal without the Aboriginal youth worker there. That is not to protect the vice-principal. That is not to do anything other than to let the student feel that the person who is advising him and working with him is his advocate. A lot of times the vice-principals work through the youth workers and will tell the youth worker to phone that parent and to explain the situation in a culturally appropriate way.

The community program leader added: "We help our youth be accountable, and we understand there are ways in which to do that, and it is not in isolation." The administrators also discussed how the counsellors' relationships with the Aboriginal students were intended to foster a sense of responsibility in the latter. According to the program leader: "[The counsellors are] ready to be there and support them [i.e., Aboriginal students] and understand why the behaviours happened and work with them so that they can be in a position to determine the choices that they make." The relationship between the counsellors and Aboriginal students encourages positive personal choices. Relationships, according to the community program leader, cannot be successful unless the Aboriginal counsellors understand the unique circumstances of their students:

> These kids are coming from homes and environments where a lot of the issues that we are seeing are survival techniques. You have to respect that, but you also have to work really hard and long to change those things, and I know that we all know this. If they [i.e., Aboriginal students] are spending more time in [an] environment where the skills that they are learning are

what is perceived as lying, stealing, high-risk behaviour ... We are their immediate supports ... saying let's send Johnny back home and [tell him] do not dare do drugs in a house that is responsible for drug trading. Okay, how is this a realistic option? ... Let us look at understanding how to create a new pathway out of this type of predicament, and that is what we do with our kids. If they continue to keep making poor choices, we still continue to let them know that we are here for them. They are not [let] off scot-free, but we are here for them. You are still a good person, and we will be here when you are ready.

According to these three administrators, although it is important to genuinely connect with and to appreciate Aboriginal student realities, it is equally important to offer these students support when they are ready to receive it. They explained that the ASP does not impose beliefs, lifeways, or practices on Aboriginal students. The community program leader referred to the complex dynamics that challenge Aboriginal students: "[They] are constantly relocating and coming from unstable homes. The trauma [is the result of] intergenerational effects of residential schools [and] intergenerational effects of cyclical poverty." Like the Aboriginal youth counsellors, who indicated the relationship between their adolescent experiences and their current roles in the ASP, the community program leader saw herself reflected not only in the ASP but also in the varying experiences of the Aboriginal students. In a most telling reflection, she stated:

Why do I drive the program? I drive the program because of my personal experience as a youth. You cannot put a price on that. I am willing to bet my last breath that there will be some kids that come out of this program that will in one way or another, whether it be through teaching, social work, or volunteering, leave their imprint on this community. They already have. But as an adult, and as a result of their experience in this program and of them reconnecting with our traditions as Indigenous persons, they are a whole person. That did not come from an academic degree – no offence as hard work as that is. That came from a self-realization.

The school administrators and the program leader attested to the strength of establishing genuine relationships with all the stakeholders in the ASP. The principal stated quite candidly: "I never met a kid who you could not get to improve by building a personal relationship with them. A personal and professional relationship. Showing an interest in them." In many instances the administrators alluded to the significance of establishing relationships that transcend issues of race and gender. In fact, the program leader cited her own observations of the principal's effectiveness in establishing relationships within the school, particularly with Aboriginal students: "There's that human contact that he [i.e., the principal] has." In reference to the principal's human contact and to the strength of the relationships throughout the program, the vice-principal added: "There is a very welcoming atmosphere [at SHSS and in the ASP], and in this program they can participate with their peers whereas in the other schools those things do not exist." Ultimately, the principal emphasized the significance of establishing positive relationships: "I make sure that I know what their cultural background is … So why wouldn't you continue to do that [i.e., speak to students and get to know them]? Because how can you teach kids and provide for kids if you do not know who you are dealing with?" The principal's comments speak directly to student identity, and he makes it clear that understanding students is at the core of establishing successful relationships.

Community and School Engagement
As the administrators described the evolution of the ASP, it became clear that its origins were very much rooted in the Aboriginal community. According to the program leader: "[We] wanted to seek out the advice of the Aboriginal community to see what the project should be. We did not want to presume to know what the project should be. The only requirement was that it would be Aboriginal-specific." Both the principal and the program leader understood the importance of engaging Aboriginal community interest and in soliciting the perspectives, advice, and counsel of that community in order to fulfill their responsibilities to it. They engaged in numerous discussions with the local Aboriginal Advisory Council in order to determine the logistics of the program and how it could best serve the needs of the Aboriginal students in this urban core. The Aboriginal Advisory Council, according to the program leader, identified Aboriginal student retention as a top priority. Upon drafting the initial idea of the ASP, the administrators explained how the Aboriginal Advisory Council and various other funding agencies approached the Board of Education to propose SHSS as the site for the program. As previously mentioned, the community program leader spoke of the critical support they received from the school board and school administrators to bring the ASP to fruition. She pointed out that it was agreed that the ultimate purpose of the ASP was to

"better the community as a whole." The principal commented on how the ASP and its mandate were a good fit with SHSS:

> The staff is very ... adept at examining the cultural values and the language and the socio-economic happenstance of any cultural group that enters the halls. We have a plan that assimilates. I know "assimilate" is a bad word around the Aboriginal table, but it assimilates them into our community, not a white community. It assimilates them into a multicultural community, so the whole idea of [SHSS] is that it is multicultural, and it is accepting, and it is tolerant. When we introduced the program, that was simply another cultural program, albeit for the First Nations, the first culture of Canada.

The principal further explained not only that the program was rooted in the values, traditions, and beliefs of the Aboriginal community but also that it continues to readily incorporate various culturally respectful interventions:

> Here are the cultural values of these people, including the smudging and the drumming. These are the things that you are going to see, and here are the characteristics of their learning ... [A]lright, so now we apply it to the Aboriginal culture as far as what are the characteristics of this culture, what are their learning characteristics, what are the socio-economic characteristics?

As the principal described the impact of enabling Aboriginal students to engage in their smudging and drumming practices, the community program leader emphasized the importance of these practices for Aboriginal students:

> The drum is very much completing the circle here, and then you have everyone coming. I mean, since when do you get high-risk inner-city youth coming out for a first day of class with very strong attendance ratings? We give them breakfast, and that helps. We have one of our own community members instructing that class, and that is huge because they genuinely share leadership opportunities and support what is happening ... One experience I cannot put into words but is very powerful is what happened with the drum. To see not only the combination of each individual student's path and how they grew and healed through the drum and continue

> to heal. But I came to the first talent show in that auditorium that holds 750 people with standing room only in an inner-city high school where it's hip hop and it's hardcore talent show ... To see our kids open that show and have their peers respect them and applaud them, I will never forget that. I gave up on Kleenex I was crying so hard. That is something that I do not know how you put into a report [in terms of saying] what was given back to our kids.

The principal's, and especially the community program leader's, comments on the impact of the drum are particularly noteworthy. They described how Aboriginal students' participation in drumming enabled them to complete the circle and engage holistically in what it means to be not only an Aboriginal person but also an Aboriginal student in a mainstream, publicly funded provincial school. According to the administrators, Aboriginal students' realities are addressed through cultural practices (such as drumming) that engage Aboriginal students in formal curricular and extracurricular schooling practices. Most significantly, perhaps, they described Aboriginal students' participation with the drum as a process of healing. It is particularly interesting, for example, to learn how drumming engages students on multiple levels. According to the three administrators, the drum heals and so reconciles them not only to the socio-cultural fabric of the school but also to their traditions and origins as Aboriginal people. It was also suggested that the strength of such cultural interventions is a result of community engagement in school practices. The program leader described how

> every human resource decision has an elder at the table. We can ask questions like "where are you on your healing journey?" because that is something that is important to someone who is supporting students in crisis ... so that they are an appropriate role model and are strong enough to deal with the roller coaster ride. Because our youth counsellors take a lot. They are dealing with a lot of issues.

Just as the advice of program leaders and advisory groups is sought, so too their presence is recognized within the ASP. According to the principal: "[We] used that money to feed the community on Friday, Saturday, and Sunday. We rent tents, chairs, and barbecues and bring in elders and other people to teach Aboriginal crafts and buy materials for the kids so the kids can partake in Aboriginal or cultural activities on those days." The community program leader supported the principal's comments: "We even made our own drums." The principal further explained how community engagement in the ASP is not limited to facilitating and assisting with cultural interventions on an extracurricular basis. In fact, according to him, the Aboriginal counsellors as well as highly regarded members of the Aboriginal community often join with mainstream teachers to plan a culturally respectful approach to teaching and learning. The principal explained how, during the current semester,

> [one teacher in particular] sits down with [the Aboriginal youth counsellor] and goes through the expectations of the curriculum and goes through his lesson plans and his opinions because that is the danger of teaching Aboriginal kids a white man's opinion of history. All of that is vetted through him [i.e., the Aboriginal youth counsellor] so the Aboriginal kids are receiving education, formal education, that has been vetted by the Aboriginal community as a whole, including our elder. We have been very cognizant of that fact. And those have been very strict orders to my teachers who are teaching those courses.

Particularly interesting is that the principal clearly states that he uses a top-down managerial style to impose his expectations upon the SHSS faculty for the benefit of Aboriginal students.

All the administrators held that the ASP's strength was a result of various community and school engagements. They also identified some systemic barriers to engaging the Aboriginal community in the ASP. For example, the principal cited how the school, school board, and community advisory councils subsidize the Aboriginal youth counsellors. In essence, the Aboriginal community agencies provide the salaries of the youth counsellors, who are officially employed by the school board. In many respects, it is a matter of contracting the services of the counsellors through the mainstream school board. Although the administrators expressed their gratitude for the counsellor positions created through the ASP, they also cited their frustration at not necessarily being able to proceed through mainstream channels to hire these counsellors. According to the program leader:

> My understanding is that if I had to go through the teacher unions I would not necessarily get an Aboriginal candidate that is suited for this role. The selection criteria [are] quite different. Even the interview criteria would be different. What I can ask them, what my expectations are of them, what

their priorities are with the students ... With all due respect to the unions, I do not see that happening.

According to the principal, if more funding becomes available through the various initiatives that he and other ASP stakeholders have engineered, their priority is to hire more culturally relevant advocates to directly address the multiple needs of Aboriginal students: "We should be allowed to hire more culturally appropriate supports for the kids." Much to the detriment of the funding formula that sustains the ASP, however, is the fact that, although the program has grown exponentially in terms of its population, its funding has not kept pace. According to the community program leader: "We are a victim of our own success. Now we had all of these kids here and we did not want to water down the program, so we had to keep up the pace with the program and keep the quality there." The principal and program leader explained how, in order to sustain the program, the non-Aboriginal community became involved in the delivery of the ASP. The program leader explained: "[We] leveraged with food banks. The community food bank used to do a delivery once a week, and other people would donate." The principal undertook various "speaking tours" and wrote applications for numerous provincial grants in order to get the financing to sustain the nutritional supports and other cultural interventions that have become an integral part of the ASP.

Strategic Recommendations
Just as the three administrators outlined the relationships crucial to the ASP and the influence of both the Aboriginal and the school communities, so too they offered strategic recommendations for enabling the program to be self-sustainable. These recommendations would be useful for ministry/state officials, policy makers, and district and school leaders alike. Many times the principal, vice-principal, and community program leader spoke of the need for further funding from the Ministry of Education in order to alleviate the stresses imposed upon the facilitators of the ASP. While the generosity of the various private donors was acknowledged, it was pointed out that additional funding was necessary if the ASP was to continue to offer the same level of cultural intervention and support for its growing number of students. The principal explained that, although the program receives a specific grant for the cultural support it offers to Aboriginal students: "The grant that the ministry gives every board is on a per-pupil basis for Aboriginal students. Those announced last year were based on the 2001

census data." Funding affects all components of the ASP, and the principal and the community program leader approached various stakeholders for financial assistance. The principal referred to various "small budgets" that helped to sustain, for example, the ASP's lunch program. As program enrolment rises, so, too, does the cost of providing lunches to the Aboriginal students.

A second recommendation was related to the notion of accountability. Like the Aboriginal youth counsellors, who spoke about the conflict inherent in attempting to quantify the success of the program, the administrators stressed that accountability cannot be reduced to statistics, numbers, and reports. And, like the Aboriginal counsellors, the administrators indicated that attendance, academic achievement, and suspensions are all very carefully tracked. However, as the community program leader suggested:

> All of the youth counsellors track statistics in graduation rates. I mean that the story of the students themselves is what is important. As I told you before, the student that has just graduated from my college program was a student here [i.e., at SHSS]. Our kids are graduating this year that started out in the ASP when they were in Grade 9 ... That is so exciting.

It was made clear that real success transcends statistics. Thus, the administrators were not immune to the conflict between mainstream measures of success and more culturally relevant measures.

Third, the principal and the community program leader recommended that more Aboriginal youth counsellors need to be hired not only to properly serve the interests of the Aboriginal students but also to protect the counsellors from the emotionally draining work of tending to adolescent needs. The principal suggested that the ASP's success rests largely upon the shoulders of these counsellors: "As long as you have the cultural supports in place and you have the youth workers working with the kids ... [teachers, both Aboriginal and non-Aboriginal] do not have the time to contribute to the success of the students in the way that the youth workers have contributed to this program." The principal recommended that, as the key conduits between Aboriginal students and the rest of the school culture, Aboriginal youth counsellors should be further supported in their roles. He insisted that teachers, given their commitments and responsibilities, do not have the time to do the work of the counsellors. In this he differed from the community program leader, who recommended that more Aboriginal teachers (who would have an understanding and appreciation of

Aboriginal student realities) should be hired in mainstream schools. According to the principal, however, regardless of one's ethnicity, the roles and responsibilities of being a professional teacher do not change. He believed that the youth counsellors were better able to tend to some of the non-curricular issues that challenge Aboriginal students than were regular teachers as the latter simply did not have the capacity, time, or resources to do so.

The principal described the nature of the responsibility that he gives to the Aboriginal youth counsellors. For readers who are school administrators, it might be interesting to note how this principal devolves some aspects of his authority. For example, he recommended that a new mainstream teacher at SHSS should be introduced to one of the Aboriginal counsellors because, as "coordinators of the program," they are in the best position to "deliver the message" regarding the ASP's mandate. The principal explained that the counsellor

> would simply provide a synopsis of the program [to the new teacher] and [explain] what the purpose of the program was. If you as the new teacher had any questions about the program, or if you have difficulty with any of the Aboriginal students, then you are to contact him. It is a graveyard concept. It is one body at a time, and every kid is different, and that is why it consumes so much time. You cannot make a blanket statement like "this is the way it is." It is going to be an individual counsellor talking with that teacher.

For the principal, it is critical that the Aboriginal youth counsellors have the capacity not only to fully endorse the ASP but also to ensure that the Aboriginal students receive adequate culturally relevant support. He insisted that a program like the ASP, which is growing both within the school and beyond, cannot be in a state of flux in terms of financial security. If an ASP is to be self-sustaining, then funding has to be secured so that proper decisions can be made both for current students and for future ones. A guaranteed source of funding would ensure that the program could be sustainable and that decisions could be made based on a vision of what could be rather than simply on everyday realities. According to the principal: "Money just cannot be thrown at it [i.e., the ASP]. It needs systematic money, like a budget, a yearly guaranteed budget, because we cannot plan into the future without it." Similarly, the community program leader suggested: "At this point, with the expansion of the program, I would say we need some further administrative supports to help sustain it." She was referring to the need for more support to help her to oversee the success of the program.

The administrators recommended that programs similar to the ASP be instituted in other secondary schools across the urban core, but they acknowledged the financial challenges of sustaining them. Perhaps of more concern, however, was the challenge of sustaining their ASP at SHSS in light of the fact that one other school (under the same school board) would soon be offering a similar program. The principal showed his concern:

> While we used to get the whole amount of money to fund the program, I now have programs at [another school] so there [are] going to be budget needs, and we are going to apply for this grant and so on ... Now we are carving into the pie smaller and smaller. It is great that we have moved the program into another high school, but they have not increased the resources in the system as a whole to create more funding for us.

The three administrators also recommended that an Aboriginal community liaison person be hired to strategically network among all the key stakeholders in order to service the administrative and systemic needs of the program. Such a person would render the program far more efficient than it is now. As the community program leader suggested:

> We need an Aboriginal liaison that works between the school board, trustee, program, and community levels. You know, they [i.e., the recommended liaison] are the people that meet and understand the evolving priorities of Aboriginal people with regards to education, so they can inform and move things forward in that respect. And they would meet with the Ministry of Education as well.

The above recommendation is concerned with proper communication between all of the significant stakeholders, the idea being that the liaison be as culturally informed as the Aboriginal youth counsellors. Indeed, the liaison would have an even stronger impact than the Aboriginal youth counsellors, and it would be on a larger scale. As the program leader stated:

> You would see an impact. I would like to see the ASP be strong and be coordinated by regular monitoring, support, and connectivity. Further, more outreach into all of the schools, especially the elementary schools, [is recommended]. But also some of the secondary schools that do not have our

program for Aboriginal students [could be contacted] because, when we do that cultural outreach part, it is sharing our culture and helping non-Aboriginal people understand what we are about. And the other part is about Aboriginal kids self-identifying and feeling that pride. It would accomplish two big goals. And to do all of that you need someone to coordinate administratively and be a champion that keeps furthering all of these opportunities so that they do not get lost.

The community program leader understood the profound influence of the ASP's cultural relevance and how it ripples into the community itself. She, like the school administrators, understood that the success of current and future programs demands a significant cost – both concrete and symbolic. As she suggested: "We are trying to get our kids educated so that they can be the teachers. I think that that Aboriginal liaison would be hammering at the board level to change some of the human resource hiring practices."

Parent(s)/Caregiver(s)/Community Members

Just as it is critical to solicit the voices of Aboriginal students, youth counsellors, and school/program administrators, so it is critical to account for the perspectives of the parents, caregivers, and community members associated with SHSS. The ten individuals who attended the research conversation Circle of parent/caregiver/community perspectives spoke freely of the importance of connection to self, connection to Aboriginal cultural identity, and connection to intellect. They attested to the varied connections their children and dependants experienced through their participation in the ASP. Emphasizing these connections, they shared their stories of the procedural, organizational, academic, and socio-cultural influences that engaged and, in some instances, re-engaged their children in formal education and with their identities as Aboriginal persons.

Connection to Self

The Aboriginal parents, caregivers, and community members emphatically suggested that the ASP was instrumental in fostering their children's self-awareness as Aboriginal people and students. They believed that the ASP helped their children to discover their Native identity. As Sarah suggested, the ASP was "absolutely vital" in connecting Aboriginal youth to adult role models who had an awareness of Aboriginal culture and teaching. Sarah elaborated on this, stating that, despite the rather low number of Aboriginal students in any particular classroom, these youth "somehow always seem[ed] to find each other" and that there was "definitely a connection" among them. The others noted how, as Susan described, these connections often parlayed into their children "finding [their] sel[ves]." Each individual, particularly Susan, credited the perseverance and commitment of the individuals involved in the ASP to recognizing the unique talents of the students and "encouraging the kids," refusing to allow them to become complacent in their studies. According to these participants, the ASP providers refused to "give up on them [i.e., the students]" (Susan).

Along with this sense of commitment on the part of the ASP, the participants distinguished how it "buil[t] up their [children's] self-esteem" (Susan). They made it clear that these efforts to enhance and engage Aboriginal student character had not existed during their own schooling experiences. Numerous individuals used similar phrases to support Susan's observation, and they candidly admitted that their lack of self-esteem as adolescents had been a direct result of their having developed very little self-confidence while attending school. Cherry concurred with the others and added her gratitude that the ASP actively "encourage[d] self-confidence" so that her children would not have to be "kept down" by the school system, as she had been when she was a child. In various instances they contrasted their own formal education to what, by comparison, were the immeasurable benefits offered by the ASP. Mary's words are a testament to the emotionally charged experiences that were freely shared: "'There was a racial issue back then too ... It was hard back then in school. A lot of people said you will not accomplish anything. If you are Native and you are female, it was even harder." Linda related to such poignant reflections: "Within this school, it is really really important that the students have that support system in place ... I was always shy of who I was as a Native person. I was not very clear on what exactly happened to us in our history because it was never taught within the school. It was just mainstream stuff that we were taught." Linda attested to how the ASP reinforced a sense of self in her children and other students:

> The first thing they [i.e., her children] mentioned was the guys. [The Aboriginal youth counsellors] are really cool and they serve us lunch every day ... They really talked highly of them ... They have that sense of belonging within this school that I never got to experience at my school. In high school we were perceived as just the Native kids who were not going to amount to anything ... I am really grateful now that they have the courses in the school that are open to non-Natives to actually learn more about us.

Perhaps the most moving words came from Katie, a graduate of SHSS and now a parent. She attributed ASP interventions to enabling her to discover a sense of herself as an Aboriginal woman:

> There was no [ASP] when I first got here, and I was a horrible student. I pretty much never went to class. I always hung outside, and then I got involved in drugs, alcohol, skipping classes, and fighting with people ... And then the ASP opened, and I was one of the first students in the program. It was life-changing for me ... The program helped me so much. It opened my eyes to my cultural heritage that I did not know anything about ... They [i.e., Aboriginal youth counsellors] kept me in school. They helped me stay there ... It even got to the point where I would pick up the work from my class, and I would go to the [Native] Room and work around other Aboriginal students. I probably would not have been as good a person as I am right now if I did not have the support of the program and [the principal of the school].

Along with alluding to the benefits of the ASP with regard to engaging their children's sense of self, parents and caregivers also discussed how the program offered a vehicle for them and the community to have a voice in their children's education and in institutional practices that have traditionally relegated them to the margins. Andrea and Linda shared their frustration at being kept from what Linda referred to as "finding value in education." Andrea spoke to this frustration and reiterated her appreciation of the ASP's efforts to recognize the identity and presence of Aboriginal parents, caregivers, and community workers: "[The ASP] is allowing parents and students to voice any concerns about their education ... There is more parental involvement ... I think parents are more aware of the value of education ... now than ever before." Sarah, Jane, and Linda alluded to the significance of parental and community involvement by underscoring the fact that the ASP creates feelings in students that resonate through their homes and out into the entire Aboriginal community. Sarah spoke of how important it is that institutions ensure that Aboriginal people "can feel good [about] what they can accomplish." Susan referred to what she believed was a direct relationship between her children's strong sense of self and positive identity and their involvement in the ASP. She described how her children

> look forward to going to school in the morning ... Because of the program, they have that sense of belonging within this school and that their

identity is out there. And now they do not feel like they have to shy away because of who they are. Now they think our Native people are being recognized in this school, and they have a better feeling about coming to school.

Jane supported Susan's observations and added that her children's "marks ha[d] improved a whole lot" and that they had "become better students and more confident." Clearly, from the perspectives of the Aboriginal parents, caregivers, and community members, the ASP has augmented their children's sense of self as Aboriginal persons.

Connection to Cultural Identity
As the discussions continued, it became clear that the parents/caregivers considered the ASP to be critical in fostering their children's/dependants' self-esteem and in connecting Aboriginal students to their cultural roots. They offered incisive recollections of how the ASP ensured that their children's experiences as students differed from theirs. As Melissa stated, "If the cultural component had been a part of schooling when we were there, we might have been more engaged." Especially interesting were the accounts of how the ASP was both sensitive to Aboriginal cultures and careful to make cultural interventions available to students without pressuring them to take advantage of them. Jane, among others, said that the ASP "was definitely an asset" for her children due to the "cultural diversity and Aboriginal traditions" it espouses. The singing and drumming groups were mentioned, as were the activities related to the arts and the community feasts sponsored by the ASP – events that, as Susan put it, essentially created "a little community right here for them." Jane, in response to Susan's analogy, reflected: "It is pretty amazing that they [i.e., their children] can find a cultural identity in a school like this that has over eighty different languages spoken ... For the kids to be able to identify with a culture that might not necessarily have been a part of them before is huge."

Mary, too, credited the program with re-engaging her children and dependants with their cultural identity. This was particularly poignant for her as she had lacked such an opportunity in her own adolescence: "I wish back then I would have paid more attention to my culture." Linda reflected upon Mary's comments and contributed her perspective on the negative impact of having had little exposure to cultural traditions in one's adolescent years: "[I went] without cultural teachings back home because they were still in the down low. It was not in the open. The ceremonies were in secret." According to these individuals, exposing Aboriginal youths to their "Aboriginal roots" is an invaluable learning experience that sustains their cultural awareness and augments their identities as Aboriginal persons.

As noted above, in numerous instances the parent/caregiver/community participants indicated that the ASP does not impose cultural interventions upon Aboriginal students. They all acknowledged the merit of availing Aboriginal youth of opportunities for re-engaging with their culture and allowing each student to determine the extent, if any, of her/his involvement in the ASP. As Jane observed, "The involvement is different for each of them." Andrea emphasized the significance of offering program services to Aboriginal youth in a manner that does not oblige them to participate: "It is recognizing our children's baby steps." Others, like Katie, commented how she, as a former ASP student, "felt more relaxed in the [Native] Room environment where [she] knew [she] could just take a five-minute breather if [she] needed to and then get back into [her] work."

The most prominent cultural component offered by the ASP is the drum. Parents and caregivers consistently commented upon the positive influence that the drumming groups had on their children and on other Aboriginal students. Susan noted: "[My child] joined a drum group with the others, and he sings. He knows what is going on when he sees the people singing and drumming ... The drumming was huge for my son." Linda, too, talked about how the drum is very much symbolic of Aboriginal traditions and, time and again, commented on how it connected her children to a sense of pride as Aboriginal people: "I was really amazed when my boys brought home their hand drums. I was just so honoured that I came in to see [the Aboriginal youth counsellors] and say, 'Thank you for giving them that opportunity.'" Like the Aboriginal students, the youth counsellors, and school/program administrators, the parents/caregivers/community members identified the drum as a profound symbol that connected their children to their Aboriginal identity.

Particularly relevant to school leaders and teachers planning or already involved in a similar ASP is the fact that, for these individuals, the cultural influence of the drum took precedence over other ASP interventions. Cherry spoke at length of how the connection to the drum contributed to a heightened level of social and intellectual awareness:

> [I] really liked the opportunity to make a drum. I loved that because, for the first time, I made it and was so proud of myself. I can sing at home ... I started getting my voice a little more. I started getting more confident.

> The drumming has done a lot for me as well as lots of people I know. Before they learned on the drum, they were really shy. Once they got on the drum, they became more comfortable ... They spoke and socialized more often.

Connection to Intellect

Throughout the reflections, there emerged the sense that the ASP established profound connections between identity and culture and that these strengthened Aboriginal students' sense of self. Equally telling were the stories of the connections to learning and to epistemic traditions that enabled students to engage with their formal education. Linda used her son's words to describe the positive influence of the program on his education: "We are learning. Because we are Ojibwa we are learning." Mary cited how the ASP repositioned her children from being students who were on the verge of dropping out of school to being students with postsecondary aspirations: "The program gives them confidence and makes me feel more relaxed because they are thinking of their future. If they went to another high school, I do not think they would have been so positive about their future." As a graduate of the ASP, Katie candidly stated: "I probably would not have graduated without the program. I would not have." She listened attentively to the others as they shared stories of their children's connection to learning and, at one point, interjected:

> The goal that they [i.e., the ASP providers] have is to help these kids where nobody else is willing to help them. They stand up for them and teach them things that were not available before. When they had the first Aboriginal art course, it was one of the first Aboriginal courses offered in [the city] and it was amazing. I loved every day. I loved going to class after that.

Sarah's comments provide further insight into Katie's first-hand testimony. Among the strengths of the ASP, according to Sarah, is the fact that it addresses the learning preferences of Aboriginal students. It is sensitive to their learning needs and attempts to address their uniqueness through academic programming. Sarah credits the ASP's high retention rates (see Chapter 4) with the fact that the program "has expanded and is supporting more kinds of learners."

People discussed how the ASP provides for the learning needs of Aboriginal students – needs that are not met by Eurocentric teaching methods. Given the often painful memories of their own experiences as students, the participants were particularly appreciative of the positive sense of engagement that their own children/dependants displayed – a sense of engagement due, in large part, to how the ASP honoured the diversity of learning. Andrea referred to her son as an example of a learner who excels in concrete, hands-on learning rather than in abstract, theoretical learning: "You can give him anything electrical, and he can do it ... He finds it easier to put something together than to write something down." Susan supported the ASP's efforts to engage Aboriginal students in their respective learning styles and attributed their frustration in formal classroom learning environments to "European influence": "[It] changed our whole value system and how we taught each other ... [W]e are throwing them into mainstream society where we did not even have an English language when we signed all those treaties. You can see the influence of the Europeans." In the eyes of these parents, in many instances, the epistemic and systemic barriers inherent in formal education stifled their children's intellectual development. They readily spoke of the impediments posed by mainstream public educational practices that are not aligned with the learning needs of Aboriginal students. Linda's reflection was typical of others: "The class-oriented system ... Just sitting there and listening to a teacher who is not necessarily talking to you but is talking to a whole class does not give you that one-on-one. I know that I cannot be in a classroom for an hour and just sit there." The ASP offers Aboriginal students a different way to be engaged in their learning – a way that is distinct from that found in traditional Eurocentric schooling practices. Consider Jane's praise of mainstream teachers who honour the "different learning styles" of Aboriginal students and appreciate the educational value of creating "interactive learning" environments that "do not make students sit in straight rows facing the chalkboard."

While mainstream teachers who tailored their pedagogy to the intellectual needs of Aboriginal students were credited, the caregivers were fully cognizant of the fact that there are far too few Aboriginal teachers in publicly funded provincial schools: "There are not enough Aboriginal teachers, [and] there is not enough Aboriginal curriculum" (Sarah). The others fully supported Sarah's statement and freely spoke to the advantages of having teachers of Aboriginal descent who might readily connect to Aboriginal students' culture and epistemic traditions. As one individual put it, "It would be better to have a teacher that is of your culture that can understand where you are coming from and can help you." It was also recommended that, at the very least, mainstream teachers be more accountable and more attentive to Aboriginal students' problems with their schooling: "This is where we need to make the teachers more accountable ... more focused on if a student is struggling. If a student is failing the class, where are the phone calls? It is not consistent. Some teachers are totally into it, and some let the kids fall through the cracks" (Linda). In every instance, the participants commended the school administration and the Aboriginal youth counsellors for their positive influence with regard to re-engaging Aboriginal students in the learning process. They recounted their numerous encounters with school personnel. Consider Susan's comments: "[I remember the times the school principal] pulled my little family aside ... and we had a lot of conversations about my children and where they were going ... I would be crying when he called to tell me they did not show up ... I had that rapport with him. He just gathered these kids and never let go." Others, like Sarah, spoke about the sense of commitment she felt towards the school principal, who made what she described as an obvious investment in her well-being. Katie, a graduate of the program and a voice in the school community, commented, "[The principal] knew my family and he worked with me and helped me stay in school even though I did not deserve to be in school."

In a similar vein, the parents/caregivers acknowledged the contributions of the Aboriginal youth counsellors with regard to facilitating Aboriginal students' intellectual connections. Time and again the youth counsellors were described as "a big help in keeping [their children] in school" (Susan). The Aboriginal youth counsellors were perceived as being "always there" (Andrea) for their children. Sarah pointed out that students "have a different relationship" with Aboriginal youth counsellors in that they are role models who are capable of relating to the students' learning needs and cultural preferences. According to Jane, the counsellors "are really cool." As for Katie, "[The Aboriginal youth counsellors] are perfect. They are kind of like teachers, but they are not actually in the classroom teaching." In many respects, these participants believed that the roles of the counsellors were equivalent to those of the teachers, especially insofar as, thanks to their understanding of their children's life circumstances, they could nurture their learning. This group also acknowledged, however, that because the counsellors were not certified teachers, they faced significant limitations. They thought that it would be ideal if their children could feel the same level of trust, respect, and intellectual connectedness with their teachers that they did with their counsellors. As Linda said, "These kids develop a relationship [and] come to trust and respect [the youth counsellors]." Furthermore, parents/caregivers thought that the Aboriginal counsellors represented their interests. Sarah said that Aboriginal parents are often "overworked and underpaid," that they "are all very strapped," and that mainstream educators should not see them as uninterested in their children's education. She spoke of how youth counsellors could relate to these realities in the Aboriginal community and commended them for advocating for their children.

Teachers

There was also a research conversation with the two Aboriginal studies teachers at SHSS, both of whom are mainstream. The female teacher, Paula, has over twenty-five years' teaching experience, has been involved in the ASP for nearly five years, and has had exposure to Aboriginal culture, teachings, and traditions for over thirty years. The male teacher, Bob, has over six years' teaching experience and has been teaching the Native studies courses for one academic year. Through the course of the discussion the teachers stressed the importance of the following topics: (1) navigating the educational environment, (2) accounting for cultural influences, and (3) relationships.

Navigating the Educational Environment

Both of the teachers readily identified Aboriginal student learning needs as distinct from mainstream student learning needs. They suggested that Aboriginal students acquire knowledge differently than do mainstream students and, as a result, have unique learning needs that are not necessarily addressed by traditional Eurocentric educational practices and learning environments. They said that the learning environments they created in their Aboriginal studies classrooms were in many respects different from those they created in their mainstream classrooms. Paula predominantly taught Aboriginal arts courses, including visual and media arts. Bob taught Aboriginal history courses. According to Paula: "As soon as they [i.e., Aboriginal students] see printed pages, they shut down. When I get them to read out loud, a lot of them do not read well out loud. I am sure that you [i.e., Bob] have found that with the density [of the reading materials used in] the history courses." Paula, like Bob, recognized the epistemic tensions and conflicts between mainstream curricula, traditional pedagogy, and the learning needs of Aboriginal students. They both believed that it is imperative to be aware of the fact that Aboriginal students' oral traditions lend themselves to learning preferences that are not dependent upon the written word. They indicated that their students' traditional communities do not necessarily value written texts in the same manner as do mainstream communities. Particularly interesting are the accounts that both Paula and Bob shared pertaining to negotiating the OME curriculum. Both stated that it is absolutely necessary to structure curriculum, teaching, and learning to accommodate the preferences of Aboriginal students.

Both noted how the OME Aboriginal Policy Framework document (2007) distinguishes what they believe are core characteristics of both the Aboriginal learner and Aboriginal epistemologies. However, they spoke to the document's inability to "deal with a very broad range of social origins, whether it be different clans, different tribes, different localities in Ontario and other site-specific things ... It has been fortunate that we are where we are, and we have lots of people in the community who are willing to give of their time" (Paula). According to Paula, she and Bob knew that the Framework existed, but it was not always of paramount importance in their planning. Bob explained the process of negotiating the curriculum to accommodate Aboriginal student needs: "I have taken the ministry documents, and I have looked at them and adapted them for what I feel my students are capable of being the most successful at ... I am trying to get the most success out of my students and to see the students pass and get the most out of it." Both educators tailor their pedagogy and use of the OME curriculum documents, including the subject-specific standardized provincial documents, in order to provide engaging learning environments for their students. They prioritize students' needs over the OME's recommended means of delivery. In other words, both Paula and Bob are willing to revise their pedagogical practices in order to establish classrooms that are more suitable for Aboriginal students. At different times they emphasized the importance of employing strategies that complement Aboriginal students' values and beliefs. According to Bob: "[The Aboriginal students in my class] are very respectful and listen to the different viewpoints that I offer. I always give them a chance to disagree if they disagree or if they find something that they do not agree with or have a different viewpoint. I am sure to add it as we discuss it and bring it into the conversation." For Paula, the key is to engage students in a learning environment that is conducive to their preferences:

> I start every course in making sure that students understand that sense of community and the spiritual teachings ... Also, to ground them by enlarging [their perspectives] because they are still urban Aboriginal youth, and

they do not have a large amount of connection with their grandmothers or with their teachings. For a lot of them this is the first time that they encounter that, and there are some kids who have been into a longhouse or into a sweat but lots of kids who have not.

The educational environment has to be authentic, and this can only happen if the teachers respect the Aboriginal students' sense of self. As Paula explained:

> They have a quiet awe. There is a silence about them that is not in any other part of the curriculum. When there is somebody doing teachings, they just get that you are present for that, and it takes a little bit of cajoling initially to know what the protocols are around that, but once they learn that then they are very there.

According to these mainstream educators, engaging Aboriginal students in the standardized provincial curriculum involves directly engaging their uniqueness as Aboriginal youth. Learning environments must incorporate Aboriginal values and beliefs so that Aboriginal students will find it easier to relate to their schooling. Paula commented on how her journey as an educator has led her to recognize the importance of creating learning environments within which Aboriginal students can comfortably engage in the learning process. She suggested that the Aboriginal learner "learns slightly different than a lot of other students that [she had] encountered."

Not only do Paula and Bob understand the epistemic differences between Aboriginal and non-Aboriginal students, but they also refuse to privilege the Eurocentric approach to teaching and learning. This is particularly admirable, given that both Paula and Bob are products of the Eurocentric educational system. Consider Paula's description of how, very much in defiance of the model of education common to mainstream classrooms, she allows her Aboriginal students a degree of autonomy as learners:

> First of all, you have to get their attention, and sometimes that is a very subtle thing to do. You start from a place of quiet instead of pushing out and questioning, and you just leave them lots of space to think and respond orally. I think that they are generally always wanting to play, so there are lots of ways that you can creatively put play into learning that engages them because most of us are visual and we learn by doing. I just happen to teach a subject that is very hands-on, and it is something that I

have pursued in my personal career as well. I come with a lot of bags full of tricks that you can pull out in a situation where it becomes difficult and you can just throw up your hands and say, "Okay, we are just going to draw now." I think engaging these kids is a lot about keeping them intrigued and enabling them to start the search of learning how to learn themselves and giving them the tools to do that.

Note Paula's use of the idea of "searching," which seems to parallel her own journey as both teacher and learner. Neither Paula nor Bob understands teaching as the act of delivering standardized, externally determined curricula in the same manner to all students; rather, they see it as bringing curricula to life in a contextually relevant and timely way. As Paula suggested: "There is always a way that kids can connect to something ... So there are ways in which you can make a curriculum very vital and at the same time empower kids to get better at what they are doing." For these mainstream teachers, education is about enabling Aboriginal students to carry on in, and to sustain, their own learning journeys. The focus rests neither on grades nor on proficiency in provincially determined literacy and numeracy skills; rather, it is on empowering Aboriginal youth as both persons and students.

Bob's pedagogical approach is similar to Paula's in theory but is often different in practice due, in large part, to the fact that the Native courses he teaches have significant literacy requirements. Given that, as Bob admitted, "there is lots of reading to be done and lots of analysis in textbooks and novels," he believed that it was imperative to "mix it up" to ensure that his pedagogy is non-mainstream in those instances when a mainstream approach would be a detriment to the learning needs of the Aboriginal student. Bob's description of his pedagogical approach is certainly worthy of note:

> I cannot just give the students readings day in and day out. Sometimes we will have a small passage, sometimes I will break things down in notes, and sometimes we will have a discussion or a debate. Sometimes we watch videos, movies, and documentaries, so it is important that I mix it up. I just cannot constantly bombard them with paragraphs and essays. A lot of the assignments that I use make them work but not to the point where it is killing them ... Smaller assignments but challenging enough. I work within the framework of what the students are capable of.

Those who are privileged to teach Aboriginal youth might benefit from Bob's and Paula's refusal to coerce Aboriginal students into a Eurocentric model of education that inevitably, as time and history have proven, fails them. Rather, they altered their pedagogy, engaging culturally sensitive teaching practices in order to address their students' needs. According to Paula:

> [I have] never met a group of kids that are so self-deprecating. You start something like a print-making project, and they say, "This is shit, I cannot do this." Yet when they are done and it is successful, they say, "Oh, I did not know I could do that. Let us do another one." So I think that they are learning a lot about themselves in that process, and I am learning a lot of where they are coming from too.

Paula and Bob also indicated that the process of customizing their pedagogical practice is time-consuming and challenging. Neither ignored the difficulty inherent in working in the ASP. As Paula explained: "It is hard bloody work ... But it is incredibly rewarding." Interestingly, Paula compared her role as a mainstream teacher in the ASP to that of a shepherd who guards her students from going astray. Like a shepherd, Paula acknowledges the difficulty of keeping track of all members of the flock and stresses the importance of guiding each individual student to keep him or her from peril. Bob and Paula's comments testify to the tension that exists when attempting the complex task of reconciling two very different cultures, epistemologies, and worldviews. Nonetheless, they offered many examples of educational spaces that empower the traditionally marginalized Aboriginal students in their classes. Both of them recognized the epistemic conflict faced by Aboriginal students and made informed decisions to employ pedagogical strategies that were better suited to their needs.

Cultural Influences
Throughout the conversation with Paula and Bob, it was clear that they believed that the cultural components offered by the ASP were integral to the success of the Aboriginal students in their classrooms. Though these teachers were mainstream, they distinguished drumming as having a powerful influence on Aboriginal students. As Bob explained: "It has become part of the school culture. Every year when we have the talent show it starts off with Aboriginal drumming, and it has been like that for five, maybe six, years now." Paula also attested to the ASP's various cultural influences. She spoke to the same memorable incident as did the program leader:

> I remember the first time that we did it [i.e., Aboriginal student drumming at the talent show]. You have to know there are at least seventy-five different languages spoken at this school. Everybody plows into the auditorium because it is the talent show, and the kids see all of our friends. All of a sudden the room went dead silent. As soon as we started to drum, it was like, "Oh, they really are paying attention." I think that this set [a] precedent that it is something to honour as opposed to just bland entertainment. It has seemed to work that way ever since.

It is interesting to note how, according to these mainstream educators, drumming is not only a significant cultural element for Aboriginal students but also a ceremony that cuts across cultural boundaries in this multicultural urban secondary school. School administrators and classroom teachers should not underestimate the symbolic significance of the drum for Aboriginal students. Interestingly, both teachers discussed how they have incorporated drumming into their curricula, despite the fact that it is not mentioned in the OME documents. Both Paula and Bob chose to include the drum in their classrooms because it is of fundamental importance to Aboriginal students. However, for both educators, the significance of the drum extends beyond the four walls of their classrooms. According to Paula:

> [Aboriginal students] develop allegiances and alliances based upon drumming. Initially, it is just bringing everybody around the drum. I lucked out the first year I taught it, and [an Aboriginal youth counsellor] presented himself and said, "We will do you first." And I think that is what started the heartbeat and really taught them to rely on each other. It is like a giant trust exercise. Learning how to anticipate and learning how to watch and learning how to be respectful.

The drum, from Paula's perspective, is the metaphoric heartbeat that unites Aboriginal students. As Bob suggested: "[It] brings them together towards a common cultural bond."

The teachers also mentioned the cultural influence of the Native Room, indicating that it is a safe haven for Aboriginal students. As Paula commented:

> If they are having difficulty in the class, they will ask to go to the Native Room and go and cool off and chill out or do some work. Depending on the

situation, often if I see kids really blow out, it is because there is so much going on outside of school that being there [i.e., the Native Room] is probably the safest place for them.

Bob saw the Native Room as a resource that could support teachers' efforts in the mainstream classrooms. He believed that the intervention and support provided by the Aboriginal youth counsellors were critical to furthering Aboriginal students' success. The success of the Native Room is largely due to the professional relationships established between the Aboriginal counsellors, the Aboriginal students, and the school faculty. According to Bob, the Native Room is strategically situated within the school and is not considered a separate entity. Bob, like the students and youth counsellors, suggested that the Native Room, like the ASP, is not

> ghettoized [because] a lot of the students are aware of it in the school and a lot of the Aboriginal students here have friends outside of their own culture. So other students know about it, and they know about the Native Room and the program and the different things that are run in the school. It has become part of the school culture.

Because the Native Room is recognized by Aboriginal and non-Aboriginal students alike, it has a most credible place within mainstream school culture.

Relationships

Strewn throughout the conversation regarding Paula's and Bob's experiences in the ASP are examples of how they appreciate the varying learning needs and styles of Aboriginal students. Paula and Bob teach both Aboriginal and non-Aboriginal students and, as a result, can attest to the pedagogical practices that authentically engage Aboriginal students' various learning needs. Further, both teachers understand that Aboriginal student learning is enhanced by practices that have cultural relevance. They also discussed the critical professional relationships that exist between Aboriginal students, their teachers, other students, and (most telling perhaps) the Aboriginal youth counsellors. From a personal perspective, Paula described how, as a teacher, she was compelled to "do a lot of negotiation for and with the Aboriginal kids. You end up doing a lot of character education." To both Paula and Bob, the concept of relationship-building is paramount when it comes to Aboriginal student learning. These teachers understand that it is crucial to establish a trusting and respectful relationship with Aboriginal students before attempting to engage them in the standardized provincial curriculum. On countless occasions, Bob spoke about his efforts to earn the trust of his Aboriginal students and to make sure they saw him as a teacher who genuinely cared about their realities. This is not to suggest that these teachers are naive with regard to the tension between some of their colleagues and Aboriginal students. As Bob stated:

> Some teachers seem a little resistant with the way they treat the Aboriginal learner, and some teachers are a lot more supportive. Some teachers may not like certain concessions that some of the Aboriginal students are given, and they think that this is unfair and that the Aboriginal students should be treated just like every other student. So when they see that [Aboriginal students are being allowed to go to the Native Room] they wonder why is this student getting to do this or getting to do that and getting away with this when the other students cannot. Sometimes this raises ... a little bit of friction or resistance. But for the most part teachers are supportive.

It is noteworthy that Bob refers to mainstream teachers who believe that Aboriginal students have a privileged status due to their participation in the ASP. He points out that some teachers comment on the inequity of school practices that grant certain privileges to Aboriginal students and not to others. These sentiments also surface in the comments made in the faculty survey (see Chapter 4). Both Paula and Bob suggested that these teachers, who are generally well intentioned, may not understand Aboriginal students' realities. Unlike some of their colleagues, who have doubts about the ASP and sometimes resist it, Paula and Bob try not only to understand Aboriginal student realities but also to accept the Aboriginal youth counsellors as student advocates and use them to help to deliver and shape their teaching. As Bob explained: "I have gone to them [i.e., Aboriginal counsellors] and said that there is this one student who's been missing a couple of days. 'You should see their home life,' they tell me. 'You know, they are dealing with this and that.' Then it really takes you back." It is imperative to account for students' personal circumstances when making plans for Aboriginal student learning. Paula reiterated Bob's impressions: "You know this is already a really impoverished area of Canada and add to that any kind of family disruption, which most of these kids are living in ... They are dealing with stuff outside of school that even the regular population here is not dealing with." According to these educators, Aboriginal students' situations not only differ from but also are often worse than the already impoverished circumstances that confront the majority of students at SHSS. Paula and Bob suggested that if teachers are not willing to account for the epistemic differences between Aboriginal and non-Aboriginal students, then they will never be able to engage Aboriginal students in their classrooms. In many respects, Paula and Bob do not understand why the Aboriginal counsellors are not unanimously accepted by faculty. According to Bob:

> [The Aboriginal counsellors] fulfill an important need in the school, and they seem to be a very important go-between not only with other teachers that students are having a problem with but also by bringing the students' family into it. They are calling home a lot of times, and they know the different situations of a lot of these students. That is where a lot of contact is made by bringing the parents in. They are talking to parents. They are also talking to the teachers and looking after them. I mean, they really fill an important role for these Aboriginal students.

Interestingly, these teachers not only express a genuine respect for the counsellors' roles within the larger school culture but also recognize their ability to bridge the relationships between the Aboriginal students, their communities, and their teachers. They recognize that the Aboriginal youth counsellors play a professional role within SHSS. Paula and Bob also attested to the critical role that the youth counsellors serve in bringing the Aboriginal community into the school. According to them, relatively few Aboriginal parents attend teacher conferences to discuss their children's academic progress; however, when the Aboriginal counsellors host a cultural feast, with drumming and various other traditional performances, Aboriginal parents "are there in support of" their children's participation. Here, the teachers identified another example of epistemic conflict. Clearly, parental involvement is understood quite differently, depending on whether one is taking an Aboriginal or a mainstream perspective. As they explained, from a mainstream perspective, parental involvement consists of being actively present at the school and becoming familiar with one's children's teachers; from an Aboriginal perspective, parental involvement consists of attending cultural feasts and traditional ceremonies. This is an important distinction, and it should be understood by school administrators and teachers alike.

According to Paula and Bob, there are a small number of teachers who do not always support the ASP. They explained that these colleagues saw the Native Room as a place where Aboriginal students could opt out of being accountable for their academic progress. It would seem that these teachers do not acknowledge or recognize the safety and security that the Aboriginal youth counsellors provide in the Native Room. As Paula described it: "[The Aboriginal youth counsellors] acknowledge, think, and walk their [i.e., Aboriginal students'] road."

Paula and Bob also described the relationships that Aboriginal students nurtured among themselves. Both teachers credited the Aboriginal counsellors with being the "right personalities to be involved with the program" (Paula) as they are able to facilitate respectful relationships among students. The teachers noted how pleasantly surprised they were when they observed how Aboriginal students conducted themselves among their peers:

> I was thinking about the kids helping each other [in my classroom]. We were just doing some vinyl cuts, and it was all I could do to stop them from helping each other work on things. You know, I thought, wait a minute. Are they going to share the marks? They are very familial, and it does not seem to matter whether they are from [remote communities] or local[...]. They develop allegiances and alliances that are based upon drumming. (Paula)

The teachers cited examples of Aboriginal students looking beyond the competitiveness of individual grades and coming together to nurture one another's learning journeys. Paula and Bob described how Aboriginal students created a sense of belonging within the classroom. Bob also noted how the Aboriginal students in his mainstream classroom related to one another in a positive manner:

> I find the Aboriginal students get along with each other very well in the classes and, to me, I think they almost form a family. They look out for one another. They know each other very well and hang out with each other outside of the classroom and through the ASP program and the Native Room. They help each other out, and there is a real sense of community with the students and the teacher that are involved with them specifically.

These mainstream teachers described the ASP as being culturally sensitive and culturally appropriate. The ASP provides students with opportunities to avoid the pressures of individual competition and to focus more on the communal benefits of education. This approach is, of course, very different from the mark-driven system most familiar to traditional mainstream students. Interestingly, both Paula and Bob indicated that it is no surprise that, when Aboriginal students are taken away from learning environments that nurture collectivity and collaboration, the end result is profound isolation and extreme frustration.

4
Subplots

It is common for stories to have subplots that are meant to develop character, further the main plot, and appeal to the main action. The story of the Aboriginal Student Program at Soaring Heights Secondary includes a number of subplots in the form of documents and surveys related to the program that move the discussion to a wider audience. Chapter 4 presents the eleven program reports and various attendance records and enrolment data collected between 2006 and 2008. It illustrates a significant and positive trend along a number of indices related to academic success. Increases in the student body of the ASP, credit accumulation, incidences of parental engagement and student attendance, and decreases in interventions, suspensions, and withdrawals contribute to a success story that speaks of an effective program tailored to the individual realities of participating students. The results of the faculty survey are included because they show that mainstream teachers see the ASP as being essentially remote from the practice and pedagogy of mainstream classrooms and offices. This presents a significant challenge to the ASP, and it is important that teachers, principals, and school board administrators consider it in relation to their own schools, communities, and districts.

The subplots serve to enhance the reader's understanding of the stories within the story of the ASP at SHSS. The documents chronicle how the story of the ASP has evolved, as do the records and reports. The survey subplots add yet more layers of perception that serve to further illuminate the details of this program. While the story of the ASP can stand alone, the stories contained within the subplots contribute significantly to the reader's appreciation of the topics at hand as well as to a broader discussion of Aboriginal education.

Student Enrolment, Attendance, and School Records
Six students were enrolled in the program at SHSS at its inception in September 2003. Data indicate that one year later fifty-two Aboriginal students were enrolled. This number remained consistent for the two subsequent years. The academic year of 2006-07 marked another dramatic increase in enrolment as the population grew to eighty students. Over the next two years (2007 to 2008), the program enrolment rose to ninety-five students (see Appendix 2). The rise in student enrolment can be attributed to two primary factors. First, some Aboriginal students residing outside the jurisdiction of SHSS and attending public secondary schools that do not offer this program were able to transfer to SHSS as a result of its being identified as a Program of Choice school. Second, students who had not previously self-identified as Aboriginal asked to be officially registered in the program. Both these factors signify the importance of program exposure across SHSS and the school district itself. The effectiveness of these kinds of programs needs to be well publicized so that the greater community, particularly Aboriginal communities, can learn from its successes and inquire about the feasibility of similar programs in their own areas. Students are drawn to SHSS for the support the ASP offers. More adolescents who were already enrolled at SHSS are self-identifying as Aboriginal and are willing to declare themselves to be Aboriginal people. This corroborates the research that suggests that individuals vary in the extent to which they associate with their ethnic identity (Greig 2003; Verkuyten 2003). Ethnic self-identification, for the students who chose to self-identify as Aboriginal after the start of the ASP, had not been a fixed part of their previous self-perceptions (Hallett et al. 2008).

The program also tracked the number of students who were regularly attending classes at SHSS (see Appendix 2). Like the enrolment statistics for the ASP, those for the SHSS indicated a steady, albeit more gradual, rise in the number of students. This increase in attendance translated into a credit accumulation average increase of 22.5 percent for the total population of SHSS students. The positive trends in the data have been partially attributed to the school's formalized intake procedure. School administrators and counsellors working with Aboriginal students in public education may find the intake procedure helpful. Aboriginal students who express an interest in enrolling at SHSS meet privately with an Aboriginal youth counsellor to discuss their goals for the academic year. After the interview, the youth counsellor drafts a contract that indicates the supports that are needed if the student is to be successful. This process means that each student is accountable for adhering to the responsibilities delineated in the contract.

Just as telling as the rise in student enrolment in the ASP since 2003 is the decrease in the withdrawal rate. In the nineteen reporting periods between September 2003 and October 2008, the maximum number of students who withdrew from the program was four (September 2004 and February 2007). In the remaining seventeen reporting periods, only six students withdrew from the program. The most consistent number of students to withdraw from the program was zero, accounting for fourteen reporting periods. The remarkably low number of students withdrawing from the ASP (fourteen from 2003 to 2008) is testament to the fact that the program has successfully managed to engage Aboriginal students in formal education. The low number of students withdrawing from the program stands in marked contrast to the disproportionately high number of Aboriginal secondary school dropouts across Canada (see introduction). Aboriginal students attending SHSS have discovered that it is to their advantage to stay in school. A vital part of these outcomes is the series of interventions in place to support Aboriginal students in rekindling a sense of pride in their identity and in their being a part of the school culture. In a national context, wherein the mainstream educational system is not sufficiently meeting the needs of Aboriginal youth (Nawagesic and Domansky 2000), the ASP has sustained their interest in school, supported their academic success, and fostered their cultural identity as Aboriginal people.

The school records document the frequency and nature of the various program interventions associated with the ASP from September 2006 to October 2008 (see Appendix 3). Six interventions were tracked, having to do with (1) volunteer activities, (2) Aboriginal parental involvement, (3) education, (4) nutrition, (5) social support, and (6) cultural and language matters. The results of these six interventions are extremely significant as they indicate the wide array of services and supports that the ASP offers to Aboriginal students on a regular and consistent basis. They suggest that the program provides for the multifaceted needs of each Aboriginal student and her/his community and that it understands the importance of each student's formative development. Furthermore, as program coordinators and district leaders note, the program interventions point to a resurgence of student interest in Aboriginal culture. To take two examples, the educational and social interventions speak to the dynamic balance of support systems offered to students in a culturally appropriate manner. The document titled *In a Voice of Their Own: Urban Aboriginal Community Development* suggests that it is imperative to "rebuild Aboriginal peoples' identity, and create a pride in their being Aboriginal" (Silver et al. 2006, 2). The recommendation to involve urban Aboriginal communities in the educational system is reflected in the success of the program interventions at SHSS. Just as *Voice of Their Own* states that a strong sense of community must exist to enable Aboriginal culture to flourish, so the ASP regularly incorporates culturally rich interventions to nurture Aboriginal students' socio-cultural awareness. It extends Aboriginal student involvement in traditional community pursuits by attempting to involve students in the Aboriginal community at large. The educational interventions in particular strengthen students' abilities to advocate for themselves. Aboriginal youth counsellors liaison with parents, teachers, and administrators in order to assist students in developing a "personal capacity [and] agency in [their] life" (Ontario Federation of Indian Friendship Centres 2005, 6).

Program Reports
The Aboriginal youth counsellors authored eleven school reports between December 2006 and October 2008. As a subplot to the larger narrative of the ASP, the program reports document the successes as well as, and perhaps just as significantly, the various challenges that arose as the program evolved. In this subplot, as in that of the faculty surveys, the reader who happens to be a teacher is privy to these conflicts and can take heed of them with regard to her or his own programs and classrooms. The first report (December 2006) emphasizes "the growing demand for youth drum performances" as well as "students' commitment to regalia, dance, and drum programs" offered through the program. It notes the success of the traditional feast that was celebrated during the first semester. Significantly, it also documents "the growth of the program as a result of positive community [support] and school reputation."

In terms of challenges, the report states that, during the late fall, various students demonstrated a lack of coping skills that required "a case by case" strategic intervention. It also indicates that a "liaison with administration" was needed in order to ensure that these particular students were properly supported.

The April and December 2007 reports highlight Aboriginal students' involvement, "knowledge, and proficiency" (April) in various extracurricular workshops as well as their participation in "traditional performances" and "feasts" (December). The challenges they discuss include the "overall aggressive nature of some female students coupled with numerous suspensions." The December report recommends "a greater need for support" during November and December as these months are typically "hard for our students and the Aboriginal community as a whole." Teachers should not overlook this observation but, rather, determine whether or not it is relevant to their own program development.

The highlights from the January, February, March, and April 2008 reports include "performances" by Aboriginal students at local elementary schools (January), "five new students joining [the] program" (February), "15 students making moccasins during March break holidays" (March), a "parent information slide show" to showcase the program services to the community, and securing "a big drum" for the school (April).

The final three reports in May, September, and October 2008 identify the increasing number of Aboriginal students at traditional feasts and community socials and document their interest in "different forms of Aboriginal music" (May). It was noted that the presence of the elder at SHSS had a significant positive influence on Aboriginal youth: "It is great that the students have an Elder that they can talk to because she has a vast array of traditional teachings" (October). The beginning of the academic school year (September) created the challenge of "getting all of [the] youth settled into their classes" given the dramatic increase in enrolment in the ASP. Although a "good problem" to have, this nevertheless points to the logistical challenges of accounting for Aboriginal students' needs within an often rigid semester-based schedule.

Documented throughout the series of reports is the sense of inclusiveness the program fostered within the Aboriginal student community. The accomplishments identified in the reports recognize the importance of soliciting positive support from the extended Aboriginal community. Policy makers and district leaders will mark that sustaining the interest of Aboriginal communities in formal education is often a daunting task, given Aboriginal people's lack of trust in Western educational institutions. Ogbu, as cited in Goulet (2001, 69), states that Aboriginal peoples "do not believe that education and individual effort will eliminate discrimination because it is institutionalized and enduring. They do not trust the schools or the people that control them." Aboriginal peoples see schools as hostile environments. If members of the Aboriginal community are invited to participate in the ASP, they can experience at first hand students' commitment to regalia, drumming, and dance programs as well as the revitalization of socio-cultural traditions in a culturally sensitive environment. The feasts, which Aboriginal communities see as both ceremonial and respectful activities, offer community members opportunities to return to school under favourable circumstances and, in so doing, to avail themselves of a new experience of education. Parental involvement in their children's education augments Aboriginal student success and increases school attendance (Minister's National Working Group on Education 2002). According to the program reports, the ASP has facilitated cultural cohesion, thus enabling Aboriginal students to take advantage of their biculturalism. It offers students opportunities to "exemplify their knowledge and proficiency" (April 2007) in areas that are meaningful for them as Aboriginal people and students in the mainstream educational system. In this way, Aboriginal students are further engaged in formal schooling. The program's accomplishments may also be partially attributed to the fact that it raises the awareness of prospective secondary school students by performing traditional music and dance at various elementary schools across the region.

School administrators and guidance counsellors will notice how the ASP works towards "accommodating students' schedules" so that they can enrol in Aboriginal courses that provide culturally relevant learning. This provides students with a further impetus to remain in school and strengthens their sense of Aboriginal identity. For years Aboriginal people have argued that their children should be privy to educational experiences that incorporate their values. Eurocentric curricula do not typically represent Aboriginal epistemologies (Dieter-Meyer 2006). Focusing on the academic development of each individual student, the ASP recognizes and celebrates Aboriginal knowledge and social traditions while being in harmony with mainstream academic expectations. The lesson for program developers is clear: the program must acknowledge Aboriginal students' distinctiveness (see, for example, Battiste 2002; Hill 2000) and honour their sense of identity while not excluding them from Eurocentric paradigms of teaching and learning. Research suggests that the implementation of solely Eurocentric academic practices, beliefs, and values further marginalizes Aboriginal children and is counterproductive to their ability to achieve academic success (Schissel and Wotherspoon 2003).

The importance of the presence of the elder at SHSS cannot be overstated. She heightens Aboriginal students' sense of identity and represents a spiritual and symbolic link to traditional values and teachings. She ensures that Aboriginal students have immediate access to culturally relevant guidance. Just as the ASP provides for students' physical, intellectual, and emotional development, so, too, it supports their spiritual growth. The reports describe how the ASP offers a comprehensive, culturally aligned, and developmental approach to addressing Aboriginal students' needs. Such a holistic approach creates an environment for Aboriginal students that challenges the inequities inherent in mainstream schools and, in so doing, meets their multifaceted needs. The reports acknowledge the "disappointment" with regard to the absence of various students "from Drum group" (April 2008). Yet they attest to the flexibility of the ASP and its ability to tend to the specific issues that make it difficult for some students to make extracurricular or curricular commitments. The program respects the distinct challenges facing Aboriginal students, and the reports document those interventions that are most responsive to students' needs without threatening their engagement in school.

Student Survey

The student survey consisted of seven questions and was administered internally by school personnel. Aboriginal students' responses were overwhelmingly favourable: they cited their reliance on the Native Room as both a social and an academically friendly environment and referred to the ASP as beneficial to their academic achievement. They also distinguished the culturally relevant field trips as contributing to their Aboriginal student identity (see Appendix 4).

The results of the Aboriginal student survey are significant to those considering or currently implementing an ASP as they provide a strong indication of student satisfaction. All of the students said that they "always or sometimes" use the Native Room to do school work, and 90 percent of the sample said that they always or sometimes use the Native Room to take advantage of the various supports and services it offers. The culturally friendly resource assistance is clearly accepted by the Aboriginal students who frequently take advantage of the sense of security it offers. Students recognized that the ASP supports and provides for their unique social, cultural, and epistemic preferences. The fact that each student indicated that the program was helping her or him complete graduation requirements, achieve better grades, and go to school suggests an exceptionally positive outcome. Students not only feel a sense of belonging in the culturally receptive Native Room but also feel more equipped to succeed in school. Their ability to determine their educational outcomes is heightened. Aboriginal students clearly see the ASP as being instrumental to their academic development and achievement. Given that, according to the literature, many Aboriginal people have internalized a sense of inferiority due to the ravages of colonialism (Silver et al. 2006), the ASP focuses on helping Aboriginal students to develop a sense of themselves as self-identified Aboriginal persons capable of succeeding in mainstream schools.

The ASP is successful because students believe that it can sustain their cultural identity and foster their abilities as learners. Although enrolled in a public educational system, these Aboriginal students recognize that their intellectual, emotional, spiritual, and physical experiences are heightened by the ASP's ability to build their capacities as Aboriginal people and learners. They overwhelmingly indicated that they see the ASP as relevant both inside and outside the classroom.

Faculty Survey

The faculty survey, as another subplot, presents the reader with what I believe to be valuable insights. It was meant to bring more individuals involved in the ASP into a larger discussion. The faculty voices were insightful, especially with regard to their views on teacher education programs. For the most part, they disagreed with the statement that their teacher education programs were successful in preparing them to address the bicultural needs of Aboriginal students. Not one of the survey participants strongly agreed with this statement. And they strongly disagreed that their teacher education programs prepared them to represent Aboriginal students' values and worldviews. As to the statements regarding the teacher education program's ability to encourage them to examine their own biases, nearly half of all faculty indicated that they either strongly disagreed, disagreed, or were indifferent.

Faculty members were just as critical when the statements shifted from pre-service to board-led in-service professional development. Nearly half strongly disagreed, disagreed, or were indifferent with regard to whether they were better able to adopt a variety of instructional methods to teach Aboriginal students as a result of school board initiatives. The same number had adverse reactions to the statement regarding the ability of school board initiatives to develop their awareness of Aboriginal student learning styles. Over half of the faculty either strongly disagreed or disagreed that school board initiatives positively influenced their ability to implement a variety of assessment strategies in order to effectively evaluate Aboriginal students. An incredible 80 percent of the faculty either strongly disagreed or disagreed with the statement that Aboriginal parents had a strong professional relationship with the school's teachers and administrators. Nearly 60 percent did not support the statement that the school in which they taught had unaddressed cultural boundaries. For a complete discussion of the statistics, means, frequencies, and test of significant differences, please see Appendix 5.

The fact that so many teachers (73 percent) expressed their strong disagreement or disagreement with the statement that their professional education program was effective in preparing them to address the bicultural needs of Aboriginal students may reflect the possibility that teacher education programs in Ontario have not prepared them to deal with multi-epistemic traditions. Faculty members, regardless of their years of experience, the length of time they have been at the school, and, arguably most significant, how recently they graduated from their teacher education programs, reported the ineffectiveness of the latter in this regard. This may suggest to teacher educators that, among other things, topics such as student diversity and multiculturalism, which have been included in teacher education programs in this province for more than thirty years, have had little effect upon the ability of teachers to address the learning needs of Aboriginal students. While this is not to diminish the energy and attention invested in these and related topics in the faculties of education across Ontario, it does indicate that the theory learned in teacher education programs did not successfully translate into pedagogical practice.

Faculty members' agreement that their teacher education programs did not prepare them to meaningfully represent Aboriginal students' values and worldviews points to the apparent inability of professional programs to illuminate for prospective teachers the unique characteristics and identities of Aboriginal students. Nearly half of the entire faculty who participated in the survey (49 percent) reported their disagreement or indifference to the statement that their teacher education programs encouraged them to examine their own biases in terms of their teacher identity and practice. The literature suggests that prospective teachers benefit from reflective practice during their teacher education programs for two reasons: (1) it enables them to reflect upon and hence critique their epistemic traditions and experiences in public education, and (2) it provides opportunities for them to think holistically about their practice in light of varying student needs. Research tells us that the majority of students enrolled in teacher education programs in Canada are upper middle class, white, and products of the

Eurocentric curricula that they will be commissioned to teach. Hence, their emerging identities as early career professionals, if left unexamined, will ensure that they remain embedded within the same Eurocentric paradigms of traditional schooling that contributed to their initial success. Imbued with these approaches and epistemic understandings, these novice teachers tend to perpetuate the practices, pedagogy, and measures of success that further the educational experiences of the students who are most like them and that continue to marginalize everyone else.

Interestingly, nearly the same percentage of individuals disagreed with (or were indifferent to) the statement that school and school board initiatives raised their awareness of instructional methods to teach Aboriginal students effectively. This is noteworthy since the ASP has been in existence at SHSS for six years and has offered various professional development opportunities and in-services to the teaching staff. The results of the survey would suggest that these professional development initiatives had a relatively low positive effect upon the faculty members' capacities to adapt their pedagogical practices to suit Aboriginal students' needs. Less than half of the faculty agreed that board and school in-services enhanced their awareness of Aboriginal students' epistemic preferences. The results indicate that teachers' ability to implement a variety of assessment strategies in order to adequately evaluate Aboriginal students has not been strengthened as a result of the various professional development opportunities. These results are significant for district and school leaders in charge of teacher professional development.

To compound the issue, less than half of SHSS faculty members reported having benefited from school board and professional development initiatives to create more epistemically appropriate learning environments for Aboriginal students. Relatively the same number of participants acknowledged that they have not acquired assessment practices that enable them to appropriately evaluate Aboriginal student learning. In these classrooms, as one might suspect, the unique learning needs of Aboriginal students are not necessarily represented in the teachers' pedagogy, nor do Aboriginal students perceive themselves to be represented in the mainstream curriculum. Teachers may be employing assessment and evaluation practices that are generally not conducive to Aboriginal students' epistemologies. However, the school board has supported, and the school has delivered, professional development initiatives for teachers that are intended to bridge these understandings. Such initiatives are in line with the literature that suggests that professional development should focus teachers' attention on the unique characteristics of the Aboriginal learner as well as on the tangible benefits of practising in multi-epistemic classrooms. In fact, the OME Policy Framework (2007) states that Ontario public school teachers will have a better understanding of Aboriginal students' needs, values, and worldviews and will reflect these understandings in Ontario classrooms and schools (OME 2007). It would seem that, despite the opportunities for professional development, neither teachers' awareness of such issues nor their pedagogical and assessment practices are particularly strong.

Teachers' perceptions that the parents of Aboriginal students have a weak professional relationship with the teachers and administrators of the school is troubling. Here, too, the OME Framework points to the importance of schools establishing strong community relations with Aboriginal parents who, as it aptly states, have been traditionally marginalized within the educational landscape. The literature shows that parents of Aboriginal children have a profound distrust of educational institutions due, in large part, to the consequences of colonialism, including the well-chronicled horrors of residential schools. The fact that Aboriginal community members willingly enter the school to attend the feasts indicates a degree of acceptance on their part; yet, according to faculty members, there are very few instances of strong professional relationships between faculty and the parents of Aboriginal students.

The results of the tests of significant differences (Bonferroni repeated measures) are also telling, both in the few statistically significant differences that existed between participant groups and in the lack of significant differences. The fact that there were no statistically significant differences reported across all eight of the Likert-scale responses in a comparison of participants' current positions deserves further discussion. To begin, the results suggest that teachers' responses were not statistically significantly different when compared with department chairpersons and counsellors: this despite the fact that, in view of their subject specialty, department chairpersons are traditionally assigned responsibilities over various instructional units (or sections). As part of their responsibilities, department chairpersons oversee curriculum review and evaluation procedures across all grades and academic streams and, hence, are usually privy to more in-service professional development opportunities at the school board level. Similarly, guidance counsellors and special education teachers have additional qualifications related to student learning and student services, yet, in comparison with classroom teachers and department chairs, there were no statistically significant differences in their responses.

In a comparison of participants' experiences (in terms of the number of years employed in their current role), only one statistically significant difference emerged in the responses to the question concerning the efficacy of their teacher education programs with regard to preparing them to represent Aboriginal students' values and worldviews in their teaching. The less experienced participant cohort (one to three years) had a higher mean than the ten-years-or-more cohort. The statistically significant difference between these populations suggests that the one-to-three-years cohort perceived more value in its teacher education program's ability to prepare teachers to meaningfully represent Aboriginal worldviews in their teaching; however, and noteworthy, even though the less experienced sample cohort represents the higher value of this significant statistical difference, its mean value is positioned in the disagree category on the Likert scale. Therefore, the more experienced sample population strongly disagreed with the statement, and the less experienced teachers, based on their mean score, disagreed with the statement. Given this qualification, the statistical difference is less convincing since both populations essentially testified to their teacher education programs' ineffectiveness in this regard.

Furthermore, since there were no statistically significant differences between participants' responses in any of the other seven statements, the result further reinforces the apparent ineffectiveness of teacher education programs with regard to preparing teachers to meet Aboriginal students' needs and encouraging them to examine their biases, regardless of the number of years since they graduated. To reiterate, whether a teacher has been teaching for two or twenty years, the results suggest that the various school and school board professional development initiatives had relatively little effect upon their practice and assessment strategies as they relate to Aboriginal students. The result also suggests that the number of years of teaching experience has no relationship to teachers' perceptions of the professional relationship between Aboriginal parents and teachers/administrators. All cohorts reported that Aboriginal parents do not have a strong professional relationship with teachers/administrators.

The fact that, across all eight statement responses, there were no statistically significant differences when we compared the number of years participants had worked in SHSS has specific implications. First, since the inception of the program, various professional development opportunities have been offered at SHSS that deal specifically with the ASP, its youth counsellors, and its objective of improving Aboriginal student engagement in public school. According to the comparative results of responses to statements 4, 5, and 6 (dealing with school board and school initiatives to assist teachers with culturally appropriate instructional methods, students' learning needs, and assessment strategies, respectively) no differences existed between faculty who have been working at the school for only two years, since the ASP began over seven years ago, or before and during the implementation of the ASP. Once again, this finding calls into question the effectiveness of the in-service initiatives with regard to preparing faculty to meet the unique needs of Aboriginal students.

Given the above findings, it is not so surprising that no statistically significant differences emerged across all eight statement responses when we compared the percentage of Aboriginal students in the participants' respective classrooms and offices. Simply put, a teacher whose Aboriginal students constitute 60 percent of the total student population is not adapting his or her instructional and assessment methods to meet Aboriginal student needs any more or less significantly than is a teacher whose Aboriginal students constitute 5 percent of the total student population. Here, too, the results call into question the success of school and professional development initiatives to equip teachers with the necessary skills and capacities to tailor their practice to the needs of Aboriginal students.

Conversely, however, the lack of statistically significant differences across cohorts with regard to the three statements related to professional development initiatives may also be indicative of their resistance to such in-services. Although merely speculative, it may be significant to consider participants' attendance at in-services, their attentiveness, and/or their willingness to act on any of the recommendations of the various in-service providers.

The qualitative responses to the survey were significant. Faculty wrote readily about "lack of student engagement." They cited Aboriginal students' "sense of segregation and difference" in what many of them referred to as "non-conducive learning environments." In effect, faculty pointed to major tensions due to "the existence of conceptual divides" in their school. These tensions should not be taken lightly.

One department head suggested that Eurocentric pedagogical practices render Aboriginal students "disconnected in the classroom and [result in their] have trouble focusing." Typically, another department head stated: "The Aboriginal students that I have taught at the 4U level [i.e., Grade 12 university stream] tend not to have a fund of broad general knowledge so are insecure in completing assignments." Interestingly, one of the counsellors suggested that the responsibility for the pedagogical challenges that face Aboriginal students in mainstream classrooms rests not with the students, as some of the department heads and teachers implied, but with the "non-invitational Socratic teachers" who refused to modify their practices to suit the diverse learning needs of their students. In various instances, the teacher cohort, like the department heads, stated that Aboriginal students are simply "not used to the traditional classroom setting." One teacher commented: "Traditional classrooms are inadequate to serve Aboriginal students' needs – frequently, despite being very able, they are unable to learn effectively in this environment." Other teachers attributed the challenges faced by Aboriginal students to the fact that "they have trouble fitting into the traditional mould," while yet another recognized that traditional pedagogical practice is simply not conducive to creating an inviting and engaging learning environment for Aboriginal students: "Using a didactic teaching model, common in most curricula, is a bad fit with kids who often learn better by inference and experiential lessons. Writing and reading skills are weak in most [Aboriginal] students."

Just as traditional pedagogical practices represent a conceptual divide for Aboriginal students, so, too, does the mainstream provincial curriculum. According to department heads, it is a profound challenge to "find curriculum that is aware of Aboriginal perspectives, awareness, and affirmation." A survey participant from the counsellor cohort thought that Aboriginal students lacked the "study skills [and] homework [skills] – the routes to success in school" – and that this was an obstacle to their "goals, dreams, [and] plans to achieve their goals." Teachers, too, recognized the conceptual divide in the standardized curriculum. One teacher explained that Aboriginal students "are not represented in the curriculum. There are too many paper/pencil types of tasks. Courses do not reflect their worldview." The majority of teachers readily admitted that such a conceptual divide negatively affects Aboriginal students' engagement with the curriculum: "Most of my Aboriginal students do not enjoy coming to class ... [They] would rather hang out in the Native Room. As a teacher, I do not agree with this." A different teacher made a similar claim: "Most of my Aboriginal students do not enjoy attending class and prefer to work in the Native Room. The students should be in the classroom socializing with others."

Faculty also saw a conceptual divide between Aboriginal students and the protocols and expectations of mainstream public schools. Common in the responses of department heads were observations that Aboriginal students, as one participant suggested, "have difficulty following school rules and routines." A different department head observed: "Aboriginal students at our school find attendance and punctuality challenging." The teachers' voice was strongest with regard to this conceptual divide. One teacher commented on how Aboriginal students did "not conform [...] to school structures such as seating charts, bells, etc." Other teachers referred to the large number of Aboriginal students who do not attend their classes, a fact that one teacher accounted for as follows: "When parents do not value education and enforce this upon their children at a young age, they have lost a sense of control upon their children as they enter secondary school, thereby resulting in a lack of good study habits, work habits. Skipping classes often results without the parents' awareness." Typically, teachers associated the schooling challenges faced by Aboriginal students with a lack of parental support. One teacher suggested: "[The] number one problem [of Aboriginal students] is attendance and feeling comfortable in the traditional classroom setting ... In most cases, contact with the home can help combat this, but in many instances there is little or no support from home." A different individual candidly stated that, when it comes to Aboriginal students, "home does not value or support school initiatives – especially attendance." As a result, according to the majority of teachers, Aboriginal students "have different ideas of how to deal with deadlines, attendance, motivation, etc." Teachers overwhelmingly cited the challenges Aboriginal students faced with regard to "adhering to the basic expectations of regular school life (attending classes regularly and punctually), completing/submitting class work regularly, and a consistent effort throughout the school year."

Faculty members readily described the conceptual divide that alienates Aboriginal students from contemporary public schooling practices, traditional classrooms, and the standardized provincial curriculum. In many respects, they distinguished the cognitive dissonance that Aboriginal students experience in their classrooms. They described how traditional instructional designs do not engage Aboriginal learners and, in numerous accounts, noted how Aboriginal student growth is stifled by standardized literacy practices. They shared their perceptions of how Aboriginal student learning often manifested itself in instances of fragmented learning that were not connected to traditional Eurocentric pedagogical landscapes. While faculty were aware of Aboriginal students' apparent inability to cultivate traditional pedagogy and assessment practices, this was not associated with the possibility that such a conceptual disconnect had to do with the mono-epistemic learning environments within which they existed. Faculty were broadly aware of this apparent disconnect, yet they tended to attribute it to Aboriginal students' inability to learn. Such assumptions present Aboriginal learners in a negative light and imply that their lack of achievement in public school is a consequence of their lack of ability, commitment, and competence. Generally speaking, faculty did not discuss Aboriginal students' bicultural identity issues; instead, they placed responsibility for not achieving better learning outcomes squarely on their shoulders, implying that it was up to Aboriginal students themselves to bridge the conceptual divide. Ironically, they had no trouble identifying these students as marginalized within the public school environment.

The vast majority of faculty members commented on the importance of the "physical and human resources" of the Native Room and the Aboriginal youth counsellors. They consistently identified the "culturally appropriate support services" available to Aboriginal students. Typically, one department head stated: "We have a Native Room on the second floor with support workers who provide for and address the needs of our Aboriginal students." Other department heads held that the Native Room functioned as a venue in which Aboriginal students could "congregate ... study, and plan activities," while others said that it provided students with "help with their courses, snacks and lunch, and just a general hang-out place." The faculty counsellors also saw the Native Room as a strategic locale for Aboriginal students within the mainstream public school. Characteristic of the rest of the responses, one counsellor suggested that the Native Room represents "a home-base for students with lots of resources and food." Unique among participants, one counsellor said that the Native Room was instrumental not only in tending to Aboriginal students' academic and nutritional needs but also in "building relationships [and] acknowledging that some students learn in a different way or format." The teachers' observations reflected those of the department heads. Teachers described the Native Room as representing "a self-contained program with numerous supports." They credited it for offering "extensive" support in a "welcoming and educational environment for Aboriginal students." They often cited how the Native Room benefited Aboriginal students by "offering support, food, counselling, and access to trips and elders." However, nearly half of the teachers thought that some Aboriginal students abused the privilege of going to the Native Room. Consider this teacher's observations: "[Aboriginal students] are generally able to learn in the Native Room. It is an oasis for the majority where they can work in a more stress-free environment. For some (a minority) it is an excuse not to work." Another teacher stated: "We have a Native Room for students to go to [that is] sometimes helpful [and] often abused." Still others were even more candid: "[Aboriginal students] like to leave to go to the Native Room, but when they return (if they even do) work is rarely complete. So it may help them make friends and have a positive self-identification, but it hinders their academic progress sometimes."

All of the faculty said that the Aboriginal youth counsellors supported Aboriginal students in acquiring positive self-images and enhancing their cultural identification (although, interestingly, they referred to these individuals as "support workers," "Aboriginal educational assistants," and "Aboriginal youth workers" rather than as "counsellors"). The faculty counsellors credited the "culturally appropriate support workers" and "[Aboriginal youth] counsellors" with providing culturally significant support to Aboriginal students. The teachers stated that the "support staff," "the two Aboriginal workers," and the "Aboriginal youth workers" provided a culturally respectful space for Aboriginal students who choose "to leave the regular classroom when they cannot cope." According to one teacher, the "Aboriginal youth advisors" are facilitators of the Native Room, "which allows Aboriginal students to go where they can work quietly, get help, and even have lunch. The workers within this room prepare lunch daily, and all Aboriginal students are allowed to come to this room and have lunch free." Some teachers commented that SHSS

> has many programs and supports available ... towards helping Aboriginal students acquire self- and cultural identification, more so than any other cultural group within the school. We have an Aboriginal classroom which caters to the Aboriginal students ... if they do not want to be in the regular classroom. This classroom has Aboriginal workers that help the students in whatever capacity the students need.

Last, the faculty indicated that the ASP provided culturally relevant curricular and extracurricular activities for Aboriginal students that enabled them to share and learn about their culture and traditions. They pointed to the "classes in place that bring Aboriginal culture into the classroom," the "four Native courses taught at the school," and the hosting of "pow wows and other cultural events such as dinners and visits to local areas of cultural significance." They noted the value of "drumming circles [as] empowering for the students as they can share and display their talents through presentations." Teachers cited the ASP's "recognition of and allowance for traditional ceremonies and teachings," such as the "drum group, consisting of Aboriginal students, that performs and holds weekly practices [as well as] consistently performing during our yearly talent shows." Other teachers indicated that the "frequent guest speakers from the Aboriginal community" helped Aboriginal students to acquire positive self-images and to proudly identify with their cultural heritage. Some teachers observed: "Aboriginal culture is celebrated at our annual Artsfest, [at] cultural events, and at a number of other events at the school over the year." More generally, various teachers concluded that the ASP provided "support for Aboriginal students that connects them to their heritage." As one teacher succinctly put it, the ASP "encourage[s] Native kids to help themselves and each other and [to] feel good about being Native."

Faculty acknowledged the value of the Native Room and the instrumental support and guidance offered by the Aboriginal youth counsellors and elder. They credited the Aboriginal youth counsellors with providing students with a safe, welcoming, and culturally reflective space within the school. They recognized that the Aboriginal youth counsellors and the Native Room provided culturally appropriate resources for Aboriginal students. Faculty also described the pivotal role the youth counsellors played in providing food for Aboriginal students in the early morning and at noon, thus acknowledging the various difficulties Aboriginal students experienced prior to the existence of the ASP in terms of meeting basic needs.

Although faculty credited the Aboriginal youth counsellors with providing a culturally respectful space for Aboriginal students, they also said that some Aboriginal students abused the privileges of the Native Room. In a number of contexts, participants indicated how Aboriginal students chose to leave their regular classrooms to go and complete their assignments in the Native Room. At times, faculty tended to frame their descriptions of Aboriginal students' decisions to choose the Native Room as a sort of default mode. In other words, they saw such decisions as reflecting a lack of motivation to remain in the traditional classroom. This suggests that some teachers viewed the choice to work in the Native Room as a disinclination to do what is necessary to succeed in mainstream classrooms.

The juxtaposition of various faculty perceptions of the Native Room is quite intriguing. It seems that some teachers, department chairs, and counsellors recognize the value of the Native Room with regard to fostering a positive student identity but also take a dim view of Aboriginal students' decisions to work in the Native Room rather than in the traditional classroom. For some, the decision to work in the Native Room seems to undermine its positive effects. Some teachers refer to the Native Room as a "party room" and as a reprieve from the rigours of the mainstream classroom. While acknowledging the Native Room as a resource for Aboriginal students who are struggling to locate their sense of self in public school culture, faculty members also thought that some Aboriginal students perceived it as an entitlement rather than as a privilege.

Clearly, the symbolic meaning that the Native Room holds for Aboriginal students, the youth counsellors, and the Aboriginal community is not consistently reflected in the faculty's responses. While faculty recognized how the drum and the various drumming groups enabled Aboriginal students to experience their culture, they (perhaps through no fault of their own) did not consistently convey an understanding of what drumming meant to Aboriginal students, parents, and youth counsellors. For the teachers, the drumming circles and singing groups were extensions of the Native Room and were seen as extracurricular activities, much like the school's athletic teams and clubs. For Aboriginal students, parents, and counsellors/program administrators, however, the beat of the drum reverberated throughout all the social and academic relationships that were nurtured in the Native Room and awakened in Aboriginal adolescents an appreciation of their ancestral histories.

Those who are working with Aboriginal students may gain much from the recommendations offered by faculty members. Department heads recommended "attendance and intensive support" for Aboriginal students to enable them to reach their potential. Counsellors recommended "fostering staff engagement," while teachers called for "increased teacher and student support."

The main thrust of the recommendations concerned "professional development and specific interventions," which included student attendance and student motivation. The issue of student attendance surfaced regularly throughout the survey responses. The department heads recommended additional professional development for teachers and staff to provide "some way to get those [Aboriginal] students to class on a regular basis." Some department heads suggested that the ASP should "continue with the support in place" and recommended "more individualized support within the classroom, as opposed to students leaving the classroom for support" at the peril of being absent during instructional time. Among the recommendations offered by the department head cohort are those that reflect this participant's frustration: "Anything that will ensure that these students are in class." The counsellors' focus was on strengthening Aboriginal students' engagement in the mainstream classroom. Counsellors recommended further professional development for teachers and school staff in the hope of illuminating some of the issues that affect Aboriginal student attendance: "I do not know how to push students to excel without overstepping the boundaries." One participant suggested "clarif[ying] ... the issues" that adversely affect Aboriginal student attendance in public schools. Another suggested doing this through providing "professional in-services [for] the Aboriginal learner." Many of the teachers recommended "developing a three-part Native Learner AQ [i.e., additional qualification for the teacher] course." They suggested "develop[ing] curriculum from an Aboriginal worldview in a way that is ready to be used in the classroom [and] integrat[ing] Aboriginal works into English and Art curriculum units that are ready for classroom use." Although such curricular integration strategies may encourage students to attend classes more regularly, many teachers recommended implementing "tracking sheets for classroom work and attendance issues that are monitored on a consistent basis." According to teachers: "Attendance is a key issue [since] they [i.e., Aboriginal students] do not come to class." Some teachers attributed poor attendance to the need for more "parental support." They believed that "stronger ties to their parents/guardians" would be beneficial and would improve student attendance.

Just as significant as the recommendations to improve Aboriginal student attendance are those to improve student motivation. One department head stated: "More professional development on Aboriginal perspectives, interests, identity, and affirmation would allow us to engage Aboriginal students in a more positive manner." Another said that "more background knowledge about [Aboriginal] culture" would allow teachers to tailor their pedagogical practices in a more inclusive and culturally representative manner. One department head's recommendation, however, put responsibility squarely upon the shoulders of the students: "Anything that reduces student apathy ... Apathy goes beyond what a teacher can definitely change. Doing x, y, and/or z will definitely not change student apathy. There must be a cultural shift, and this is generational ... two to three generations." The majority of counsellors, like some of the teachers, recommended "in-services [for] the Aboriginal learner" in order to raise teachers' awareness of their students' epistemic preferences. As one counsellor explained:

> I have to say that some of the teachers do not understand that role modelling is one of the most important aspects of the programming that we offer to students ... I think we can start staff meetings with smudging

ceremonies so that we look to the good of the whole rather than the personal agenda ... I think all staff members should be invited to attend the cultural feasts that take place.

As another counsellor said, all staff members could enhance Aboriginal student engagement in public school if they attended "workshops with current information about the challenges faced by the community – strategies and tips on how to best help students, [including] a clearer understanding of how to reach/motivate/encourage them to reach their potential."

Teachers' recommendations focused on the uniqueness of the Aboriginal learner. One teacher suggested "spending a professional development day with guest speakers (some from the Native community) discussing the Aboriginal learner and related issues." Others recommended "professional development for Native education awareness that shows the kind of strategies necessary to reach Native students." Many teachers admitted to their lack of knowledge about Aboriginal socio-cultural traditions. One teacher stated: "It would be good for us to know more about local Native history and traditions and spiritual traditions so that we could try to incorporate that into our lessons." For some teachers, the issue of Aboriginal student motivation is beyond their influence:

I once had an Aboriginal student in my math class. He never did anything in class. He would come but not complete any work. He was a nice boy who had a good sense of humour. We got along fine, and he got along well with students within the class. He was just too lazy to perform any work. I asked him, "What can I do to get you a credit?" His response was "Just give me the credit." His answer shocked many of us since the students heard his response as well. His reply was very nonchalant and serious at the same time. Aboriginal students, indeed any student, must *want* to learn in order for any kind of learning to take place. They must be open and receptive to the learning. I have discovered that many Aboriginal students are not willing to do the work necessary to be successful, let alone reach their full potential. They want the easy way to obtain their goals. We have support and interventions in place to help *all* students, including Aboriginal students, but the students have to *want* it.

Here, as in other cases, it is clear that some teachers believed that issues related to motivation were predominantly the responsibility of the students themselves.

Faculty identified the need for specific interventions to improve Aboriginal student achievement. Pointing to the frustrations of dealing with spotty attendance, faculty members discussed the difficulties they experienced trying to convince students to attend class each day. Interestingly, however, various faculty members cited a poor work ethic as a contributing factor to chronic absenteeism. They also expressed their frustration with the lack of Aboriginal parental support in ensuring their children's attendance at school. If they were to be provided with meaningful in-service opportunities that would give them insight into Aboriginal values and worldviews, faculty members felt that they would be better equipped to motivate Aboriginal students to attend their classes. They tended to conclude that in-service teacher education with regard to Aboriginal student issues has been far removed from the practice and pedagogy practised in their classrooms and offices. In many instances, faculty were preoccupied with Aboriginal students' perceived deficiencies as learners, their apparent uninterest in adapting to mainstream schooling practices, and their lack of motivation to become more engaged in their studies. While faculty admitted to the multiple factors that negatively influence Aboriginal learners and their families, they did so in the context of mainstream epistemic, societal, and historical expectations. Faculty perceptions attest to the fundamental dichotomy of some educators' understanding of Aboriginal students' experiences in public education.

There is much for educational leaders to learn from these subplots within the main story of the ASP at SHSS. The faculty survey results make it clear that teachers, department chairs, and counsellors need to be involved in the development of such programs from the outset. If all faculty members are invested with a sense of ownership in the scope and design of the program, they may more readily buy into its mandate and objectives. In the process, they may be able to identify the specific areas and topics related to Aboriginal student learning that are most pertinent to their own needs. In this manner, the ASP and its interventions would not be externally mandated; rather, they would be identified by faculty members as having intrinsic professional value. Prospective program developers should consider how faculty-wide participation can serve as a vehicle to enable all educators to examine their own biases. An intimate involvement in the program design may spark educators to consider the sources of their own privilege.

5
Climax: Learning from the Stories

This chapter, in many ways the climax of the story, emerges from the complex narratives that explore the diverse perspectives of those involved in creating, actualizing, and sustaining the Aboriginal Student Program at Soaring Heights Secondary School. It organizes the voices of the participants within the External Medicine Wheel, which includes (1) vision, (2) relationships, (3) knowledge, and (4) action (see below for a further explication of the Medicine Wheel; see also Figure 2). Grounded in these stories are student perceptions of inviting and non-inviting school spaces, conducive and non-conducive learning environments, and the importance of establishing trusting relationships with Aboriginal youth counsellors.

This chapter offers a key observation – namely, that Aboriginal students in the ASP came to realize that they learn best when they recognize and appreciate the skills, attitudes, and values that are unique to them and their communities. It argues that creating educational relevance in the lives of the students participating in the ASP involves connecting them to their culture, which, in turn, reinforces and (in some instances) creates a positive self-image that speaks to their everyday realities. It further suggests that this positive self-image is connected to academic success.

The experiences of all the participants may be seen through the lens of the External Medicine Wheel; however, as the students are of the utmost importance, I honour them by seeing them through the lens of the Internal

FIGURE 2 Engaging two medicine wheels

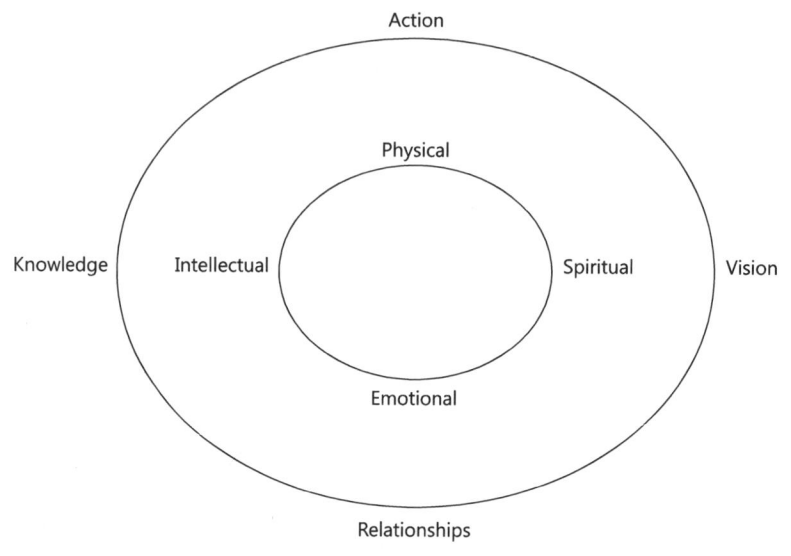

Medicine Wheel. My colleague and friend Lyn Trudeau refers to the Internal Medicine Wheel as the voice of the spiritual, emotional, intellectual, and physical aspects of the self and as what connects the students to their past, present, and future. Trudeau, an Ojibway woman, was an integral member of the team and speaks brilliantly to the recognition that Aboriginal students must be considered from both external and internal perspectives if we are to appreciate their unique engagement in each. Grounded within the Internal and External Medicine Wheels, Aboriginal students may make a place for themselves within the greater society while maintaining a healthy sense of self.

Aboriginal students, youth counsellors, community members, teachers, and school and program administrators all said that community, trust, and identity contributed to the complexity of the unique educational space known as Soaring Heights Secondary School. In the Medicine Wheel, their stories are contextualized in a culturally appropriate manner.

The four components of the External Medicine Wheel reflect the ASP's vision: (1) to provide Aboriginal students with opportunities to take meaningful action, (2) to establish cross- and intercultural relationships, (3) to heighten their traditional knowledge, and (4) to foster their development as self-determining individuals. The following pages offer a glimpse of each component of the External Medicine Wheel from a twofold perspective: (1) that of the Aboriginal student participants and (2) that of the non-student participants. It provides critical information for educators, policy makers, and the community, regardless of the lens through which they are viewing the story.

Vision
The Aboriginal students. It is critical that all program developers and policy makers realize that programs like the ASP must align themselves with Aboriginal students' vision of themselves as Aboriginal persons and learners. The female students often positively referred to the importance of being able to leave their mainstream classrooms during uneasy circumstances. Students, at their own discretion, could decide whether the Native Room was better suited to their learning needs than was the regular classroom: "The program makes it easier for me because I struggled with my classes in math, and with the Room you can get one-to-one help or whatever if you need it. Or if you have trouble working in the classroom with other students you can go down there, and there is [someone] if you need to talk" (Grade 10 female student). The school administration made it clear to faculty that the Native Room provides Aboriginal students with a respite from the challenges and tensions of the mainstream curriculum and classroom. Teachers may take from this that educational spaces like the Native Room complement mainstream classrooms. If they recognize that some Aboriginal students work better in a more culturally respectful place, teachers might be able to structure their lessons so that those Aboriginal students who choose to work elsewhere may do so without being seen as functioning outside regular classroom practice. Here we see the importance of the ASP's vision of empowering Aboriginal students to request access to various cultural supports and trusting them to leave the classroom and tend to their school work in the Native Room.

District and school leaders would be well served to observe that, given their shared vision, Aboriginal students perceive the Aboriginal youth counsellors as their literal and figurative advocates. For the female students in particular, the counsellors' vision is instrumental in guiding them towards making positive choices, especially when in conflict with teachers, administrators, or outside community agencies. As one Grade 9 female student confessed: "You can go to them, and they will stand up for you if you are in trouble. They will help you in any way ... I feel more comfortable with them than I would a normal teacher." Students see the Aboriginal youth counsellors as having the power to advocate for them both inside and outside the school. They did not always perceive their mainstream teachers in the same light. Speaking pragmatically, principals, counsellors, and teachers who are planning or already working in an ASP may benefit from recognizing how, at the ASP at SHSS, the youth counsellors are seen as authority figures. For example, whenever an Aboriginal student meets with a vice-principal, a youth counsellor is present and helps the school administrator communicate with parents/guardians, classroom teachers, community services personnel, and/or legal agencies. When necessary and appropriate, the counsellor helps the student to explain any mitigating circumstances to the other parties. This allows the students to feel they have a strong Aboriginal advocate. Such an advocacy role is only possible if the school administration publicly recognizes it. In the ASP, the Aboriginal counsellors are empowered to speak on behalf of the students during conflict resolution. They have the authority to address teachers when Aboriginal students ask them to do so. In order for this authority to be properly exercised, the counsellor's role must be firmly established and recognized by all school faculty. While there is no indication that Aboriginal students do not respect their mainstream teachers, there is every indication that they are particularly respectful of their counsellors. The fact that the counsellors "are there" and accessible provides Aboriginal students with a voice and a common vision within the mainstream school culture.

The ASP recognizes that Aboriginal students typically withdraw from conflict; consequently, it employs counsellors to serve as intermediaries between students and teachers. This is a vital component of the program. Students feel that the counsellors make teachers aware of the legitimacy of their concerns and thus help to keep them engaged in their classrooms. There is an implicit understanding of shared power between student and teacher, student and counsellor, and counsellor and teacher. Those readers who are currently working in mainstream schools would do well to appreciate the challenges of establishing such power relations. Consider the instances at SHSS when mainstream teachers considered student requests to go to the Native Room as frivolous and as excuses to avoid the expectations of the classroom. One of the students attributed this resistance to teachers "just see[ing] what they see" (Grade 11) and not understanding the epistemic conflict that Aboriginal students encounter within mainstream learning environments. In these instances, some faculty seem to stifle the ASP's vision.

Throughout the discussions, everyone referenced how the vision of the ASP was reflected in the Native Room and the Aboriginal youth counsellors who worked there. For the male students, the Aboriginal youth counsellors were instrumental in creating a welcoming space. In a number of instances, they suggested that the Native Room was a distinct place within the school where their culture, art, and traditions were especially visible and celebrated. This is a realization of the ASP's vision. In each case, the male students expressed their appreciation of the fact that neither the ASP coordinators nor the Aboriginal youth counsellors forced them to participate in the program; rather, they were made to understand that assistance was available "when [they] ask" (Grade 9). Program developers and school leaders should recognize the importance of having supports offered through the Native Room as ASP's vision is to avail Aboriginal students of opportunities but not to force them to take advantage of them. The Native Room is successful because it does just this. According to the male students, the Native Room provided them with inclusive and culturally reflective educational practices that were attentive to their distinct learning, physical, emotional, and spiritual needs. It invites students to work, study, and learn in a more culturally friendly way than do the mainstream classrooms. For these students, the Native Room offers sustenance and support. It offers an option to students who are struggling to discover meaningful learning in the school's classrooms. All students readily distinguished it as a positive influence.

While the male students were aware of the Native Room's benefits, they were also aware that some teachers questioned its viability as a means of providing academic support. In their estimation, this undercut the ASP's vision. Students sometimes sensed a teacher's cynicism when they requested permission to leave the classroom to work in the Native Room. They resented this reluctance to allow them to fully participate in the ASP. Students believed that those teachers who refused to allow them to go to the Native Room did not understand its usefulness. In the students' eyes, this weakened the integrity of the ASP's vision.

According to the oldest male student, teachers who do not perceive the utility of the Native Room do not understand that it is an integral resource for Aboriginal students and that it symbolizes the ASP's vision. District and school leaders should consider the usefulness of establishing an inviting space that provides academic support in culturally relevant ways. The students argued that the Native Room complements their learning. "I have a hard time," the oldest male student confessed, "sitting in a classroom with a bunch of people because they always talk. So, I go down to [the Native Room] and I get my work done. I have computer access; I have books and dictionaries. I have everything I need right there to do a project, a collage, or anything." A space like the Native Room would be useful for any program that wants to enhance cross-cultural student relationships and let students know that culturally respectful schooling practices can co-exist within the larger school culture.

The non-student participants. The non-student responses point to the challenges that Aboriginal students face when attempting to discover a sense of self and a respectful view of their culture within the public school system. Just as noteworthy, though, and also common across non-student participant responses, was an undeniable sense of hope. Although there were many comments regarding the difficulty of meeting certain statistically significant thresholds to prove the success of the ASP, everyone spoke to the need to establish collaborative relationships among all professional roles in the school. The principal and community program leader served as examples of individuals whose agency informed the ASP every step of the way. These players are testament to the importance of establishing strong school and program leadership. Neither of these individuals shied away from the sophisticated challenges that presented themselves; instead, they remained hopeful that they could respond in culturally relevant ways. This reflects the importance of continuing to hope for good educational outcomes despite the fact that these are rare for Aboriginal students (Moss et al. 2008; Perle et al. 2005). It is critical for district and school leaders to manoeuvre the human capital afforded to them by virtue of their authority to seek counsel, to engage in community discussion, to assist in facilitating authentic learning between educators and the Aboriginal community, and to question the legitimacy and fairness of embedded school procedures.

Equally noteworthy is the process by which the youth counsellors and program administrators distinguished instances of what Giroux (1991) refers to as political and cultural contestations in public schools. While the non-student participants certainly believed that the school provided the necessary support for the ASP's vision to flourish, this did not negate their acute awareness of the conceptual boundaries that existed for some mainstream teachers. These participants applauded those teachers who embraced the ASP's ideology and practised the type of pedagogical awareness that the OME advocates in its policies related to Aboriginal education. The counsellors and teachers distinguished how, in those classrooms, Aboriginal students did not have to compromise their values. The counsellors' experiences serve as examples of how to navigate the ASP and the school culture to illuminate for Aboriginal students the complexity of living in two worlds. The experiences of the counsellors and program administrators affirm Giroux, who claims that "it is imperative to develop a language that locates schooling within a moral and social context in order to assess how a politics and pedagogy of difference might be engaged" (508). Program administrators, like counsellors, need to have a profound understanding of the program's vision.

The stories told by the counsellors and teachers introduce readers to educators who are open to the epistemic realities faced by Aboriginal students and who offer them the opportunity to discover meaningful learning across different classrooms. Readers are also introduced to teachers who seemingly cling to the security of more mainstream teaching methods and do not understand the value the Native Room has for Aboriginal students.

The pedagogical details that can be taken from the mainstream educators who made deliberate decisions to represent Aboriginal student identity and epistemology reflect culturally responsive schooling practices (see Castagno and Brayboy 2008; Demmert, Grissmer, and Towner 2006). Whether it involves focusing more on oral traditions than on written histories, creating art and art forms from Indigenous perspectives, or having students sit in Circle to discuss specific concepts mentioned in the lesson, teachers of culturally responsive schooling practices metaphorically "build a bridge" between a student's lived realities and the school curriculum (Pewewardy and Hammer 2003, 1). In all of these examples and those cited in Chapter 1, culturally responsive teachers not only acknowledge the backgrounds of Aboriginal students but also use their unique identities to optimize their learning (Gay 2000).

Teachers who can refashion their pedagogical practice and, in so doing, offer inclusive learning environments are testament to the fact that dominant traditions can coexist with competing ideologies. In these instances, students were offered opportunities

> to be border crossers; as border crossers, students not only re-figure the boundaries of academic disciplines in order to engage in new forms of critical inquiry, they also are offered the opportunities to negotiate and translate the multiple references that construct different cultural codes, experiences and histories. In this context, a pedagogy of difference provides the basis for students to cross over into diverse cultural

zones that offer a critical resource for rethinking how the relations between dominant and subordinate groups are organized, how they are implicated and often structured in dominance, and how such relationships might be transformed in order to promote a democratic and just society. (Giroux 1991, 509)

For educators, program leaders, and Aboriginal community members, the vision of a program like the ASP was most tangible when it facilitated the ability of Aboriginal students to critically negotiate their personal experiences, histories, and epistemic conflicts.

School and program leaders cannot deny that some teachers may not support the ASP's vision. These teachers may not believe that the holistic and collaborative learning environment offered in spaces like the Native Room is a legitimate alternative to a more traditional Eurocentric learning environment. Community members might wonder about teachers who discount the culturally sensitive assistance offered by youth counsellors, especially when some teachers in the ASP saw Aboriginal students' requests to work in the Native Room as an excuse to leave class. All stakeholders who envision an ASP of their own must accept the significance of the program's vision and cultural interventions, both of which enable Aboriginal students to see themselves as represented in their public school experience. Their identities as Aboriginal youth and students, according to participants in this case story, were consistently manifested through the ASP's vision. Parents and caregivers paid attention to the culturally appropriate interventions offered to their children – interventions that facilitated trusting relationships with the youth counsellors and their peers and contributed to self-understanding. The ASP allowed Aboriginal students to categorize and negotiate their experiences with mainstream teachers, the standardized provincial curriculum, and traditional teacher-directed pedagogical practices. It gave students a way of dealing with the reality of being Aboriginal students in a public secondary school, and it offered a viable alternative to what, prior to their enrolling at SHSS, they described as their anxiety-ridden and disconnected experiences of education.

Another key learning to be taken from the story of the ASP, and one that is consistent among all voices, is the importance of establishing a vision of an educational program that is driven by justice issues and that is both equitable and multicultural (see Darling-Hammond, French, and Garcia-Lopez 2002). On various occasions the principal referred to situations in which students (and not necessarily just Aboriginal students) faced difficulties that he considered unacceptable if they were to become authentically engaged in their school work. Citing what could be seen as a moral imperative of caring (as discussed in Ghosh and Abdi 2004), the principal's vision included providing students with equitable opportunities to learn.

Of particular significance to the vision component of the External Medicine Wheel, and something that relates to the Medicine Wheel in its entirety, is the manner in which all of the voices touched upon the notion of self-determination. It would be prudent for readers, regardless of their respective interests in this topic, to conceive of an ASP that facilitates self-identity among Aboriginal students and leads to positive educational, social, spiritual, and cultural experiences. The collective narratives presented here testify to the emergence of self-identity as Aboriginal students gained a sense of themselves as distinct persons and students. They and their youth counsellors described how they were able to succeed in different circles within the mainstream school culture. The counsellors and program leader complemented and corroborated the stories of empowerment told by Aboriginal students who felt in control of their educational experiences.

Castagno and Brayboy (2008), among others (see Beaulieu, Sparks, and Alonzo 2005; Deloria and Wildcat 2001), note the significant relationships between education and self-determination for Aboriginal peoples. Battiste (2002) and A. Wilson (2004) link the concept of self-determination to the process of reclaiming Indigenous knowledge. It is necessary for Aboriginal students, youth counsellors, and community participants to share experiences that enable Aboriginal students to orchestrate their intellectual, social, cultural, and spiritual development according to Aboriginal worldviews. Consider, for example, Aboriginal students' descriptions of how the sound of the drum amplified so that it echoed as loudly in the auditorium as it did in their hearts and homes. They benefited from power and social relationships that existed outside the mainstream school. They were thoughtful about how they approached educational spaces and paid great attention to the perils of dominant educational practices and protocols.

Just as the youth counsellors identified the ability of Aboriginal students to adapt to both mainstream and Aboriginal traditions, so Aboriginal students wove unique understandings of what it means to learn in traditional, culturally relevant, and empowered ways. Where once their experiences in public education were profoundly fragmented, these Aboriginal students now serve as examples of the importance of successfully transgressing social and symbolic boundaries. This enabled them to understand their relationships with their traditions, culture, peers, community, and themselves. As the literature suggests, programs like the ASP can provide Aboriginal students with the resiliency needed to function successfully in their bicultural environments. They do this by ensuring that Aboriginal culture has a central place in the public school (Klug and Whitfield 2003; Reyhner and Jacobs 2002). Students have the opportunity to drum and to speak to its significance. They can showcase their dancing and singing during school assemblies and performances. They and their community can gather in the hallways and large spaces of the school to celebrate traditions and feasts. These are examples of the initiatives that validate the cultures, languages, and traditions of Aboriginal students and, in so doing, allow them to co-create knowledge in public schools (Belgarde, Mitchell, and Arquero 2002). Such programs represent models of bicultural learning environments that enable Aboriginal students to distinguish meaning and purpose in both worlds.

Relationships
The Aboriginal students. The female students involved in the ASP serve to remind principals and teachers of the importance of providing a secure space within mainstream school cultures. These students believed that their values as Aboriginal people were reflected in the culture of the school and that this had a positive impact on their sense of academic engagement. Whereas in the past they tended to, as one of the students stated, "sit there ... and just stare at" their classroom assignments, the ASP gave them the opportunity to go to the Native Room and complete their assignments in a welcoming environment. The female students made numerous references to the impact of the cultural interventions offered by the Aboriginal counsellors: "Everybody is there, and they will explain just what you have to do to get your work done" (Grade 10). Prior to their participation in the ASP, these students felt marginalized in the mainstream school culture and disengaged from their academic commitments. The ASP offered them culturally relevant learning environments that were generally accepted within the broader school culture. At SHSS, the ASP "really ma[de] a difference" (Grade 9 student).

The students' descriptions of authentic relationships testify to the strength of school environments that honour their values and beliefs and so enable purposeful learning. For those teachers of Aboriginal students who are reading these stories, you might take special note of the fact that the students at SHSS spoke at length about how the influence exerted by mainstream teachers who effectively incorporated their epistemic realities into their pedagogy and celebrated Aboriginal traditions permeated the entire school culture. As one Grade 10 female student explained: "She [the classroom teacher] does not talk at you. She gives you a project and she will teach you. Other teachers will talk at you forever until the end of the period then give you your work and be, like, here you go and do it. Ms [referring to Paula] will help you." Culturally respectful teachers, combined with the availability of a space like the Native Room, encourage inclusive learning environments. The potential result is a respectful school culture that supports the social, spiritual, and epistemic uniqueness of Aboriginal students without ghettoizing them. This is important to all stakeholders, from policy makers to students, teachers, and community members. The significance of culturally receptive learning environments, of interventions that re-engage students with their studies, and of the impact of relationships with mainstream teachers who practise culturally inclusive pedagogy should not be ignored.

The female students' reflections on the ASP's impact on school culture are significant. The Native Room and the ASP are accepted components of the school culture, and they facilitate culturally respectful relationships that honour the epistemic and socio-cultural realities of Aboriginal students. The students hold the Aboriginal youth counsellors in high regard. They regularly observe counsellors interacting with mainstream staff as part of school culture. One Grade 11 female student described her relationship with the youth counsellors as instrumental to her re-engagement in public school:

They [mainstream teachers] send you to class, and I used to skip a lot. Being in there [i.e., the Native Room] the counsellors tell you to go to class, and they will talk to you about why you should go to class and why it is important to go to class ... I never used to have this ... The way they [i.e., counsellors] talk to you it makes you realize why you should go to class.

Readers who are currently serving as public school guidance counsellors will no doubt relate to the significance of Aboriginal counsellors to Aboriginal students. The counsellors represent professional relationships that are not only authentic but also able to reconnect students to the broader school culture. As one student suggested, the counsellor represents "someone who cares that is watching and knowing what is going on" in their and in the rest of the school community. Through the counsellors, the Aboriginal students feel they can exert their influence across the entire school culture.

It is interesting that all five of the female students mentioned the impact of the mainstream teachers who incorporated the ASP into their classroom culture. The Grade 12 student proclaimed: "We all skipped to go to her class." And one of the Grade 11 students added: "My teacher knows that I go there." The students recognized that their relationships with the teachers who willingly addressed their learning needs directly affected their learning environment: they felt the difference in those classrooms in which their epistemic preferences were as valued as were mainstream preferences. Equally clear was the impact of allowing Aboriginal and non-Aboriginal students to share their stories as peoples and learners at the beginning of the term. Such practices, as recognized by both the literature and the Aboriginal students, established each person's unique identity. The Grade 12 female student commented:

> Mostly everyone knows we go there, even my first period teacher. There are three other Native kids in my class, but two of them really like to go drumming. So lots of times they will just go and ask the teacher if they can go and drum ... instead of being in his class, and lots of times he lets us ... He is really understanding about it.

These students readily distinguish the positive relationships they have with mainstream teachers whose practice takes account of their cultural realities. Students perceive the value of the teachers who "know most of the students ... and [with whom] everyone is comfortable" (Grade 12 student). If an ASP is to be effective, it must afford students opportunities to explore their epistemic preferences in culturally rich learning environments that are not seen as distinct cultures.

Male Aboriginal students' perceptions of the Native Room and of the Aboriginal counsellors are similar to those of the female students. One of the male students described the benefits of the ASP's cultural interventions in this way: "You get extra help there from people that you know and trust" (Grade 11). One can easily deduce that this sense of familiarity with counsellors who have a genuine understanding of Aboriginal epistemic, historical, and cultural realities is critical if students are to establish nurturing, professional, and trusting relationships with them. In many respects, the trust students invest in their counsellors is at the centre of their academic success. It enables them to feel that they belong in mainstream secondary school culture. Note the impact not only of the support offered by Aboriginal counsellors but also of their interest in a student's welfare and academic achievement. The counsellors earned the students' trust, and students established a strong relationship with them: "You just have to get to know them and what kind of people they are" (Grade 11).

While it is true that the Aboriginal youth counsellors do not have to be certified teachers (as is the case at SHSS), their impact on students' experiences can be profound if they form trusting and supportive relationships. The students who had been enrolled in other Aboriginal programs observed that their former programs were unable to further their epistemic and cultural traditions within sustaining relationships. This speaks to the significant role that counsellors have in establishing themselves as trustworthy advocates of student welfare. All of the students perceived the Aboriginal youth counsellors differently than they did their teachers, and this was mainly because of the higher trust they had for the former. The counsellors were perceived as neither formal "counsellors [n]or teachers" (Grade 12 male); rather, they were perceived as advocates who cared for students' well-being and who offered respectful cultural interventions: "A teacher would just help you, but [counsellors' names are mentioned] would actually come and see us on the weekend if we asked them to help. They are more of a friend than a teacher or a counsellor" (Grade 12 male).

The mainstream classroom environment is not always conducive to Aboriginal students' establishing relationships with their mainstream peers. However, a Native Room, like the one offered by the ASP, functions as the centre of cultural celebrations and feasts that contribute to the creation of positive relationships between Aboriginal and non-Aboriginal students. These events and services enable Aboriginal students to reflect upon themselves, to identify with their traditions, and to appreciate culturally relevant pedagogical practices.

The non-student participants. The voices of the Aboriginal youth counsellors, program administrators, teachers, and parent/community participants tell us that school cultures can be inclusive and respectful. Educators should notice how Aboriginal students negotiated their relationship with their histories, traditions, and ceremonies. Counsellors and community members shared stories about how students embraced the study of history when they could learn it orally rather than from a textbook. According to the youth counsellors and parent/community participants, it was imperative that the ASP not coerce students into participating in any of its components. Teachers can learn from the ASP's ability to build trusting relationships among students, their peers, and their teachers when its vision is realized in the school's classrooms. Programs like the ASP can be an accepted component of the hidden curriculum (Wint 2002) if their resources are incorporated within regular school practice and protocol. The relatives of Aboriginal students can take heart in knowing that such programs do not socially isolate Aboriginal students or make spectacles of them.

The program administrators and youth counsellors indicated the importance of students feeling at liberty to interrogate their sense of self and community within cross- and intercultural relationships. Although the ASP differs ideologically from mainstream schooling practices, Aboriginal parents and counsellors do not perceive it as an instrument for resisting mainstream school culture; rather, they see it as representing culturally respectful practices that locate them and their communities within the school culture. In many respects, parents described the influence of the youth counsellors in much the same way as the literature describes effective teacher-student relationships. Parents cited the genuine care that the youth counsellors demonstrate for Aboriginal students, which is similar to the type of care that Cummins (2000) and Nieto (2003) argue is central to teaching and learning. The stories within the story of the ASP speak of Aboriginal counsellors as persons of influence who can give students the incentive to remain in school. Readers should be particularly impressed by the fact that students exercised their capacities both as Aboriginal people and as students functioning within a mainstream institutional space. The community and program administrator noted the potential of such a program to reconcile students both to their personal histories and to their relationships with their peers.

The stories of the Aboriginal counsellors indicate the positive professional relationships that can be established with Aboriginal youth. Counsellors who are immersed in mainstream school cultures can understand how Aboriginal students are hampered by various schooling practices that perpetuate systemic racism. Practising school counsellors will appreciate the sometimes difficult task of broadening the scope of mainstream teachers' knowledge of programs such as the ASP as well as of the learning needs of Aboriginal students. They might also appreciate the sensitive nature of establishing positive relationships with school faculty. Particularly compelling in these stories is the sophistication of the Aboriginal youth counsellors' descriptions of their relationships with staff members. The youth counsellors professed their awareness that Aboriginal students are challenged by two variables: (1) Aboriginal students have to cope with the physiological and emotional challenges of being teenagers, and (2) they have to deal with what Spencer (2000) identifies as the unique challenges of being members of a stigmatized and marginalized population. It is up to readers to make sense of these observations in the context of their own realities as educators and community members.

The youth counsellors tactfully engaged in conversations with school faculty across what they identified as very different conceptual boundaries. They served as sources of information for mainstream educators, presenting them with discursive frames that enabled them to think about the issues that challenge Aboriginal youth, and they understood that these dialogues often shaped teachers' decisions, behaviours, and attitudes. Thus, the counsellors' role concerns the socio-political and socio-cultural relationships that span the various demographics of the school population. Counsellors can urge educators to be responsive to the complex social systems within which Aboriginal students find themselves and to note the fragile interplay between these systems and each Aboriginal student. In doing this, the youth counsellors can show mainstream teachers how social relations shape the norms, values, obligations, and trust that exist between teachers and students.

The Aboriginal youth counsellors also identified the barrier between the Aboriginal caregiver community and some of the mainstream faculty members. It is important for district and school leaders to account for the sense of distrust that the Aboriginal community might have for public educational institutions. The youth counsellors maintained regular communication with the Aboriginal community, and, by hosting various Aboriginal community feasts at the school, attempted to make that institution a more inviting locale. With respect to their relationship with the school faculty, counsellors realized that some faculty members saw the Aboriginal community's lack of involvement in school issues as uninterest in their children's education. This perception is corroborated by Hauser-Cram, Sirin, and Stipek's (2003) research, which concludes that the more teachers believed that their educational values differed from those of minority parents, the more inadequate was their support for minority students. Counsellors realized such beliefs had the potential to problematize the relationships between student and teacher.

Knowledge and Action

The Aboriginal students. The ASP was instrumental in furthering Aboriginal students' knowledge. The female Aboriginal students credited the program with connecting them to Aboriginal traditions, values, and beliefs, which, in turn, illuminated their identity as Aboriginal women: "Before I came here [i.e., SHSS] I did not know anything about it ... my culture ... I learned a lot more. Now I know how to sing some songs and drum. We made some drums and everything, so that was good" (Grade 10). The reader will note the positive influence that such programs can exert on students' cultural knowledge and its impact on their identity as Aboriginal people. These programs not only re-engage students academically but also enhance both their self-perception and the traditions unique to them as Aboriginal people. As one Grade 10 female student said: "It is nice to know about my background and the history behind everything. It is interesting too and good to learn about."

Participants also discussed the ASP in terms of how it rekindled familial connections through the celebration of traditions and feasts. District and school leaders will notice that students derived satisfaction from bringing their families to the feasts housed at the school and coordinated by the ASP and the Aboriginal community. They spoke of how younger siblings, who had little knowledge of Aboriginal traditions, benefited from being exposed to the ceremonies and feasts given at the school. Similar programs could further the knowledge and self-identity of other Aboriginal parents and siblings. Students benefited from a sense of engagement that enabled them to discover a greater sense of identity. Program coordinators should appreciate the value of such programs, which honour the traditional teachings and stories of the elders. Typical of others, one Aboriginal student observed: "It makes you think ... I think it is good to learn about it even though we are living the way we are and things were the way they were back then. It makes you think in a positive way."

A central tenet of such programs concerns their potential to further students' knowledge of traditional teachings and to positively influence their sense of identity. The students explained that they chose to attend SHSS rather than some other secondary schools because it enabled them to identify with members of their own community and to engage in the process of knowledge-sharing with other Aboriginal youth. Whether it is as simple as hanging student art in a dedicated space, or as involved as arranging for an Aboriginal student singing group to attend an out-of-town powwow, it is clear that principals, teachers, and counsellors should take note of the significance of having access to visual, artistic, and traditional representations of Aboriginal students' worldviews. "Being with our own people," as one student said, makes it much easier to learn about one's cultural values and beliefs. The opportunity to self-identify due to the collective knowledge made available through the ASP led students to conclude that one's identity thrives in an environment in which "everyone has something in common." It is clear that the presence of the elders and other community leaders is a critical component of the ASP. The students "try to learn as much as they can" (Grade 12). According to one female student, the stories and traditional teachings offered by the community "tell us things about ourselves. It's like having a grandma around. It's really comfortable and awesome" (Grade 11). It would be good for readers to make note of the obvious solace that students experienced in the presence of the elder (see below).

It is also necessary to mark the relationship between self-identity and language. Students shared examples of their memorable experiences, giving opening addresses in their own language and discussing how they discovered the significance of language to both their past and present realities as Aboriginal peoples. The combination of learning about their heritage and learning about their socio-linguistic traditions led the students to feel more grounded in their traditions and more a part of the ASP and school culture. Similar programs can also further Aboriginal student identity. Aboriginal students find comfort in sharing their experiences with their own people. Educational leaders should be aware that ASP programs can re-engage alienated students with their educational endeavours.

Policy makers and educators should also be aware of the potential of such programs to align Aboriginal students with culturally sensitive epistemic practices. As we see in the stories of the ASP, the potential exists for students to define their learning preferences and to appreciate their learning strengths. This observation needs to be underscored. Programs such as the ASP can help Aboriginal students make better sense of traditional teacher-directed pedagogical practices and help them understand why they might find formal education problematic. By providing them with a Native Room, the ASP enables Aboriginal students to engage in collaborative and intimate learning environments that are inclusive of their worldviews and more conducive to a culturally aligned process of knowledge generation than is the mainstream classroom. The Native Room and the culturally appropriate counselling associated with it offer Aboriginal students a preferred learning environment.

Aboriginal students' preferences for cultural interventions can be structured to be in line with their epistemic traditions. Aboriginal counsellors can provide clear instructions for assignments, and Aboriginal students can take advantage of a culturally sensitive learning environment that is more suited to their learning styles, less threatening than mainstream classrooms, and non-judgmental. Those reading this book through a teacher's lens should take note that the pedagogy offered in these welcoming spaces is often identity-based, allowing students' stories to factor into their learning.

By becoming aware of their learning preferences, Aboriginal students may become more engaged in their schooling. Whereas in their previous schools students felt isolated, this was not – policy makers and educators take note – the case in the ASP at SHSS. However, it is critical that such a program be a part of the public school and not require students to be relocated to another building. Students should feel connected to the school and engaged in its classes.

The non-student participants. According to the program administrators, the community, teachers, and youth counsellors, Aboriginal students' experiences in culturally respectful learning environments (including the Native Room and their other classrooms) were examples of how competing epistemologies can be used to extend learning. Throughout the discussions, participants commented upon the notion of power and how the representation of knowledge affects Aboriginal students' schooling experiences. I invite you to consider how, as figurative "border crossers," Aboriginal students experienced the complicated and often contradictory manifestations of power within the socio-political reality of knowledge systems and school organizations. The conversations in the Circle often touched upon how, ideally, power is positioned in mainstream schooling to fulfill both teacher and student (Jackson 2004; Toomey 1999). This implies that teacher and student identities are co-constructed, often in accordance with the particular classroom circumstances that govern their interaction (Hendrix, Jackson, and Warren 2003). The issue, regardless of the lens through which you read these stories, is that, in the context of Aboriginal learning, the expected patterns of action, the social and political norms, and the process of knowledge generation are not necessarily acceptable to both parties.

From the ASP, one might learn how power can be positioned so as to establish a relationship between mainstream teachers and Aboriginal students that enables each to respect the other's ideology and epistemology. In the ASP, cultural differences were recognized, appreciated, and fashioned to engage in meaningful action. Aboriginal students, as border crossers with co-created contracts, must be engaged in fluid discourse and thoughtful scholarship that is able to reconnect them to formal education. Aboriginal students' awareness of themselves and their community became more sophisticated, as did their proficiency at navigating the social, political, and cultural milieux of public school. Their experiences resulted in new possibilities. Consider Giroux's (2004, 84) particularly insightful observation:

> Refusing to decouple politics from pedagogy means, in part, that teaching in classrooms or in any other public sphere should not only simply honour the experiences students bring to such sites, including the classroom, but should also connect their experiences to specific problems that emanate from the material contexts of their everyday life. Pedagogy in this sense becomes performative in that it is not merely about deconstructing texts but about situating politics itself within a broader set of relations that addresses what it might mean to create modes of individual and social agency that enable rather than shut down democratic values, practices and social relations.

Programs like the ASP can facilitate opportunities for Aboriginal students to purposefully and successfully mediate their situations.

The centrality of the relationships between teachers and Aboriginal students is of utmost importance. Throughout the stories of the teachers, we can see their willingness to reform their pedagogical practice to meet the needs of Aboriginal students. For the most part, they understood the cultural and epistemic discontinuity between Aboriginal students' realities and traditional teacher-directed classroom instruction and institutional expectations (Ndura 2004; Parsons, Travis, and Simpson 2005). The emphasis must be upon the engagement between teacher, student, and curriculum, and the students must be enabled to learn to understand who they are as people and as learners. What the stories make clear is that there cannot be either one exclusive conception of a student or one notion of learning. Teaching should engage Aboriginal students in reflective thinking and in a dialectical learning process. Classrooms could be reconceived as spaces that cultivate mindful actions and intersubjective understandings that are central to the identities of Aboriginal people and students. Such a pedagogical approach differs considerably from those identified in the literature as reflecting mainstream cultural values rooted in Western worldviews (Baker 2005; Loewen 2007). Aboriginal students' culturally informed behaviour, which is often shunned in mainstream classrooms, is frequently invited and accepted by the teachers at SHSS and is considered a central component of the learning process (Boykin, Tyler, and Miller 2005). In the conversations with non-student participants, we see the consequences for Aboriginal students when mainstream teachers assume a monolithic identity and do not reflect upon the effect of institutionalized power upon marginalized student populations.

Furthermore, the community program leader as well as the counsellors and community participants recognized that the knowledge and action espoused by the ASP and its respective components honoured students' life experiences as Aboriginal youth and students. Community participants noted how their children felt affirmed by the Aboriginal youth counsellors, who related to their worldviews and offered culturally appropriate support to enable them to improve their educational experiences. The parent/caregiver participants spoke of how students' life experiences, whether on a reserve in northern Ontario or in other urban centres across the province, were readily acknowledged by the ASP providers and that this enabled their children to actively participate in their learning. Feeling self-empowered by the culturally appropriate supports and by the relationships with the youth counsellors and their peers, students were able to reflect upon and account for the influence of their past life circumstances and to internalize their uniqueness as people and as learners. Interestingly, the community participants articulated these intensely private experiences while they themselves were making sense of their epistemic and cultural identities in relation to their experiences in public education.

Such awareness on the part of the community and counsellors reminds one of Freire's (1970) concept of praxis, which describes an individual's ability to reflect upon her or his particular circumstances and take actions to change them. The community and counsellor participants stated that students' learning includes a culturally reflective space in which they can internalize knowledge according to their worldviews and value systems. Programs like the ASP offer Aboriginal students the opportunity to reflect upon different learning environments and to translate these into an understanding of what it means to be an engaged learner. Such programs enable Aboriginal students to be better positioned to examine mainstream schooling practices that render them quiescent. The reader can appreciate the complex patterns of interaction that exist between students, teachers, and peers and the challenges Aboriginal students face in attempting to negotiate the epistemic tensions in their schools.

Readers might also consider how the principal of SHSS did what he could to facilitate the most desirable outcomes for Aboriginal students. It is necessary for principals to articulate their belief in the importance of listening to students. Consultation with students is crucial if educators are to accurately assess their curricular and extracurricular needs as Aboriginal learners. There is little evidence in the literature to suggest that such consultations are commonplace (Nieto 2010). The principal must ensure that Aboriginal students are free to choose whether or not to take part in social gatherings and traditional feasts. In this way, students may be drawn to traditional teachings and social behaviours that complement an emerging pride in Aboriginal worldviews and customs.

The community participants noted how their children saw the purpose of traditional ceremonies and perceived the drum as a central symbol of their realities as Aboriginal youth. Similar programs could awaken other Aboriginal students to their epistemic, historical, and socio-cultural values and beliefs as they are encouraged to develop an awareness of traditional knowledge and teachings. They will be able to realize their preferred learning styles and, as they do so, to discover the relevance of traditional knowledge. Given the example and testimonies of the case story of the ASP, Aboriginal students are inclined to interrogate their self- and collective understandings of what it means to be an Aboriginal person first and an Aboriginal student second. Their involvement in such programs encourages them to continue setting their sights on social and academic goals.

It is imperative to discuss the details of how the ASP was implemented in a public school. These stories within the larger story of the ASP provide examples of how a public school can be inclusive of Aboriginal students and encourage their meaningful engagement in education. As the OME's Framework mandates, the ASP illuminates the importance of aligning Aboriginal students' epistemic worldviews with their social and cultural traditions (Cherubini 2009d). In effect, the ASP creates "a space for Aboriginal initiatives ... so that Indigenous ways of knowing can flourish and intercultural sharing can be practiced in a spirit of coexistence and mutual respect" (Castellano 2000, 23).

This notion of space, both literally and figuratively, often surfaces in the literature as *community schools* and *culturally responsive schooling*. Community schools are intended to support students who have historically not benefited from self-contained schooling models (Phillips 2008). According to Dryfoos (2008), traditional educational practices do not adequately address long-standing achievement gaps; therefore, community resources need to be enlisted to account for the effects of poverty and marginalization. Culturally responsive schooling, like community schools, honours the idea of having space for marginalized students. It, too, is a strategy to increase students' academic achievement and considers their linguistic and cultural traditions as crucial to sustaining healthy student development (Alaska Native Knowledge Network 1998). The research on community schools and culturally responsive schooling suggests that alternative models of educational practices, the purpose of which is to re-engage marginalized populations, should be introduced into public school culture.

Community Schools

Phillips's (2008) research on community schools is pivotal. Community schools solicit the support of community resources to benefit the educational experiences of students and to strengthen the connection between parents and the school. The objective is to align family and cultural roots with the aims of the school and, in so doing, to increase student motivation (Cahill 1996). Programs associated with such objectives include those of community support agencies, arts and cultural classes, and the hiring of outreach workers. In British Columbia, for example, community schools were established in various districts and provided inviting school environments that, for marginalized students, encouraged a sense of belonging (Talbot 2004). Community agencies lend their support to marginalized families, provide leadership opportunities for youth, and establish literacy programs in students' heritage languages (Woodward 2007). In Manitoba, community schools offer programs to address specific social issues in order to heighten student engagement. These programs are particularly targeted at those populations that continue to suffer from residential school experiences that have negatively affected parenting skills (Phillips 2008). In these provinces and in others, community schools and various social services work together to offer greater support for students and families living in poverty, to provide collaborative approaches to sustaining student development, to decrease the secondary school drop-out rate, and to use school buildings as community resources after school hours. As Talbot (2004, 6) states:

> Using public schools as hubs, community schools can knit together inventive, enduring relationships among educators, families, volunteers, and

community partners. Health and social service agencies, family support groups, youth development organizations, institutions of higher education, community organizations, businesses, and civic and faith-based groups all play a part. By sharing expertise and resources, schools and communities act in concert to transform traditional schools into permanent partnerships for excellence.

Although the characteristics of community schools vary from site to site, Dryfoos and Knauer (2002) identify some fundamental characteristics, including being inclusive of families, students, school administrators, teachers, and community members; offering culturally appropriate programming for the sake of improving Aboriginal student achievement and furthering their formative development; fostering community awareness by encouraging student involvement in the community; offering curricular and extracurricular opportunities to augment educational experiences; and providing interventions to further educational outcomes, adolescent development, family support, and community awareness. Woven throughout these characteristics is the importance of the school principal's providing sustaining relationships between the students, school, school staff, and greater community (McDougal et al. 2006). The principal's leadership capacities are integral to the success of the various interventions (Whalen 2007). The literature also emphasizes the leadership capacities of the community service coordinator as both she/he and the principal contribute to establishing a common goal for each community school (Blank and Berg 2006). Often in tandem, the principal and the community service coordinator conceive of funding development strategies to finance their interventions (Blank and Shah 2004).

Culturally Responsive Schooling

A culturally inclusive school can make a significant contribution to sustaining Aboriginal students' socio-cultural and socio-linguistic traditions, which, in turn, can further their academic engagement in public school (Ball 2004; Johansen 2004). School cultures that are inclusive of Aboriginal students' epistemic worldviews counter the experiences of discontinuity felt between colonialist and Aboriginal paradigms of knowledge and learning (Jones 2004). Culturally responsive schooling is considered to be a viable strategy for improving the academic success of Aboriginal students because it favours a pedagogy that is aligned to their epistemologies, culturally sensitive curriculum resources, heightened teacher awareness of their learning preferences, and positive relationships between Aboriginal and mainstream school communities (Castagno and Brayboy 2008).

Culturally responsive schooling practices include complex interactions between epistemic theory, culturally based practices, historical traditions, and educator dispositions. Aboriginal students, according to some scholars, demonstrate learning styles that differ from those of the mainstream student cohort (Goin 1999; Ross 1989). Mainstream schools, however, generally do not address these learning preferences and thus place Aboriginal students at a disadvantage (Gilliland 1995). This is not to suggest that Aboriginal students' learning styles and epistemic preferences can be reduced to a single and sweeping generality, as Lomawaima and McCarty (2006) caution against, but it does suggest that student achievement is enhanced when educators tailor curriculum and pedagogy to better suit the needs of individual students (Klump and McNeir 2005). Culturally responsive schooling practices respect the intergenerational teachings inherent in Aboriginal epistemologies (Battiste 2002), which, among other things, are rooted in a sense of community, interrelatedness (Burkhart 2004), and responsibility (Medicine and Jacobs 2001).

The literature warns that attention to cultural practices must stem from a sound understanding of the systemic racism that continues to alienate Aboriginal learners within formal educational institutions (Sparks 2000). By attending to Aboriginal students' cultural practices in mainstream classrooms and schools, educators can draw upon local knowledge to motivate their interest (Demmert 2001). One way of including local knowledge within the standard curriculum involves inviting community members, including elders and other community leaders, to serve as resources in the classroom (Deloria and Wildcat 2001). Aboriginal parents can provide elements of cultural inclusion that will lend a greater degree of significance to Aboriginal student learning. For Aboriginal students, the presence of elders reinforces cultural representation (Fayden 2005), while their storytelling embodies traditional and culturally appropriate teaching and learning strategies (Cajete 1994). The inclusion of Aboriginal student learning styles and cultural practices in mainstream schools and classrooms has the potential to lower the drop-out rate of Aboriginal students and further their interpersonal and individual development.

The ASP at SHSS provides a good example of an educational model that is a hybrid of both community schooling and culturally responsive schooling. Although it does not directly mirror either schooling concept, it has adapted its human and social capital to include some of the key characteristics of both. Although not all readers will relate to each and every detail of the program, there are enough examples of how to implement such programs and interventions that there should be something for everyone.

SHSS has adapted some of the core characteristics of community schools to better serve Aboriginal student needs. The ASP has solicited community resources from the local friendship and Aboriginal health centres. Although none of these institutions occupies office space in the school, Aboriginal youth counsellors and school administrators readily refer to them, and they offer support to students in need. In this way, Aboriginal students have guided access to the professional services in their community. These resources are linked to the school services that deal with the technical core of education. The alignment between school personnel and Aboriginal community resources reinforces a connection between the Aboriginal community and the school itself. Parents see the school as recognizing and relying upon culturally appropriate support services for their children – something that did not happen in the past. In many ways, the inclusion of culturally sensitive community resources in the protocols and practices of formal schooling is an attempt to address the adverse consequences of residential schooling.

The literature on community schools stresses that students should be provided with arts and culture classes, literacy programs, and leadership opportunities. SHSS invites traditional teachers from Aboriginal communities to teach crafts during after-school and weekend hours. It offers Native language courses to students who want to learn about their socio-linguistic traditions, and it encourages Aboriginal youth to learn traditional dancing so that they can fully participate in the powwows offered at the school and elsewhere. These curricular and extracurricular activities are intended to reinforce students' involvement in their community and to foster their engagement in schooling.

At SHSS, the literature's focus on culturally sensitive programming is represented by the full-time Aboriginal youth counsellors. These people serve as advocates for Aboriginal students not only with school personnel but also with outside agencies. The youth counsellors are familiar with the substantial barriers that Aboriginal students face when attending mainstream educational institutions, including the social and epistemic tensions that contribute to Aboriginal student disengagement. SHSS has a dedicated space – the Native Room – that symbolizes the presence of the community within the school. This room stores the traditional drum, showcases Aboriginal art, and affords students a respite from the dominant Eurocentric ideologies of school practices.

Although SHSS does not employ a community service coordinator, as do most community schools, it does rely upon a program coordinator to oversee the effect of the ASP at the student level. The program coordinator is from the Aboriginal community and, like the youth counsellors, is acutely aware of the tensions inherent in the prevailing assumptions about public education. In many ways, this individual functions as a conduit between community services and the school. She oversees the logistical operations of the program and ensures that they are compatible with OME policies and with SHSS functions. Community resources and financing are channelled through the program coordinator in order to establish the general parameters of the various ASP services.

As the literature insists is crucial, both the program coordinator and the school principal at SHSS exercise strong leadership capacities and are committed to the ASP. In keeping with the practice of community schools, the principal and program coordinator collaborate to establish meaningful and thoughtful program goals that are accountable to provincial policy, school board protocol, and all of the concerned communities. Furthermore, the ASP at SHSS has adapted some of the practices of culturally responsive schooling to better address Aboriginal students' learning experiences. The literature on culturally responsive schooling recognizes the significance of honouring the socio-cultural and socio-linguistic traditions of Aboriginal students. SHSS not only includes Native language courses as a curriculum option but also, through the ASP, facilitates various traditional feasts and celebrations throughout the calendar year, all of which involve community participation. Various student body assemblies include Aboriginal drumming and other cultural activities as a regular feature. Aboriginal parents and the community at large recognize what amounts to a shift in educational priority as the school regularly enlarges its capacity to include their traditions. This enables Aboriginal students and their families to feel that they have some influence and to notice that the once overwhelming and frightening school spaces are being transformed into shared and welcoming spaces. This is not to suggest that the honouring of Aboriginal traditions has erased all the distrust that resulted from colonialist practices; nonetheless, the ASP at SHSS has shown the community how Aboriginal perspectives and traditions can be honoured within the school. This is critical to engaging Aboriginal students and their families in the practices of public schooling.

Equally critical, according to the literature, are pedagogical practices that are aligned with Aboriginal student epistemologies, culturally sensitive curricular resources, and a heightened sense of teacher awareness regarding Aboriginal student learning preferences. Although the ASP does not claim to extend its influence into each and every teacher's pedagogy (as the literature suggests is reflective of culturally responsive schooling), the youth counsellors advise teachers of culturally appropriate strategies that will help them to better engage Aboriginal learners. Similarly, although the ASP does not directly provide culturally sensitive curricular resources for each course offered at the school, the Aboriginal youth counsellors and community support services share their knowledge of particular intellectual traditions with both teachers and students. Through the counsellors, school personnel have the opportunity to become informed and to actively participate in the program. The counsellors make it clear that they are prepared to tend to teachers' needs and to assist them in negotiating critical understandings of Aboriginal worldviews.

The ASP encourages a greater consideration of Aboriginal learning styles. In keeping with culturally responsive schooling, individual Aboriginal student needs are addressed on a case-by-case basis. Aboriginal student frustration and disengagement in the classroom are openly discussed with the youth counsellors, who, with the students, reflect on the barriers and construct a basis for response. The counsellor assists in mediating the competing interests of the student and the teacher and helps the student to formulate a course of action. The intent is for both the student and the teacher to discover how different epistemic learning needs can coexist. The regular presence of the elder in the school not only symbolizes this peaceful coexistence of different worldviews but also ensures that students can seek culturally appropriate guidance during the school day. The elder is the link between traditional Aboriginal teachings and Western educational practices.

The ASP is engineered, first and foremost, to meet the needs of Aboriginal students. While it exists within the larger context of public school culture, it harnesses the capacities of individuals to manage resources, respect differences, and commit to its success. It establishes spaces that are culturally relevant, sensitive, and appropriate and that honour Aboriginal people's worldviews and meaningfully engage Aboriginal students in their education.

Across Canada, Aboriginal students in mainstream public schools have lagged behind their mainstream counterparts. Public school protocol, traditional teacher-directed pedagogy, and standardized curricula and assessment and evaluation practices have been in conflict with Aboriginal students' values, beliefs, and epistemic traditions. The stories within the story of the ASP bring to the fore the impact on Aboriginal students of one program in one inner-city public secondary school. The voices of the ASP's key stakeholders describe inviting and uninviting school spaces, environments that are conducive to learning and those that are not, and the importance of establishing trusting intercultural relationships. It is up to the readers to apply all this to their own particular contexts.

The story of the ASP serves as an example of how the life experiences and knowledge that students have accumulated by attending SHSS can contribute to their critical reflections and subsequent personal and social behaviours. In similarly structured programs, Aboriginal students can learn about how they learn best. They can discover the skills, attitudes, and values that are unique to them and their communities. Aboriginal students' awareness of their epistemic preferences and values can lead them to a sense of their self-identity and allow them to express their pride in their uniqueness as Aboriginal peoples and learners.

The ASP's success in fostering the self-identities of Aboriginal students, attracting students to SHSS, providing them with various supports, creating inviting and safe educational spaces, and meaningfully involving community members should not be underestimated. These successes represent a major step towards accomplishing yet more fundamental changes to how curricula and Indigenous knowledge are interpreted in public schools.

The larger debate posits that cultural knowledge must exist and thrive in school curricula. Brant-Castellano suggests that Indigenous knowledge emanates from a variety of sources that include traditional teachings, critical observations, and intuition (see Steinhauer 2002). It is not enough for public schools to offer interventions to Aboriginal students in order to assist them in their journeys through public education; rather, public school culture needs to acknowledge and meaningfully represent Aboriginal languages, orthographies, and Indigenous knowledge in general (Battiste and McLean 2005). Curricula, broadly understood as the programs offered across public educational institutions, must take into account Indigenous knowledge and be mindful of Aboriginal ancestry and respectful of relationships.

The stories within the story of the ASP serve as a starting point from which policy makers, educators, and community members can begin to determine what can be done to honour Aboriginal knowledge and values in public school curricula (Cohen 2001; Norris 2006; Norris and MacCon 2003). A key possibility rests in teacher education. While school and school board professional development initiatives concerning bicultural issues and the learning needs of Aboriginal students were delivered to faculty at SHSS, a disconcertingly large number of faculty members did not recognize the significance of these initiatives to their professional practice. They may have gained some level of awareness of Indigenous knowledge but clearly had issues with incorporating it into the school's curriculum and recognizing it as a legitimate epistemic practice. Teacher education, both pre- and in-service, might do better to provide teachers with opportunities to confront their ontological assumptions about teaching, learning, knowledge, and curricula. Professional development might be targeted, at least initially, not so much on raising teachers' awareness of Aboriginal student learning but more on opportunities for teachers to reflect critically upon their taken-for-granted assumptions. The OME Policy Framework gives licence to provincial school boards to ask educators to recognize how, historically, Aboriginal knowledge has been silenced in public school curricula and how it continues to be excluded. As Battiste and Youngblood Henderson (2000, 88-89) observe: "[Canadian educational systems] teach this double consciousness to Indigenous students. Canadian educational systems view Indigenous heritage, identity and thought as inferior to Eurocentric heritage, identity and thought ... Educators still know very little about how Indigenous students are raised and socialized in their homes and communities, and even less about how Indigenous heritage is traditionally transmitted." Teachers, principals, and school board administrators must point out that Indigenous knowledge is not a recognized aspect of curricular and policy ideologies.

But teacher education is only one possible way to Indigenize the curriculum and to honour Aboriginal knowledge. Another possible way of doing so is to more directly involve elders. As previously stated, elders are the traditional gatekeepers of knowledge. Schools might consider having an elder present in classrooms to function as a conduit between Aboriginal students, the curriculum, and the teacher. Elders can be instrumental in presenting education on a holistic level for Aboriginal students and perhaps for others. Given that Indigenous knowledge is largely experiential, elders can be critical co-instructors and can help to unpack the standardized curriculum and to develop an Indigenized curriculum. Teacher federations would, of course, be consulted extensively and would be involved in the development of such a co-instructional model. I suspect, however, that until such time as the scripted curriculum is entirely Indigenous-based, educators would welcome the elders' capacity to situate Western knowledge within a broad socio-cultural context.

Elders could also serve on district school boards to oversee educational policy, as they could on provincial and state governing agencies. In these roles, elders could ensure that educational policies and school board practices are respectful of the respective community's expectations. In the process, they can reverse the oppressive practices that exclude Aboriginal knowledge from, or marginalize it within, mainstream schooling practices (Battiste 2002; Duggan 2003). Elders could serve in these positions on school councils and during faculty meetings. The point is to fully engage them in the processes and protocols involved in creating educational curricula.

The Story in Retrospect: The Internal Medicine Wheel

I have said that there is profound learning to be gained from the stories within the story of the Aboriginal Student Program at Soaring Heights Secondary School. This being the case, I want to conclude the story in the same way it began in the foreword: through the voice of Lyn Trudeau, an Ojibway woman and scholar. It is important to me that the story be framed in a traditional voice so that it does not lose any of its richness.

The following pages provide a retrospective angle on the story. I rely on Trudeau's observations to bring to the fore the heartfelt experiences shared by the Aboriginal students. In this way, policy makers, educators, students, and community members can better appreciate the power of the Circles throughout the research conversations if they choose to honour the voices of those who try to plan and implement similar programs. The Circle provides individuals with an intimate opportunity to search for their essential selves, and I am grateful to Trudeau for guiding us through these explorations, beginning with the following reflection. Consider the following words of renowned elder Black Elk of the Oglala Sioux Nation:

> You have noticed that everything an Indian does is in a circle, and that is because the Power of the World always works in circles, and everything tries to be round ... The Sky is round, and I have heard that the earth is round like a ball, and so are all the stars. The wind, in its greatest power, whirls. Birds make their nest in circles, for theirs is the same religion as ours ... Even the seasons form a great circle in their changing, and always come back again to where they were. The life of a man is a circle from

childhood to childhood, and so it is in everything where power moves. (Sutton 2007, 346)

Trudeau contends that the Circle is full of meaning when viewed through Aboriginal people's eyes and felt in Aboriginal people's hearts. Earlier, I discuss the Aboriginal students' and non-Aboriginal participants' voices in the context of an Aboriginal belief system known as the Medicine Wheel. One should understand its teachings as a series of interrelated circles that reside within and form a larger circle. Each circle is an independent teaching that connects and relates to the circle on either side. Each circle is divided into four quadrants and helps one to come to wholeness (Graveline 2000). I have learned that the Medicine Wheel is used as a tool to help one understand one's place among, and relationship with, all beings.

As the students' voices are directly reflective of the notion of self, it is both necessary and appropriate to situate them within the Inner Medicine Wheel. As Lyn Trudeau describes it, the Inner Medicine Wheel is concerned with the search for the essential self. There are four aspects of the Internal Medicine Wheel, just as there are four aspects of the self: the spiritual, the emotional, the intellectual, and the physical. It is critical to recognize and to address these four aspects of the self, which are meant to be understood as an inward journey. They represent how one views and understands oneself and how one deals with one's own inner world – the internal connections. For Trudeau, engaging both the External and the Internal Medicine Wheels gives rise to the wellness and healing of the Aboriginal student. Readers should note how Trudeau's explanations (see below) represent a moving forward and, hence, a beginning of something new. Another circle – all interrelated and interconnected (see Figure 2).

The Internal

According to Trudeau, the Internal Medicine Wheel reflects the Aboriginal students' sense of their own inner being. This is considered to involve the four aspects of the self shown in the smaller circle: the spiritual, the emotional, the intellectual, and the physical. The relationship between these four aspects of the self makes up one whole. This may give the reader further insight into how the Aboriginal students at SHSS see themselves. Without this internal fullness, the student is left with an inner void that, if not adequately addressed, will eventually result in disconnect, disinterest, and disengagement.

The internal and external are viewed as existing synonymously, each constantly interacting with and dependent upon the other for guidance throughout the trials of life. According to Trudeau, the key point is that the two medicine wheels are interconnected and that each is a bridge to the other. From an Aboriginal perspective, they are interconnected and flow in unison.

Internal Teaching
Spiritual. Aboriginal people's culture is steeped in spirituality. For Trudeau, spirituality involves turning inward to the heart, where one makes a connection to the spiritual world. Many Aboriginal people know this as it is embedded within their culture; perhaps it is indicative of the SHSS students' desire to find this space, this inward path that must be travelled if one is to have the inner strength to face the challenges that obstruct one's journey. It is important for readers to understand that, according to Trudeau, it is an Aboriginal person's spiritual centredness that enables her or him to be open to the past and the present and that allows her or him a degree of control over the future. This is crucial for the success of Aboriginal students as colonialism crosses all generations and continues to have a negative impact on Aboriginal culture and people (Castellano, Davis, and Lahache 2000; Hampton 1988). As Prime Minister Harper stated in his June 2008 apology to Aboriginal peoples, acknowledging the past means no longer having to live with the shame of slogans such as "kill the Indian, save the child." With this horrific philosophy no longer in force, young Aboriginal people can come to understand their traditional ways. To deal with the present means recognizing the injustices committed in the name of forced assimilation, particularly through residential schools. For Trudeau, although it is important to acknowledge these injustices, it is just as important not to dwell on them. Today is about focusing on the healing process and on making good decisions. This new focus is concerned not only with the academic realm but also, as Trudeau explains, with furthering all aspects of Aboriginal students' sense of self so that they may determine their future as powerful Aboriginal youth. An education that encompasses the whole person and makes room for inner spirituality greatly enhances the chances for Aboriginal students' academic success. This is indicated throughout the students' narratives (a most relevant point regardless of the lens through which you are reading this story).

According to Trudeau, a key component of self that is born out of spirituality is identity. This was certainly corroborated by the Aboriginal students who participated in the research conversation Circles. For Aboriginal students, identity plays a role in being successful as it concerns how they see themselves. As Trudeau comments or suggests, three key elements contribute to Aboriginal students' identity and are embedded within their stories: drumming, dance, and Native studies courses. Principals and teachers saw the implementation of culturally related activities in an overwhelmingly positive light since it meant that more Aboriginal students became involved in their education and were reconnected with their culture.

For Trudeau, Aboriginal culture involves ceremony and connecting with the natural and spiritual realms. Furthermore, drumming is fundamental to most Aboriginal teachings. Trudeau believes that the drumbeat is the heartbeat of "Mother Earth." The drumbeat reaffirms our oneness with the land and with the natural and spiritual worlds. It is because of such beliefs that the ASP at SHSS brought traditional drumming into the classroom and supported it as an after-school activity. Despite the fact that students came from various Aboriginal communities, the school formed a Big Drum (a Grandfather Drum as it is known to the Anishnawbe Nation). It was the common cultural bond of drumming that led to the elimination of many of the boundaries among the students. The drumming group was very successful with the Aboriginal students, who decided to make a drum themselves. Throughout the process of making this drum, they followed traditional teachings and ceremonies associated with creating and giving birth to the drum. Trudeau points out how the students learned about the respect one must have for drumming and its significance in all Aboriginal cultures. As is clear from their stories, the drum offered a rewarding spiritual connection among the Aboriginal students who became involved with it.

The Aboriginal student drum group was the first act at the school talent show at SHSS. It was met with cheers from the entire student body, which allowed the members of the group to feel a sense of pride and accomplishment. These feelings extended into the everyday routines of Aboriginal students. I am certain the reader will agree with Trudeau that there is much to be learned from schools that embrace Aboriginal students' culture and allow Aboriginal spirituality to complement the academic setting.

Prospective program leaders might also benefit from how the Aboriginal students who participated in the drum ceremonies were encouraged to venture into various local and provincial communities: "They put us in powwows and everything so we can drum and things like that" (Grade 9 female). Enacting Aboriginal spirituality across numerous communities can enable students to experience traditional ceremonies and to be witness to the fact that their culture is alive and thriving. As Trudeau observes, whenever the topic of drumming arose, the students' eyes lit up, and they were suddenly alert and willing to share their experiences of drumming: "Now I know how to sing some songs and drum. We made some drums and everything, so that was good" (Grade 10 female). Re-establishing traditional practices in programs like the ASP can be rewarding experiences for students. Trudeau explains that drumming is a spiritual journey and suggests that its heartbeat reverberates in all Aboriginal people, reminding them of who they essentially are.

The second key element of Aboriginal students' identity is dance. Dance is significant to Aboriginal communities as it is a connection to the spirit world and forms part of all Aboriginal celebrations and ceremonies. Trudeau describes the fluid movement of bodies and feet keeping time with the drumbeat and how the heartbeat of Mother Earth connects dancer and earth. Dance is recognized as establishing and reinforcing a spiritual relationship between the dancer and Mother Earth. For Aboriginal peoples, dance is more than physical movements: it helps the dancers stay true to who they are by enabling them to experience their unity with the natural world. As Trudeau beautifully describes it, dance is movement that expresses the emotion of life.

Students at SHSS benefited from dance because the ASP understood the spiritual connection between Aboriginal traditions and dance. Principals, teachers, and counsellors considering a similar program should pay attention to the student programs and extracurricular activities involving dance and regalia. People wear regalia when they perform in ceremonies as this identifies them to the Creator. The ASP at SHSS assisted students not only with the fees associated with attending various celebrations but also by getting those knowledgeable about such customs to teach students how to make their own regalia.

Dance became a part of the Aboriginal students' lives at SHSS and can be considered an instrumental component of program development. For some students, dance illustrates cultural awareness. Some students were well versed in traditional dance and taught other students who were not as knowledgeable. The students were happy to share their cultural knowledge and were willing to learn from others. Trudeau acknowledges that, in dance, the spiritual realm is close at hand as one lets go of the physical world, as, through the drumming, one moves in time to the heartbeat of Mother Earth. In this way, outer being and inner being find harmony.

The Native studies courses provided at SHSS comprise the third key element of Aboriginal students' identity. As one Grade 12 female Aboriginal student explained: "It's eas[ier] going in [teacher's name] class than it is other classes." This comment was corroborated by statements such as "Everyone is comfortable" (Grade 12 female) and "I don't really have a favourite subject besides Native arts" (Grade 11 female). Aboriginal students valued culturally relevant studies. Teachers working with Aboriginal students should consider the merit of making drums and conveying information about the importance of the drum to Aboriginal spirituality. To help with this, traditional knowledge keepers could be invited to classrooms as guest speakers. The students who participated in Native studies courses expressed their joy in learning more about their own histories and teachings – something that brought them closer to self-knowledge. Seeing their own culture represented in the curriculum contributed to their acceptance of their own Aboriginal ancestry and gave them a reason to care about their education.

Nevertheless, students also noted that not enough culturally relevant courses were offered at SHSS. The absence of Native language courses was keenly felt. According to Trudeau, Aboriginal people have a spiritual connection to their language as it is through language that they present themselves to the Creator. All readers who can influence program decisions should seriously consider recommending that their school offer a variety of Native language courses.

Emotional. According to Trudeau, Aboriginal people consider emotional connectedness to be fundamental to true understanding. The emotional aspect of the Internal Medicine Wheel, as SHSS students recognize, is embodied by the community. Readers will note the sense of community that emerged from students who sought comfort and belonging in order to eventually be able to contribute to their own people. Community extended beyond immediate families and home communities to include the support base at the school itself – the community that the Aboriginal students created at SHSS.

In search of their own sense of place, the Aboriginal students established emotional connections within the school environment. Trudeau notes with what affection Aboriginal students describe the Native Room: "It's comfortable"; "Everyone has something in common"; "You are with your own people." The students considered the security resulting from well-balanced emotional connections to be a contributing factor to their ability to achieve and maintain better grades and to remain engaged in their education. They gained a greater acceptance of self by knowing they were not alone in their educational journey. Upon entering into a positive relationship with the self, Aboriginal students became more confident in their ability to give back to their own people.

> I see [counsellor name] and [counsellor name] and everyone, I see other people that went to postsecondary school, and they studied their own people, and then they can go and get a career with their people to help their people, and I think that has helped me a lot because that is what I am going to do. I am going to grow up, and I am going to learn about my people, and I am going to go out there and help my people out. (Grade 12 female)

The students felt a sense of responsibility to their communities and intended to take the knowledge they acquired back to them. Readers will mark the influence of the ASP in this regard. As Trudeau describes it, throughout Aboriginal communities, the elders prophesize that Aboriginal peoples need to look to the younger generations to regain and revive their culture, to keep it rooted in the old ways and not allow it to be appropriated by other cultures. The Aboriginal students at SHSS exemplify this prophecy. It was evident that, for varying reasons (including the residual effects of colonialism), some of their families had fallen away from their traditional lifestyle. A number of the students revealed that they carried what they had learned through the ASP back to their families. Such programs provide Aboriginal students with the potential to keep their culture alive by letting older generations know that, despite the colonialist past, Aboriginal culture and ceremonial practices need not be kept shrouded in darkness and hidden within a cloud of shame and fear (Chrisjohn, Maraun, and Young 1997). Aboriginal youth can both give back to their communities and draw strength from them. And this applies to youth from Aboriginal communities located a great distance from SHSS. A student from northern Ontario came to SHSS because a student at the school suggested he do so: "I recommended this school because of the [Aboriginal] program, and now he just loves it" (Grade 10 female). The reach of programs such as the ASP can be long, and this speaks to their value.

For Aboriginal students, the ASP, the Native Room, and the people involved in them have become a community unto itself. Trudeau describes it as their home away from home – a family: "And you have someone who cares that is watching and knows what is going on" (Grade 12 male). The camaraderie helps students to feel safe and welcome. For all stakeholders in

Aboriginal education, it is imperative to ensure that students are allowed to embrace their culture and are not made to feel like outsiders within the greater school environment. Trust is extremely important in getting Aboriginal students to utilize the ASP, and building a supportive environment is certainly conducive to gaining that trust: "It's useful, because you get extra help there from people that you know and trust" (Grade 11 male). Trust allows students to move forward. When they begin to trust, they discover that they can benefit from their time in public schools. This overarching sense of community, comfort, and trust can leave Aboriginal students emotionally rejuvenated and feeling that their success can be unlimited.

Intellectual. Ancestral knowledge has been passed down throughout the generations in Aboriginal communities, keeping the cultures alive and thriving. Trudeau suggests that it is staying true to traditional ways and adhering to the teachings of the ancestors that have sustained Aboriginal cultures in the modern world. The intellectual aspect of the Internal Medicine Wheel includes seeing beyond the standard curricula and reaching back to the ancestors for the wisdom they possess. In Aboriginal communities, these traditional teachings are considered to be relevant and worth teaching to the younger generations (S. Wilson 2008). The Aboriginal students attending SHSS recognize the significance of maintaining this connection to the past while living in the present and preparing for the future. These types of programs enable students to acknowledge their own learning styles and to understand that they do not always coincide with Eurocentric pedagogy. As Trudeau aptly explains, the intellectual dimension of the Internal Medicine Wheel acknowledges that students have to make sense of two worlds – the mainstream and the traditional – if they are to find a place of peace.

The first step in the process of taking a two-worlds approach to living is understanding and acquiring knowledge; however, as Trudeau suggests, Aboriginal students must also often determine what constitutes worthy knowledge. Traditional knowledge is as relevant and as important as are academic skills. Asked whether or not traditional teachers were important in her life, one female Grade 11 student stated: "I try to learn as much as I can, as much as possible." The relevance of ancestral knowledge to the Aboriginal students who participated in the ASP is significant for educators who must, in turn, recognize the importance of addressing the intellect of Aboriginal students apart from the standardized curriculum. As a Grade 12 male student suggested: "Yeah, it's good that we are getting our culture back." Clearly, the students taking part in the ASP recognize and appreciate the importance of academic learning, but their intellect rests in cultural knowing.

Particularly interesting are Trudeau's observations regarding how the student participants discussed their histories, which are very much embedded in their consciousness. The students situate themselves as Aboriginal people who are learning the history of their homeland in the context of a mainstream provincial school curriculum. In the ASP, the students realize that the history of Aboriginal peoples continues to affect them but that it does not have to victimize them. The culturally aligned perspective that programs like the ASP provide is of great benefit to these students. As one of them stated: "Yeah, it's nice to know about my background and the history behind everything, it's interesting too, and it's good to learn about" (Grade 11 female). It stands to reason that, through such appropriate cultural supports, students can gain a better appreciation of the relevance of their culture. It gives Aboriginal students strength to see their own culture represented and supported within a public school framework. As one Grade 11 female student suggested: "I think I have changed. Like, I am a better student. I never used to be the 'best' student in Grades 9 and 10 and 11. But I think I changed." Another and related success attributed to culturally sensitive programming involves the fact that the ASP welcomes students back into the school system so that they can graduate. A Grade 12 male student stated: "I am doing good. I dropped out . . . then I came back because they have the program here. Ever since then I have been getting good grades, and I am out of the school this year." Trudeau is emphatic that it is as crucial to offer these students traditional Aboriginal ways as it is to offer them academic skills. There must be a sharing of the knowledge associated with both cultures.

Physical. Trudeau describes the physical being as the materialized presence that houses the collective energies of a person. This corporeal space needs to be sustained as it literally carries an individual throughout her or his journey. According to Trudeau, this facet of the Internal Medicine Wheel must be maintained and treated with the same respect as the others, for it is understood that it is a gift to be able to walk on Mother Earth and to enjoy the tangible as well as the intangible beauty that the Creator has given to all living beings. It is this understanding of the need to keep the physical body healthy that led the ASP at SHSS to implement initiatives to provide students with supports that relate directly to physical wellness.

For example, the ASP provides a daily lunch for students. Only when one is physically fed and one's body is nourished can one focus on one's school work. Some of the Aboriginal students do not always have the luxury of daily meals, so it is good for them to be able to depend on the meals offered by the program. The availability of food as part of the program is also directly related to certain Aboriginal traditions, according to which food plays a part in the many ceremonies that give thanks to the Creator. According to Trudeau, these ceremonies acknowledge the spirit and other natural elements that provide life's nourishment. They are a time for sharing and for coming together to socialize, reflect, and celebrate. In keeping with this, the SHSS offers clothes (donated by the community) to students in need. The students may take any of the garments for their own personal use and are free to donate some of their own. It is what Trudeau describes as a cycle of giving and receiving, and it supports the whole student body. It should also be noted that some students have to travel long distances to attend ASPs and to benefit from their culturally sensitive interventions. This being the case, program developers should include bus/subway travel expenses in their budgets.

Trudeau also reflects upon another factor associated with the physical element of the Inner Medicine Wheel – the actual location in which the ASP operates. The Native Room is not hidden away or located in a separate building but, rather, is situated within the school itself. Some of the Aboriginal students said that programs with which they had previously been affiliated were located in basements and were not readily visible within the greater school atmosphere. This made them feel isolated and excluded. A Grade 10 male remarked on this type of predicament: "Yeah, it didn't really feel like a school, it just felt like, I don't know – a bowl." This idea of being physically separated from most of the school can have a negative impact on students. Trudeau believes that a space that is visibly apparent, like the Native Room, tells Aboriginal students that their culture is not something to be ashamed of but, rather, is welcomed within the overall structure of the school: "I am honestly happy that this program is in a real school. That is a definite plus" (Grade 12 male student).

A Conclusion to the Story
I am captivated by Lyn Trudeau's vision of wellness and healing. She explains that wellness and healing encompass all facets of the Medicine Wheel and embrace the teachings therein. This curative process is about personal growth, about striving to establish a sense of well-being throughout one's life. It is important that readers understand that the path to wellness must begin as early as possible if it is to enable a strong sense of self,

thereby enabling one to journey along the road with a greater understanding of oneself and of one's place in society.

It is from this mindset that the question emerges: "What is education?" Is education associated only with recognizing and developing our cognitive functions and intellectual capacities? Aboriginal peoples often view education holistically, addressing all aspects of the Medicine Wheels: vision/spiritual, relationships/emotional, knowledge/intellectual, and action/physical. All of these need to be nurtured in order to have a healthy interaction with the external world. It stands to reason that students' inner personal growth goes hand-in-hand with the successes associated with academia. This, in turn, leads to an overall state of well-being – the harmonious balance of the internal and external circles. These circles should never be far from educators' minds while they are engaged in planning and development.

Community involvement, as Trudeau explains, is key in helping Aboriginal students to keep their cultural identity intact. In this context, "community" refers to the local Aboriginal community in which students can understand and appreciate their own cultures – something that leads to an improved ability to function within the larger society.

I certainly concur with Trudeau's observation that the stories shared by the young Aboriginal men and women in the ASP at SHSS shed new light on educating Aboriginal students within mainstream school systems. Since the inception of this program, students have shared stories about getting to know, maintain, and further their own cultural teachings and understanding, thereby increasing student retention and graduation rates. The collective outcome, as we have seen, is the realization of self-determining individuals. This is a direct manifestation of what happens when all aspects of the self are nurtured. A lesson for every reader!

The story of the ASP would not be complete without a comment about the influential role that the elder associated with it played in Aboriginal students' formative development. The elder had a soft and gentle spirit and was an influential presence. She represented the broad support for culturally relevant programming that tended to the diverse and unique needs of Aboriginal students. According to one female student: "[The presence of the elder is] like having a grandma around ... and it's really comfortable and awesome." In order to encapsulate the authentic flavour of the elder's thoughts, I rely again on Lyn Trudeau's cultural expertise.

According to Trudeau, an elder is a person of great significance who is respected throughout Aboriginal communities for the traditional knowledge he or she possesses. It is because of this knowledge and wisdom that elders are seen as ethical, moral, and spiritual leaders. Elders pass shared memories of a collective history on to the next generation; thus, they are honoured for their connection to the ancestral past and for their ability to provide and perpetuate a framework for Aboriginal cultures.

Given the elder's role in Aboriginal culture, there is no reason that it should not be incorporated into public education. Such carriers of culture can be crucial resources for educators and can be central in representing Aboriginal culture within educational institutions. An elder's participation assists Aboriginal students in realizing that their culture is not only very much alive but also still relevant. As the stories coming out of SHSS indicate, Aboriginal students need to have the support of those in their community who know their histories. Elders help Aboriginal youth find and keep their balance while forging their own paths in an ever-evolving society. The elder involved in the ASP commented: "I feel that just the idea of having an elder there is comforting for them as well." The elder's presence plays a fundamental role in Aboriginal students' education, especially as, in Aboriginal cultures, it is life experiences and traditional knowledge that constitute "education." All those with a stake in Aboriginal education would be well served to ensure that elders are included as significant partners in the development and implementation of such programs.

The elder associated with the ASP at SHSS spoke of valuing traditional Aboriginal knowledge, being true to oneself, recognizing epistemic conflict, and displaying mutual respect. The elder had been involved with the program since its inception, and she spoke for the community. She reflected on the need to understand the importance of keeping alive and valuing traditional Aboriginal knowledge, of "bringing in the drums, bringing the traditions, bringing the speakers, and bringing the elders in and making the kids understand what it is to be an Aboriginal person." Trudeau agrees that educating Aboriginal students in their own cultural ways ensures that they will be more engaged and responsive within the educational environment. According to the elder: "The kids were changing, more kids were coming. Like, we started with four, and now there is a hundred. That makes a big difference." The elder was also involved in extracurricular activities involving Aboriginal traditions. These activities were ceremonial occasions and included drum feasts, powwows, and drumming. The elder commented: "I think the drum is the centrepiece of Aboriginal life." She explained that the sound of the drum resonates within everyone because it echoes the first sound we hear – our mother's heartbeat. The elder appreciates traditional knowledge and ignites a spark within the Aboriginal students. When this is incorporated into their formal education, the results speak for themselves.

The elder's response when asked what distinguished her work with Aboriginal students has implications for policy makers, educators, and community members alike:

> The only thing that stands out to me is when we have feasts and the parents and the little ones come and they hear the drum and they hear the singing and we talk to them and we visit with them and it is like family coming to dinner. And that has been just a wonderful experience because everybody seems to be on the same page and they listen and they enjoy being there and the little ones are dancing around when the drum is going and it's like a party and they just have such a great time, and I think that would have never happened if it hadn't been for this program. It is also the dedication of the people that work the program, and you have to have that, otherwise it won't go.

Having a sense of community and of being embedded in one's learning environment inculcates a sense of awareness in Aboriginal students who are in the process of regaining their culture. The elder maintained that being true to oneself is as vital as breathing. When students become aware that they and their cultural background are valuable and crucial to their education, they can better focus on their life journeys. The elder is very much aware that being Aboriginal has not always been perceived in a positive manner and that there continue to be harsh stereotypes:

> There are many, many times in life when, if you look Native and you're Native, you get kind of pushed aside because either Natives are drunks or they are, you know, they just live on the government and ... all of that stuff that you hear which is not true, but there is a perception out there that Aboriginal people are kinda lazy and drunks and violent.

In the eyes of the elder, the youth of today need help to build a strong sense of self and to overcome racist stereotypes. Once Aboriginal students recognize who they are, they are better situated to be successful. As the elder commented: "It is encouraging to think that those kids, all that they needed was somebody to be interested enough in them, to invite them, I guess, or to make them feel that it is good to be here, and it is all right to be an Indian,

Learning from the Stories

you know. You can be Indian and educated at the same time." According to her, the spirit knows each individual's true self, and Aboriginal people must find harmony if they are to live successfully: "It is sitting right there in your spirit ... Your spirit says that is who you are, and it doesn't make you any better than anybody else, but that is who you are, that is your identity, and we can't lose our identity." The presence of an elder and her or his wisdom is crucial to Aboriginal students. The elder constantly reminds students that they can be educated and yet remain true to themselves.

Just as significantly, Trudeau noted that the elder can deal with epistemic conflicts and issues of mutual respect. The elder spoke of how Aboriginal students need to find a way to participate in both the Aboriginal world and the Western world. She noted: "[Aboriginal people] have left the natural world to the point that [they] are all [relying on] technology ... [They] cannot have only one. It has to balance." In other words, Aboriginal students need to find a way to balance the two worlds and not be overwhelmed by the dominant society. This is particularly the case for Aboriginal students who live far from their home territories and now reside in urban centres. It is in these instances that an elder can ease the tensions that result from a clash between Aboriginal and Western epistemologies. When both worlds come together in a spirit of harmony and attempt to appreciate each other's culture, they (i.e., educators, administrators, school boards, elders, Aboriginal community members) can bridge conceptual gaps and create mutual respect. On this issue the elder acknowledged the ASP:

> Well, I don't think that it can be all for everybody because again there are different cultures, right, and we don't want to impose [the ASP] on people ... It would be nice to be able to have it so that others understand it, respect it, and agree that it is a good thing to be there, to have here, but I wouldn't want to think that it was imposed on somebody, it shouldn't be. Other cultures are raised in their culture, and that is great, as I have said before, that your spirit, that is you, so ... it should be. I don't think that we need to hide if somebody would like to come to the feast and listen to the drum and see what is going on, that is perfectly okay. We have powwows, and we invite everybody.

From the elder's perspective, an understanding and appreciation of diversity "is so important for [Aboriginal students] because it is not only the Aboriginal people who benefit, it is everybody."

The elder spoke eloquently of these Aboriginal students and of how the ASP was established to assist them to become well-adjusted young men and women. The elder made it clear that Aboriginal teachings and activities have to exist alongside mainstream academic curriculum.

Although the story of the ASP at SHSS concludes with these words, it is my hope that, for all readers, regardless of their personal and professional interests in Aboriginal education, the learning is just beginning. Your story is yet to be told.

A Postscript

Provincial educational policy in Ontario has brought to light the importance of distinguishing Aboriginal students' learning needs and preferences in mainstream classrooms. In the process, teachers, principals, senior school board administrators, and school communities at large have been made aware of the tensions between Eurocentric and Aboriginal epistemologies in public schools. *Aboriginal Student Engagement and Achievement* offers an example of a publicly funded provincial secondary school that provides an exemplary Aboriginal student program.

The ASP at SHSS is an example of the successful transfer of policy into practice – an initial, but significant, first step towards Indigenizing curriculum and knowledge in schools. The stories account for a myriad of educational, cultural, physical, epistemic, emotional, and spiritual complexities. The depth of participants' experiences and perceptions positions this book on the frontier of educational reform. The stories discussed in these pages address educational experiences for Aboriginal youth and their communities in a formal school context, which, traditionally, has not been receptive to Aboriginal epistemology.

Aboriginal Student Engagement and Achievement describes an experiential shift on the part of Aboriginal students that has resulted in their genuine engagement with educational and cultural matters. The process of interpreting these experiences has tugged on the heartstrings of each member of the research team. There were many poignant stories that told of genuine connections to Aboriginal youth counsellors; of the assistance offered to Aboriginal students and their caregivers by school and program administrators; of the efforts of teachers to emotionally and aesthetically tailor their pedagogy to suit the needs of their students; of the soothing voice of the elder; and of the brave students who overcame their respective obstacles to offer promise for future youth in this school, province, and country.

Learning from the Stories

Through these stories, this book delves into Aboriginal student experiences and sheds light on how students and other members of the school community internalize (1) the delicate balance involved with living in two worlds and (2) the responsibility to take social action. Certainly, the outcomes discussed in *Aboriginal Student Engagement and Achievement* attest to any number of ways that Aboriginal students can learn and thrive in provincial schools. But this is just the beginning. Successful Aboriginal student programs like the one offered at SHSS provide Aboriginal youth with the means to find their own niche. They offer hope for a better future.

This recognizes the fact that power and politics permeate publicly funded classrooms in this province and elsewhere. However, these compelling stories speak to the success of an ASP that is in tune with an understanding of the importance of shared learning. Although not a panacea for what ails school systems that, according to the literature, often reinforce societal inequity, such programs make it clear that Aboriginal youth have historically been relegated to the margins of education and have not been well served by public schools.

The stories within the story of the ASP ask you, the reader, to think carefully about the morality of acting upon the inequities that Aboriginal students face in modern-day schools. Do educators have a moral obligation to reframe and to reconsider educational spaces for Aboriginal youth so that these students might have a brighter future? It is not enough to provide teachers with the "latest and greatest" culturally informed resources and teaching kits, just as it is not enough to include token traditional Aboriginal dances in select school functions. Neither of these adequately influences the epistemic space in which educators and policy makers participate as professionals. Instead, school communities must carefully refine and critique the way they think about Aboriginal student experiences, identity, and strengths within the broader curriculum. Teachers, principals, and policy makers must be willing to consider the interconnections among Aboriginal students and between them, their cultures, their communities, and their schools. The ASP at SHSS is sustainable because of a growing understanding of the fact that how Aboriginal students think about vision, relationships, knowledge, and action has profound implications for their development as individuals and as students.

I hope that the stories in this book have captured your attention. I hope, too, that these shared experiences have provoked you to consider how the values of the dominant culture, as they relate to education, are manifested in public school classrooms. Undeniably, the cultures of schools cannot and should not be left unobserved; rather, by examining and critically considering pedagogy, school culture, curriculum, and knowledge from within an anti-oppressive paradigm, we may arrive at collaborative understandings not only of our history (and the history of others) but also of our assumptions about teaching and learning.

Appendices

APPENDIX 1: Student and Faculty Surveys

Aboriginal Student Survey

1. How frequently do you use the Aboriginal resource centre to do school work?
2. How frequently do you use the Aboriginal resource centre to take advantage of the various supports it offers?
3. Is the program helping you complete your high school graduation requirements?
4. Is the program helping you achieve better grades?
5. Is the program making it easier for you to come to school?
6. Are the field trips offered through the program positive experiences for you as a secondary school student?
7. Are the field trips offered through the program worthwhile for you as a secondary school student?

Faculty Survey

There were eight Likert-type-scale statements in the quantitative section of the survey, ranging from *strongly disagree* (1) to *strongly agree* (5). The statements were as follows:

1. My professional teacher education program (faculty of education) prepared me to address the bicultural* needs of Aboriginal students.
2. My professional teacher education program prepared me to meaningfully represent Aboriginal students' values and worldviews in my teaching.
3. My professional teacher education program encouraged me to examine my own biases and dispositions in terms of my teacher identity and teaching practice.
4. As a result of various school board or school initiatives, I am able to adopt a variety of instructional methods to teach Aboriginal students effectively.
5. As a result of various school board or school initiatives, I have developed an awareness of the learning styles of Aboriginal students.
6. As a result of various school board or school initiatives, I am able to implement a variety of assessment strategies to evaluate Aboriginal students effectively.
7. Aboriginal parents have a strong professional relationship with the teachers and administrators of their children's school.
8. There are unaddressed "cultural boundaries" in the school where I work.

Conversely, three questions were included in the qualitative component of the survey:

1. Describe in detail the kinds of bicultural identity issues that the Aboriginal students in your classroom/school find most challenging.
2. Explain the nature of the programs and supports available in your school for helping Aboriginal students acquire positive self- and cultural identification.
3. What support/intervention would you recommend be offered to teachers that would assist them in helping Aboriginal students reach their full academic potential?

---

* For the purposes of this survey, "bicultural" refers to mainstream and Aboriginal cultures.

Appendices

APPENDIX 2: School Records

TABLE A.1 School records

	Number of students			
Month/year	Enrolled in the program	Regularly attending classes*	Absent with cause**	Withdrawn from the program
09/03 ^	6	N/A	N/A	0
10/03	35	N/A	N/A	0
09/04 ^	52	N/A	N/A	4
09/05 ^				
09/06 ^	51	27	0	0
10/06	62	34	0	0
11/06	68	36	1	1
12/06	76	40	3	2
01/07	73	40	2	1
02/07	80	49	2	4
04/07	77	48	0	1
10/07 ^	80	40	7	0
11/07	80	40	4	0
12/07	80	40	10	0
01/08	80	40	N/A	0***
02/08	85	45	N/A	0***
03/08	85	45	4	0
04/08	85	45	2	0
05/08	85	45	1	0
09/08 ^	95	55	4	1
10/08	95	55	6	0

Notes:

*   This column represents the number of students who are regularly engaged in the program; the other students use the services that the program offers on a part-time basis as determined by their academic/social/physical/spiritual needs.

** "With Cause" includes family relocation, suspension, lengthy illness, and referral to the Aboriginal Alternate Education Program supervised by the same school principal.

*** One student had withdrawn from the ASP but was referred to the Aboriginal Adult Education Program supervised by the same school principal.

^   The first report of a new academic year that is scheduled from September to June.

APPENDIX 3: Program Interventions

TABLE A.2   Program interventions

Month/year	# of VA	# of PI	# of EI	# of NI	# of SS	# of CLI
09/06 ^	2	1	2	1	1	3
10/06	1	2	3	1	3	3
11/06	1	1	2	1	1	4
12/06	1	2	1	1	1	3
01/07	0	3	3	1	2	2
02/07	1	5	4	2	4	3
04/07	1	2	2	2	2	2
10/07 ^	2	2	3	2	2	3
11/07	3	0	2	2	4	4
12/07	4	3	2	2	4	4
01/08	3	1	2	2	4	4
02/08	1	3	2	2	5	3
03/08	1	2	3	2	3	4
04/08	1	1	3	3	3	4
05/08	1	1	3	2	4	4
09/08 ^	1	2	2	2	3	3
10/08	1	2	2	2	4	3

Notes:
VA   volunteer activities (e.g., activities such as classroom volunteer, teaching a craft, fundraising, and food preparation).
PI   positive parental involvement (e.g., parent-teacher night, private discussions about student progress, feasts and celebrations for students and parents, personal consultations with parents regarding student progress, and participation in Full Moon Ceremonies).
EI   educational interventions (e.g., timetable assistance to meet students' needs; meeting with parents, school administration, and teachers; Native and African American youth groups; Aboriginal culture workshops; study periods and study habits workshops; career information nights; and literacy test support).
NI   nutrition interventions (e.g., providing breakfast and snacks in a culturally friendly classroom for students before and during school hours, feasting for the drums, and workshops on healthy nutritional alternatives).
SS   social support interventions (e.g., access to Aboriginal healing and outreach programs, cultural celebrations, appointments at the Aboriginal Health Centre, and personal prayer and remembrance ceremonies).
CLI   cultural and language interventions (e.g., youth drumming program, youth dance and regalia making, female hand drum, moccasin workshops, school trips to powwows, and the presence of an elder in residence).
^   The first report of a new academic year that is scheduled from September to June.

The volunteer activities included individuals from the Aboriginal community who assisted in classrooms, taught traditional Aboriginal arts to students, helped with fundraising initiatives for the program's field trips, and assisted in the preparation of food offered to students during the school day. The number of volunteer activities ranged from zero (in only one of the seventeen reporting periods) to four (in one reporting period), with one intervention representing the most consistent number throughout all reporting periods. Occurrences of parental involvement were also documented as the program aimed to include Aboriginal parents in parent-teacher nights, private discussions about student progress with the Aboriginal youth counsellors, feasts and celebrations for both students and their parents, and culturally representative events such as the Full Moon Ceremonies. With the exception of one period, there was positive parental intervention in each of the remaining reports (ranging from one occurrence to five). Educational interventions included matching students' timetables with their unique needs and interests; private meetings between parents, school administration, and/or teachers; Native Youth Group seminars; study habits workshops; career information nights; and intensive support with the provincial OME's large-scale standardized literacy tests. Results indicate that the educational interventions significantly reduced or eliminated conflict between Aboriginal students and school staff. The range of nutritional interventions remained consistent between one and two (with the exception of one reporting period [April 2008], in which there were three). As one might expect, providing breakfast and snacks before and during school hours is a very important intervention, and it remained relatively consistent throughout each of the reporting periods. Social support interventions included Aboriginal healing and outreach programs, cultural celebrations, and personal prayer and remembrance ceremonies. These interventions ranged from one (in three separate reporting periods) to five (in one reporting period). There were, however, four occurrences in six different reporting periods. The social support interventions provided opportunities for Aboriginal students to appreciate the value of both historical and contemporary teachings. As extensions of the social support interventions, the cultural and language interventions provided opportunities for Aboriginal students to engage in culturally inclusive pathways within the public education system. The Aboriginal community acknowledged the program as supportive and relevant to their needs, and, as a result, the program offered youth drumming, youth dance and regalia making, female hand drum, moccasin workshops, school trips to powwows, and access to an elder. With the exception of one reporting period, in which two interventions were recorded (April 2007), the program offered three and four interventions in each of the remaining sixteen reporting periods.

APPENDIX 4: Results of Student Survey

Aboriginal students were asked to respond to each question on the student survey by selecting *always, sometimes,* or *never* as the response that best represented their views. In response to the first question, 20 percent of the total sample ($N = 48$) indicated that they always use the Aboriginal resource centre to complete their school work; 80 percent reported that they sometimes use the resource centre (zero student participants replied that they never use the centre). In the second question, 30 percent of the sample indicated that they always use the Aboriginal resource centre at one time or another, 60 percent responded that they sometimes use it, while 10 percent of the participants indicated that they never use the resource centre. In question 3, all of the respondents (100 percent of the sample) indicated that the Aboriginal student support program was helping them complete their graduation requirements. The results for question 4 were identical. All of the respondents (100 percent of the total sample) reported that the program was helping them achieve better grades. Similarly, in question 5, 100 percent of the total sample indicated that the program was making it easier to go to school. For question 6, 90 percent of the students surveyed indicated that the culturally relevant field trips offered through the ASP are positive experiences for them as Aboriginal students attending a mainstream public secondary school; the remaining 10 percent reported that they had not attended such excursions. Finally, 100 percent of the total sample indicated in their responses to question 7 that the field trips were a good idea and enhanced their Aboriginal student identity.

APPENDIX 5: Results of Faculty Survey

First I offer a presentation of the descriptive statistics related to the survey results and their respective frequencies (see Table A.3). The frequencies related to study participants' demographics reflect the fact that the current position of the majority of participants was in the capacity of teacher (value of 1) versus department chairperson (value of 2) or support services (value of 3). The mean for this demographic was 1.46 with a standard deviation of .868. In terms of participants' professional experience in their current roles, the mean of 3.59 indicates that they had a minimum of five years and potentially more than ten years' experience (with a standard deviation of .706). More specifically, 70.7 percent of the cumulative percentage of the total N reported to have more than ten years of experience, while 17.1 percent of the entire population reported between five and ten years of experience (N = 29 and 7, respectively). In response to the number of years that participants have been employed at SHSS, there was a mean result of 3.09 (and a standard deviation of .969). Of the total N, 29.3 percent of participants reported to have been employed at the school between five and ten years (N = 12), while 43.9 percent (N = 18) indicated that they have been at the school for more than ten years. The last self-reported demographic frequency asked participants about the percentage of their students who are Aboriginal or of Aboriginal descent. The mean statistic was 2.39 (with a standard deviation of .833). Of the total N, 75.6 percent indicated that they have a 1 percent to 20 percent presence of Aboriginal students in their classrooms and school offices (N = 31), while 17.1 percent suggested a presence of between 21 percent and 40 percent (N = 7). None of the participants reported a 0 percent value to this question.

TABLE A.3 Descriptive means and frequencies

	Current position	Experience in the role	Years in the school	% of Aboriginal students
N	41.00	41.00	41.00	41.00
Mean	1.46	3.58	3.09	2.39
Standard deviation	0.86884	0.70624	0.96966	0.83301
Variance	0.755	0.499	0.940	0.694
Skewness	1.801	−1.437	−0.722	2.413
Minimum	1.00	2.00	1.00	2.00
Maximum	3.00	4.00	4.00	5.00

Frequencies: Likert-Scale Responses

The eight Likert-scale statements required participants to rate their perspectives on various issues related to their roles as professional educators in light of Aboriginal students' epistemologies, school culture, and OME policy. What follows is my analysis of frequencies based on the entire population of the faculty survey participants (see Table A.4).

In response to the first statement, which concerns the effectiveness of participants' professional teacher education program in preparing them to address the bicultural needs of Aboriginal students, the 2.02 mean score (and the 1.01 standard deviation) indicates that the study population *disagreed* with the statement that their teacher education programs were successful in preparing them in this regard. Zero participants indicated that they *strongly agreed* that their teacher education programs prepared them to address Aboriginal students' bicultural needs, while 12.2 percent of the total N (N = 5) reported their *agreement* with the statement. Of the total N, 73.2 percent of participants indicated their *strong disagreement* or *disagreement* with the statement (N = 15 for both category responses).

The second statement requires participants to report on the extent to which their teacher education programs prepared them to meaningfully represent Aboriginal students' values and worldviews in their teaching. The mean result of 1.97 (and a standard deviation of 1.01) convincingly indicates participants' *strong disagreement* with this statement; approximately 5.6 percent of the total N (N = 31) reported their *strong disagreement* and *disagreement* (N = 15 and 16, respectively). Two participants (4.9 percent of the total N) *strongly agreed* with the statement.

Statement 3 focuses on the extent to which participants' professional teacher education programs encouraged them to examine their own biases in terms of their teacher identity and practice. The mean statistic in response to this statement rested in the *indifferent* category (3.19 mean value and a 1.24 standard deviation); approximately 48.8 percent of the total population reported either their *strong disagreement* with (N = 5), *disagreement* with (N = 8), or *indifference* to (N = 7) this statement. Conversely, 39 percent of the population (N = 16) *agreed* with the statement.

The 3.29 mean value (and the 1.12 standard deviation) in response to statement 4 was also situated in the *indifferent* category. This statement shifts the attention from the previous three statements, which focus on participants' teacher education programs, to school board and school initiatives in response to the expectations and responsibilities placed on teachers in the context of the OME's policy. The fourth statement concerns whether the participants were better able to adopt a variety of instructional methods to teach Aboriginal students differently as a direct result of various board or school initiatives. In this case, 43.9 percent of the total N either *strongly disagreed* ($N = 4$), *disagreed* ($N = 6$), or were *indifferent* ($N = 8$), while 48.8 percent of the entire population ($N = 20$) *agreed* with the statement.

Statement 5 represents the highest mean value of the eight statements (mean of 3.31 and a standard deviation of 1.14). It requires participants to consider whether the various school board or school initiatives have developed their awareness of the learning styles of Aboriginal students. Cumulatively, 43.9 percent of the total sample either *strongly disagreed* ($N = 4$), *disagreed* ($N = 6$), or were *indifferent* ($N = 8$); 46.3 percent ($N = 19$) *agreed* with the above statement.

Like the mean values for the previous three statements, the mean for statement 6 belongs in the 3-value range – 3.07 (with a 1.08 standard deviation). The cumulative percentage for those participants who either *strongly disagreed* ($N = 4$), *disagreed* ($N = 9$), or were *indifferent* ($N = 9$) was 53.7 percent; 43.9 percent of participants *agreed* with the statement ($N = 18$). One participant (representing 2.4 percent of the cumulative percentage) *strongly agreed* with the statement that school board or school initiatives positively influenced their ability to implement a variety of assessment strategies to evaluate Aboriginal students effectively.

The focus of the seventh statement is educators' perceptions of Aboriginal parent involvement in their children's school. The statement is "Aboriginal parents have a strong professional relationship with the teachers and administrators of their children's school." The responses represented the lowest mean value across all the study statements. Participants reported a 1.87 mean (and a .927 standard deviation). Cumulatively, 80.5 percent of the entire population reported that they either *strongly disagreed* ($N = 14$), *disagreed* ($N = 18$), or were *indifferent* ($N = 5$); 7.3 percent of participants ($N = 3$) responded that they *agreed* with the statement.

The last statement requires participants to rank their perceptions of the following: "There are unaddressed cultural boundaries in the school where I work." A 2.92 mean value (and a standard deviation of 1.12) was reported; 58.5 percent of the cumulative percentage represented those participants who either *strongly disagreed* with ($N = 5$), *disagreed* with ($N = 11$), or were *indifferent* to ($N = 8$) the statement; 39 percent of the total N ($N = 16$) *agreed* that there are unaddressed cultural boundaries in the school, and 2.4 percent ($N = 1$) *strongly agreed* with the statement.

TABLE A.4 Descriptive means and frequencies (Likert-scale items)

	Bicultural	Worldviews	Biases	Instruction methods	Learning styles	Assessment	Parents	Cultural boundaries
N	41.00	41.00	41.00	41.00	41.00	41.00	41.00	41.00
Mean	2.02	1.97	3.19	3.29	3.31	3.07	1.87	2.92
Standard deviation	1.0121	1.0121	1.24	1.1234	1.1497	1.0814	0.9272	1.126
Variance	1.024	1.024	1.561	1.262	1.322	1.170	0.860	1.270
Skewness	0.710	1.267	-0.389	-0.729	-0.668	-0.525	0.648	-0.291
Minimum	1.00	1.00	1.00	1.00	1.00	1.00	0.00	1.00
Maximum	4.00	5.00	5.00	5.00	5.00	5.00	4.00	5.00

Appendices

Test of Significant Differences: Post Hoc Bonferroni
Bonferroni repeated measures (at an alpha of 0.05) were conducted for each of the eight statements according to the four variables identified by the participant demographics of the study, including (1) current position, (2) years of professional experience in their current role, (3) the number of years working in the school, and (4) the percentage of their students who are Aboriginal or from Aboriginal descent.

Current position. There were no statistically significant differences reported across all eight Likert-scale responses at a mean difference that is significant at the 0.05 level. Hence, regardless of participants' current position (be it as a teacher, department head, counsellor, or special education resource teacher), there were no statistically significant differences in their respective responses to the statements that related to their teacher education programs, school or school board of education initiatives, parents' professional relationships in their children's school, or matters related to unaddressed cultural boundaries that exist in the school.

Professional experience in current role. One statistically significant difference was reported across the eight statements. The results from statement 2 – "My professional teacher education program prepared me to meaningfully represent Aboriginal students' values and worldviews in my teaching" – reported a statistical difference of alpha = .046 (with a standard error of .44934 and F values of 2, 38 when alpha = < .05) between participant groups that had one to three years of experience in their current role and the participant group that self-reported having more than ten years' experience in their role. The mean for the less experienced sample (one to three years) was 2.77; the experienced sample (more than ten years) reported a 1.65 mean. Also noteworthy is the fact that no significant statistical differences existed in the other two statements (statements 1 and 3) related to participants' professional teacher education programs.

Number of years working in the school. Similar to the results for the variable identified as participants' current position, the third variable – the number of years working in the school – also resulted in no statistically significant differences. This underscores a significant finding as it relates particularly to those statements focused on school board and school initiatives (statements 4, 5, and 6). Essentially, the findings attest to the fact that there is no significant statistical difference in those participants who have been employed in the school for a shorter duration (one to three years) versus those who have been working at the school for, in some cases, over ten years. Thus, regardless of the nature of the professional development offered to participants over the years, its degree of receptivity on the part of the teachers, department chairpersons, counsellors, and special education teachers is consistent (at least given their responses to these survey statements).

Percentage of Aboriginal students. Here, too, no statistically significant differences were reported across the eight Likert-scale statements. Put differently, there was nothing statistically different in any of the participant responses regardless of the percentage of Aboriginal students reported to be in their classrooms and offices. This finding, when compared with the number of years participants reported to have been working in the school, sheds a rather dubious light upon the effect that school board and school initiatives have on those educators who work with a relatively substantial number of Aboriginal students.

Works Cited

Absolon, K., and C. Willett. 2004. "Aboriginal research: Berry picking and hunting in the 21st century." *First Peoples Child and Family Review* 1: 5–17.

Agbo, S. 2004. "First Nations perspectives on transforming the status of culture and languages in schooling." *Journal of American Indian Education* 43 (1): 1–31.

Aikenhead, G.S. 2006. *Science education for everyday life: Evidence-based practice.* New York: Teachers College Press.

Aikenhead, G.S., and H. Michell. 2011. *Bridging cultures: Science and Indigenous ways of knowing nature.* Toronto: Pearson.

Alaska Native Knowledge Network. 1998. *Alaska standards for culturally-responsive schools.* Fairbanks: Author. http://www.ankn.uaf.edu/publications/standards.html.

Allington, R.L. 2002. *Big brother and the national reading curriculum: How ideology trumped evidence.* Portsmouth, NH: Heinemann.

Apthorp, H., E. D'Amato, and A. Richardson. 2002. *Effective standards-based practices for Native American students: A review of research literature.* Aurora, CO: Mid-Continent Research for Education and Learning.

Archibald, J. 2008. *Indigenous storywork: Educating the heart, mind, body, and spirit.* Vancouver: UBC Press. http://dx.doi.org/10.4135/9781452226545.n31.

Baker, P.B. 2005. "The impact of cultural biases on African American students' education: A review of research literature regarding race-based schooling." *Education and Urban Society* 37 (3): 243–56. http://dx.doi.org/10.1177/0013124504274187.

Ball, J. 2004. "As if Indigenous knowledge and communities mattered." *American Indian Quarterly* 28 (3): 454–79. http://dx.doi.org/10.1353/aiq.2004.0090.

Battiste, M. 2000. "Maintaining Aboriginal identity, language, and culture in modern society." In *Reclaiming Indigenous voice and vision,* ed. M. Battiste, 192–208. Vancouver: UBC Press.

—. 2002. *Indigenous knowledge and pedagogy in First Nations education: A literature review with recommendations.* http://www.afn.ca/uploads/files/education/24._2002_oct_marie_battiste_indigenousknowledgeandpedagogy_lit_review_for_min_working_group.pdf.

Battiste, M., and S. McLean. 2005. *State of First Nations learning.* www.ccl-cca.ca/pdfs/AbLKC/StateOfFirstNationsLearning.pdf.

Battiste, M., and H.J. Youngblood Henderson. 2000. *Protecting Indigenous knowledge and heritage: A global challenge.* Saskatoon: Purich Press.

Beaulieu, D., L. Sparks, and M. Alonzo. 2005. *Preliminary report on NCLB in Indian country.* Washington, DC: National Indian Education Association.

Belgarde, M., R. Mitchell, and A. Arquero. 2002. "What do we have to do to create culturally responsive programs? The challenge of transforming American Indian teacher education." *Action in Teacher Education* 24 (2): 42–54. http://dx.doi.org/10.1080/01626620.2002.10734418.

Berg, L.D., M. Evans, and D. Fuller, and the Okanagan Urban Aboriginal Health Research Collective. 2007. "Ethics, hegemonic whiteness, and the contested imagination of Aboriginal community in social science research in Canada." *ACME: An International E-Journal for Critical Geographies* 6 (3): 395–410.

Bigelow, B. 2003. "Standards and multiculturalism." In *Rethinking school reform: Views from the classroom,* ed. L. Christiansen and S. Karp, 231–39. Milwaukee: Rethinking Schools.

Bishop, R. 1997. "Maori people's concerns about research into their lives." *History of Education Review* 26: 25–41.

Bishop, R., and T. Glynn. 2003. *Culture counts: Changing power relations in education.* London: Zed Books.

Blank, M., and A. Berg. 2006. *All together now: Sharing responsibility for the whole child.* Alexandria, VA: ASCD.

Blank, M., and B. Shah. 2004. *Educators and community sharing responsibility for student learning.* ASCD Info Brief No. 36. Alexandria, VA: ASCD.

Boykin, A.W., K.M. Tyler, and O.A. Miller. 2005. "In search of cultural themes and their expressions in the dynamics of classroom life." *Urban Education* 40 (5): 521–49. http://dx.doi.org/10.1177/0042085905278179.

Brascoupé, S., and H. Mann. 2001. *A community guide to protecting Indigenous knowledge.* Ottawa: Research and Analysis Directorate, Department of Indian Affairs and Northern Development.

Briggs, J. 2005. "The use of Indigenous knowledge in development: Problems and challenges." *Progress in Development Studies* 5 (2): 99–114. http://dx.doi.org/10.1191/1464993405ps105oa.

Bruno-Jofre, R., and D. Henley. 2000. "Public schooling in English Canada: Addressing difference in the context of globalization." *Canadian Ethnic Studies* 32 (1): 38–43.

Burkhart, B. 2004. "What Coyote and Thales can teach us." In *American Indian thought: Philosophical essays,* ed. A. Waters, 15–26. Malden, MA: Blackwell.

Cahill, M. 1996. *Schools and community.* Chicago: Cross City Campaign for Urban School Reform.

Cajete, G. 1994. *Look to the mountain: An ecology of Indigenous education*. Durango, CO: Kivakí Press.

—. 2008. "Sites of strength in Indigenous research." In *Indigenous knowledge and education*, ed. M. Villegas, S.R. Rak Neugebauer, and K.R. Venegas, 204–10. Cambridge, MA: Harvard Educational Press.

Canadian Council on Learning. 2009. *The state of Aboriginal learning in Canada: A holistic approach to measuring success*. Ottawa: Author.

Castagno, A.E., and M.J. Brayboy. 2008. "Culturally responsive schooling for Indigenous youth: A review of the literature." *Review of Educational Research* 78 (4): 941–93. http://dx.doi.org/10.3102/0034654308323036.

Castellano, M.B. 2000. "Updating Aboriginal traditions of knowledge." In *Indigenous knowledges in global contexts: Multiple readings of our world*, ed. G.J.S. Dei, B.L. Hall, and D.G. Rosenberg, 21–36. Toronto: University of Toronto Press.

Castellano, M.B., L. Davis, and L. Lahache, eds. 2000. *Aboriginal education: Fulfilling the promise*. Vancouver: UBC Press.

Charmaz, Kathy. 2000. "Constructivist and objectivist grounded theory." In *Handbook of qualitative research*, 2nd ed., ed. N.K. Denzin and Y. Lincoln, 509–35. Thousand Oaks, CA: Sage.

Cherubini, Lorenzo. 2009a. "Aboriginal identity, misrepresentation, and dependence: A survey of the literature." *Canadian Journal of Native Studies* 28 (2): 221–39.

—. 2009b. "Reforming teacher preparation: Fostering critical reflection and awareness in the context of global education." *Excelsior: Leadership in Teaching and Learning* 3 (2): 43–55.

—. 2009c. "'Taking Haig-Brown seriously': Implications of Indigenous thought on Ontario educators." *Journal of the Canadian Association for Curriculum Studies* 7 (1): 6–23.

—. 2009d. "Understanding the shifting sand in my Native Land: Crossing the cultural and conceptual divide." *Professing Education* 7 (1): 5–7.

Cherubini, L., and J. Hodson. 2008. "Ontario Ministry of Education policy and Aboriginal learners' epistemologies: A fundamental disconnect." *Canadian Journal of Educational Administration and Policy* 79: 1–33.

Cherubini, L., J. Hodson, M. Manley-Casimir, and C. Muir. 2010. "Closing the gap at the peril of widening the void: Implications of the Ontario Ministry of Education's policy for Aboriginal education." *Canadian Journal of Education* 33 (2): 329–55.

Chrisjohn, R.D., M. Maraun, and S.L. Young. 1997. *The circle game: Shadows and substance in the Indian residential school experience in Canada*. Custer, WA: Orca Books.

Cohen, B. 2001. "The spider's web: Creativity to diversity in dynamic balance." *Canadian Journal of Native Education* 25 (2): 140–48.

Cokley, K., and W. Williams. 2005. "A psychometric examination of the Africentric scale." *Journal of Black Studies* 35 (6): 827–43. http://dx.doi.org/10.1177/0021934704266596.

Cooper, I.T., and G. Stacey-Moore. 2009. *Walking in the good way: Loterihwakwarihshion Tsi Ihse*. Toronto: Canadian Scholars' Press.

Creswell, J.W., V.L. Plano Clark, M. Gutmann, and W. Hanson. 2003. "Advanced mixed methods research designs." In *Handbook of mixed methods in social and behavioral research*, ed. A. Tashakkori and C. Teddlie, 209–40. Thousand Oaks, CA: Sage.

Cummins, J. 2000. *Language, power, and pedagogy: Bilingual children in the crossfire*. Clevedon, UK: Multilingual Matters.

Deloria, V., and D. Wildcat. 2001. *Power and place: Indian education in America*. Golden, CO: Fulcrum Resources.

Demmert, W. 2001. *Improving academic performance among Native American students: A review of the research literature*. Charleston, WV: Eric Clearinghouse on Rural Education and Small Schools.

Demmert, W., D. Grissmer, and J. Towner. 2006. "A review and analysis of the research on Native American students." *Journal of American Indian Education* 45 (3): 5–23.

Dieter-Meyer, H. 2006. "The rise and decline of the common school as an institution: Taking myth and ceremony seriously." In *The new institutionalism in education*, ed. H. Dieter-Meyer and B. Rowan, 51–66. New York: State University of New York Press.

Dryfoos, J. 2008. "Centres of hope." *Educational Leadership* 65 (7): 38–43.

Dryfoos, J., and D. Knauer. 2002. *The evidence and lessons learned from fullservice community schools*. http://albany.edu/aire/urban/dryfoos-knauer.html (no longer active).

Duggan, L. 2003. *The twilight of equality? Neoliberalism, cultural politics, and the attack on democracy*. Boston: Beacon Press.

Eaves, Y.D. 2001. "A synthesis technique for grounded theory data analysis." *Journal of Advanced Nursing* 35 (5): 654–63. http://dx.doi.org/10.1046/j.1365-2648.2001.01897.x.

Elijah, M.J. 2002. "Literature review – Language and culture." Report prepared for the Minister's National Working Group on Education.

Ellis, A.K. 2004. *Exemplars of curriculum theory*. Larchmont, NY: Eye on Education.

Fayden, T. 2005. *How children learn: Getting beyond the deficit myth*. Boulder, CO: Paradigm.

Freire, P. 1970. *Pedagogy of the oppressed*. New York: Continuum.

Friesen, J.W., and V.L. Friesen. 2002. *Aboriginal education in Canada: A plea for integration*. Calgary: Detselig.

Frideres, J.S., and R.R. Gadacz. 2005. *Aboriginal peoples in Canada*. Toronto: Pearson.

Fultz, N.H., and A.R. Herzog. 1996. "Epidemiology of urinary symptoms in the geriatric population." *Urologic Clinics of North America* 23 (1): 1–10. http://dx.doi.org/10.1016/S0094-0143(05)70288-3.

Garcia, D.R. 2008. "Mixed messages: American Indian achievement before and since the implementation of NCLB." *Journal of American Indian Education* 47 (1): 136–54.

Gay, G. 2000. *Culturally responsive teaching: Theory, research, and practice*. New York: Teachers College Press.

Ghosh, R., and A.A. Abdi. 2004. *Education and the politics of difference: Canadian perspectives*. Toronto: Canadian Scholars' Press.

Gilbert, A. 2009. "Utilizing science philosophy statements to facilitate K-3 teacher candidate's development of inquiry-based science practice." *Early Childhood Education Journal* 36 (5): 431–38. http://dx.doi.org/10.1007/s10643-009-0302-7.

Gilliland, H. 1995. *Teaching the Native American*. Dubuque, IA: Kendall/Hall.

Giroux, H.A. 1991. "Postmodernism as border pedagogy." In *Postmodernism, feminism, and cultural politics: Redrawing educational boundaries*, ed. H.A. Giroux, 217–302. Albany: State University of New York Press.

–. 2004. "Cultural studies and the politics of public pedagogy: Making the political more pedagogical." *Parallax* 10 (2): 73–89. http://dx.doi.org/10.1080/1353464042000208530.

Glaser, B.G. 1978. *Theoretical sensitivity: Advances in the methodology of grounded theory*. Mill Valley, CA: Sociology Press.

Glaser, B.G., and A. Strauss. 1967. *The discovery of grounded theory: Strategies for qualitative research*. Chicago: Aldine.

Goin, L. 1999. "Planning academic programs for American Indian success: Learning strategies workshop." Workshop held at the "World Indigenous People's Conference: Education," 15-22 June 1996.

Goulet, L. 2001. "Two teachers of Aboriginal students: Effective practice in sociohistorical realities." *Canadian Journal of Native Education* 25 (1): 68–81.

Graveline, F. 2000. "Circle as methodology: Enacting an Aboriginal paradigm." *Qualitative Studies in Education* 13 (4): 361–70. http://dx.doi.org/10.1080/095183900413304.

Greig, R. 2003. "Ethnic identity development: Implications for mental health in African American and Hispanic adolescents." *Issues in Mental Health Nursing* 24 (3): 317–31. http://dx.doi.org/10.1080/01612840305278.

Haig-Brown, C. 1988. *Resistance and renewal: Surviving the Indian residential school*. Vancouver: Tillacum Library.

Hallett, D., S.C. Want, M.J. Chandler, L.L. Koopman, J.P. Flores, and E.C. Gehrke. 2008. "Identity in flux: Ethnic self-identification and school attrition in Canadian Aboriginal youth." *Journal of Applied Developmental Psychology* 29 (1): 62–75. http://dx.doi.org/10.1016/j.appdev.2007.10.008.

Halloran, M.H. 2007. "Indigenous reconciliation in Australia: Do values, identity, and collective guilt matter?" *Journal of Community and Applied Social Psychology* 17 (1): 1–18. http://dx.doi.org/10.1002/casp.876.

Hampton, E. 1988. "Towards a redefinition of Indian education." In *First Nations education in Canada: The circle unfolds*, ed. M. Battiste and J. Barman, 5–42. Vancouver: UBC Press.

Hatcher, A., C. Bartlett, and M. Marchall. 2009. "Two-eyed seeing: A cross-cultural science journey." *Green Teacher* 86: 3–6.

Hauser-Cram, P., S.R. Sirin, and D. Stipek. 2003. "When teachers' and parents' values differ: Teachers' rating of academic competence in children from low-income families." *Journal of Educational Psychology* 95 (4): 813–20. http://dx.doi.org/10.1037/0022-0663.95.4.813.

Hendrix, K.G., R.L. Jackson II, and J.R. Warren. 2003. "Shifting academic landscapes: Exploring co-identities, identity negotiation, and critical progressive pedagogy." *Communication Education* 52: 177–90. http://dx.doi.org/10.1080/0363452032000156181.

Hill, D.M. 2000. "Indigenous knowledge as a tool for self-determination and liberation." Paper presented at the National Association of Native American Studies Section of the Joint Conference of NAAAS, NAHLS, IAAS, and NANAS, Houston, 21-26 February.

Howitt, R., and S. Stevens. 2005. "Cross-cultural research: Ethics, methods and relationships." In *Qualitative research methods in human geography*, ed. I. Hay, 30–50. Melbourne: Oxford University Press.

Huffman, T. 2001. "Resistance theory and the transculturation hypothesis as explanations of college attrition and persistence among culturally traditional American Indian." *Journal of American Indian Education* 40 (3): 1–23.

Hutchison, P., and D. Hammer. 2010. "Attending to student epistemological framing in a science classroom." *Science Education* 94: 506–24.

Jackson, R.L. 2004. "Cultural contracts toward theory: Toward a critical-rhetorical identity negotiation paradigm." In *New approaches to rhetoric*, ed. P. Sullivan and S. Goldzwig, 89–108. Thousand Oaks, CA: Sage. http://dx.doi.org/10.4135/9781452233116.n4.

Johansen, B.E. 2004. "Back from the (nearly) dead: Reviving Indigenous languages across North America." *American Indian Quarterly* 28 (3): 566–82. http://dx.doi.org/10.1353/aiq.2004.0099.

Jones, H. 2004. "A research-based approach on teaching to diversity." *Journal of Instructional Psychology* 31 (1): 12–19.

Kanu, Y. 2011. *Integrating Aboriginal perspectives into the school curriculum: Purposes, possibilities, and challenges*. Toronto: University of Toronto Press.

Kavanaugh, B. 2005. "The role of parental and community involvement in the success of First Nations learners: A review of the literature." A report to the Minister's National Working Group on First Nations Education, Ottawa.

Kincheloe, J. 2005. *Critical constructivism primer*. New York: Peter Lang.

Klug, B., and P. Whitfield. 2003. *Widening the circle: Culturally relevant pedagogy for American Indian students*. New York: Routledge.

Klump, J., and G. McNeir. 2005. *Culturally responsive practices for student success: A regional sampler*. http://educationnorthwest.org/.

Kompf, M., and J. Hodson. 2000. "Keeping the seventh fire: Developing an undergraduate degree program for Aboriginal adult educators." *Canadian Journal of Native Education* 24 (2): 185–202.

Kovach, M. 2005. "Emerging from the margins: Indigenous methodologies." In *Research as resistance*, ed. L. Brown and S. Strega, 19–36. Toronto: Canadian Scholars' Press.

Kymlicka, W. 1996. "Three forms of group-differentiated citizenship in Canada." In *Democracy and difference: Contesting the boundaries of the political*, ed. S. Benhabib, 153–70. Princeton, NJ: Princeton University Press.

Loewen, J. 2007. *Lies my teacher told me: Everything your American history textbook got wrong.* New York: Simon and Schuster.

Lomawaima, K.T., and T.L. McCarty. 2006. *To remain an Indian: Lessons in democracy from a century of Native American education.* New York: Teachers College Press.

MacIvor, M. 1995. "Redefining science education for Aboriginal students." In *First Nations education in Canada: The circle unfolds,* ed. M. Battiste and J. Barman, 73–98. Vancouver: UBC Press.

Malott, C., and M. Pruyn. 2006. "Marxism and critical multicultural social studies education." In *The social studies curriculum: Purpose, problems and possibilities,* ed. W. Ross, 157–70. New York: SUNY Press.

Malott, C.S., L. Waukau, and L. Waukau-Villagomez. 2009. *Teaching Native America across the curriculum.* New York: Peter Lang.

Marshall, A. 2007. "Two-eyed seeing." Paper presented to the "Two-Eyed Seeing Workshop for Science Education for Children and Youth," Cape Breton University, NS, 24 May. http://tinyurl.com/d93qp3w.

McDougall, D., J. Gaskill, J.J. Flessa, J. Kugler, and E.E. Jang. 2006. *Improving student achievement in schools facing challenging circumstances.* Toronto: OISE/University of Toronto.

Medicine, B., and S. Jacobs. 2001. *Learning to be an anthropologist and remaining Native.* Urbana: University of Illinois Press.

Mihesuah, D. 1998. *Natives and academics: Researching and writing about American Indians.* Lincoln, NE: Bison Books.

Miller-Lachman, L., and L.S. Taylor. 1995. *Schools for all: Educating children in a diverse society.* New York: Delmar.

Minister's National Working Group on Education. 2002. *Our children: Keepers of the sacred knowledge – Final report of the Minister's National Working Group on Education.* Ottawa: Department of Indian Affairs and Northern Development Canada.

Moreton-Robinson, A. 2000. *Talkin' up to the white women.* St. Lucia: University of Queensland Press.

Moss, P., D. Pullin, J.P. Gee, E. Haertel, and L.J. Young, eds. 2008. *Assessment, equity and opportunity to learn.* Cambridge: Cambridge University Press. http://dx.doi.org/10.1017/CBO9780511802157.

Moyle, D. 2005. "Quality educators produce quality outcomes: Some thoughts on what this means in the context of teaching Aboriginal and Torres Strait Islander students in Australia's public education system." *Primary and Middle Years Educator* 3 (2): 11–15.

Nawagesic, B., and D. Domansky. 2000. *Labour market analysis.* Toronto: Federation of Indian Friendship Centres.

Ndura, E. 2004. "ESL and cultural bias: An analysis of elementary through high school textbooks in the Western United States of America." *Language, Culture and Curriculum* 17 (2): 143–53. http://dx.doi.org/10.1080/07908310408666689.

Neegan, E. 2005. "Excuse me? Who are the first peoples of Canada? A historical analysis of Aboriginal education in Canada then and now." *International*

Journal of Inclusive Education 9 (1): 3–15. http://dx.doi.org/10.1080/1360311042 000299757.

Nieto, S. 2003. *What keeps teachers going?* New York: Teachers College Press.

—. 2010. *Language, culture, and teaching.* New York: Routledge.

Norris, M.J. 2006. "Aboriginal languages in Canada: Trends and perspectives on maintenance and revitalization." In *Aboriginal policy research: Moving forward, making a difference,* ed. J.P. White, S. Wingert, D. Beavon, and P. Maxim, 197–226. Toronto: Thompson Educational.

Norris, M.J., and K. MacCon. 2003. "Aboriginal language, transmission, and maintenance in families: Results of an intergenerational and gender-based analysis for Canada, 1996." In *Aboriginal conditions: Research as a foundation for public policy,* ed. J. White, P. Maxim, and D. Beavon, 164–96. Vancouver: UBC Press.

OME (Ontario Federation of Indian Friendship Centres). 2005. *Literacy as a barrier to employment.* Toronto: Author.

—. 2007. *Ontario First Nation, Métis, and Inuit education policy framework.* Toronto: Aboriginal Education Office.

Ontario Native Affairs Secretariat. 2005. *Ontario's new approach to Aboriginal affairs: Prosperous and healthy Aboriginal communities create a better future for Aboriginal children and youth.* Toronto: Queen's Printer for Ontario.

Paquette, J., and G. Fallon. 2010. *First Nations education policy in Canada: Progress or gridlock?* Toronto: University of Toronto Press.

Parsons, E.C., C. Travis, and J. Simpson. 2005. "The black cultural ethos, students' instructional context preferences, and student achievement: An examination of culturally congruent science instruction in the eighth grade classes of one African American and one Euro-American teacher." *Negro Educational Review* 56: 183–204.

Perle, M., R. Moran, A. Lutkas, and W. Tirre. 2005. *NAEP 2004 trends in academic progress: Three decades of student performance in reading and mathematics.* Washington, DC: National Center for Education Statistics, US Department of Education, Institute of Education Sciences.

Pewewardy, C., and P. Hammer. 2003. *Culturally responsive teaching for American Indian students.* Charleston, WV: ERIC Clearinghouse on Rural Education and Small Schools.

Phillips, S.M. 2008. *Forging partnerships, opening doors.* Kelowna, BC: Society for the Advancement of Excellence in Education.

Piquemal, N. 2005. "Cultural loyalty: Aboriginal students take an ethical stance." *Reflective Practice* 6 (4): 523–38. http://dx.doi.org/10.1080/14623940500300707.

Priest, H., P. Roberts, and L. Woods. 2002. "An overview of three different approaches to the interpretation of qualitative data." *Nurse Researcher* 10 (1): 30–42. http://dx.doi.org/10.7748/nr2002.10.10.1.30.c5877.

Reyhner, J., and D.S. Hurtado. 2008. "Reading first, literacy, and American Indian/Alaska Native students." *Journal of American Indian Education* 47 (1): 82–95.

Reyhner, J., and D. Jacobs. 2002. "Preparing teachers of American Indian and Alaska Native students." *Action in Teacher Education* 24 (2): 85–93. http://dx.doi.org/10.1080/01626620.2002.10734422.

Rice, D. 2008. "Workforce focus." *Oxford Local Training Board* 2 (7): 1–4.
Richardson, G. 2008. "Within the luminal space: Repositioning global citizenship education as politics of encounter." In *Decolonizing democratic education*, ed. A. Abdi and G. Richardson, 127–38. Rotterdam, The Netherlands: Sense Publishers.
Robertson, H.J. 2003. "Decolonizing schools." *Phi Delta Kappan* 84 (7): 552–53.
Ross, A. 1989. *We are all related*. Fort Yates, ND: Bear, Inc.
Rowland, P., and C. Adkins. 2003. "Native American science education and its implications for multi-cultural science education." In *Multicultural science education: Theory, practice, and promise*, ed. S.M. Hines, 103–20. New York: Peter Lang.
Schissel, B., and T. Wotherspoon. 2003. *The legacy of school for Aboriginal people*. New York: Oxford University Press.
Sears, A., and A.S. Hughes. 1996. "Citizenship education and current educational reform." *Canadian Journal of Education* 21 (2): 123–42. http://dx.doi.org/10.2307/1495085.
Shaw, W.S., R.D.K. Herman, and G.R. Dobbs. 2006. "Encountering Indigeneity: Re-imagining and decolonizing geography." *Geografiska Annaler, Series B, Human Geography* 88 (3): 267–76. http://dx.doi.org/10.1111/j.1468-0459.2006.00220.x.
Silver, J., P. Ghoorayshi, J. Hay, and D. Klyne. 2006. *In a voice of their own: Urban Aboriginal community development*. Ottawa: Canadian Centre for Policy Alternatives.
Slavin, R.E. 2007. *Educational research: In an age of accountability*. New York: Allyn and Bacon.
Smith, L.T. 1999. *Decolonizing methodologies: Research and Indigenous peoples*. Dunedin, New Zealand: University of Otago Press.
Sparks, S. 2000. "Classroom and curriculum accommodations for Native American students." *Intervention in School and Clinic* 35 (5): 259–63. http://dx.doi.org/10.1177/105345120003500501.
Spencer, M.B. 2000. "Identity, achievement orientation and race: Lessons learned about the normative development experiences of African American males." In *Race and education*, ed. W. Watkins, J. Lewis, and V. Chou, 100–27. Needham Heights, MA: Allyn and Bacon.
St. Denis, V. 2010. *A study of Aboriginal teachers' professional knowledge and experience in Canadian schools*. Ottawa: Canadian Council on Learning.
Stake, R.E. 2000. "Case studies." In *Handbook of qualitative research*, ed. N.K. Denzin and Y.S. Lincoln, 435–51. Thousand Oaks, CA: Sage.
Steinhauer, E. 2002. "Thoughts on an Indigenous research methodology." *Canadian Journal of Native Education* 26: 69–81.
Strauss, A., and J. Corbin. 1990. *Basics of qualitative research: Grounded theory procedures and techniques*. Newbury Park, CA: Sage.
Sutton, V. 2007. "Wind and wisdom." *Environmental and Energy Law and Policy* 1: 345–72.
Taber, K.S. 2000. "Case studies and generalizability: Grounded theory and research in science education." *International Journal of Science Education* 22 (5): 469–87. http://dx.doi.org/10.1080/095006900289732.

Talbot, A. 2004. "Community school research project: Phase one report." Association for Community Education in British Columbia.

Tanner, D., and L. Tanner. 1995. *Curriculum development: Theory and practice*. New York: Merrill.

Tharp, R.G., H. Lewis, R. Hilberg, C. Bird, G. Epaloose, S.S. Dalton, D.G. Youpa, et al. 1999. "Seven more mountains and a map: Overcoming obstacles to reform in Native American schools." *Journal of Education for Students Placed at Risk* 4 (1): 5–25. http://dx.doi.org/10.1207/s15327671espr0401_2.

Tlanusta Garrett, M., M.L. Bellon-Harn, E. Torres-Rivera, J.T. Garrett, and L.C. Roberts. 2003. "Open hands, open hearts: Working with Native youth in the schools." *Intervention in School and Clinic* 38 (4): 225–35. http://dx.doi.org/10.1177/105345120303800405.

Toomey, S. 1999. *Communicating across cultures*. New York: Guilford Press.

Trudeau, L., and L. Cherubini. 2010. "Speaking our truths in 'a good way.'" *Canadian Journal of Native Education* 33 (1): 113–21.

Tyler, K.M., A.L. Uqdah, M.L. Dillihunt, R. Beatty-Hazelbaker, T. Conner, N. Gadson, A. Henchy, et al. 2008. "Cultural discontinuity: Toward a quantitative investigation of a major hypothesis." *Educational Researcher* 37 (5): 280–97. http://dx.doi.org/10.3102/0013189X08321459.

Verkuyten, M. 2003. "Positive and negative self-esteem among ethnic minority early adolescents: Social and cultural sources and threats." *Journal of Youth and Adolescence* 32 (4): 267–77. http://dx.doi.org/10.1023/A:1023032910627.

Villegas, M., S.R. Rak Neugebauer, and K.R. Venegas. 2008. *Indigenous knowledge and education*. Cambridge, MA: Harvard Educational Press.

Wee, B., D. Shepardson, J. Fast, and J. Harbor. 2007. "Teaching and learning about inquiry: Insights and challenges in professional development." *Journal of Science Teacher Education* 18 (1): 63–89. http://dx.doi.org/10.1007/s10972-006-9031-6.

White, J., P. Maxim, and N.D. Spence. 2004. "An examination of educational success." In *Aboriginal policy research: Setting the agenda for change*, ed. P. White, P. Maxim, and D. Beavon, 129–48. Toronto: Thompson Educational.

Wilson, A. 2004. "Reclaiming our humanity: Decolonization and the recovery of Indigenous knowledge." In *Indigenizing the academy: Transforming scholarship and empowering communities*, ed. D. Mihesuah and A. Wilson, 69–87. Lincoln: University of Nebraska Press.

Wilson, S. 2008. *Research Is Ceremony: Indigenous research methods*. Winnipeg: Fernwood.

Wint, A. 2002. "Competitive disadvantages and advantages of small nations: An analysis of inter-nation economic performance." *Journal of Eastern Caribbean Studies* 27 (3): 1–25.

Womack, C.S. 1999. *Red on red: Native American literary separatism*. Minneapolis: University of Minnesota Press.

Woodward, J. 2007. "Schools to be social service hubs." *Vancouver Sun*, 15 September. http://www.canada.com/vancouversun/news/westcoastnews/story.html?id=1a3548b9-745d-4900-b727-b5c864923403.

Index

Note: (f) after a page number indicates a figure. In subheadings, ASP refers to the Aboriginal Student Program at Soaring Heights Secondary School, and OME to the Ontario Ministry of Education.

Aboriginal Advisory Council, 63, 70
Aboriginal arts courses at SHSS, 83, 86, 88-89
Aboriginal caregivers. *See* Aboriginal parents and caregivers
Aboriginal community: on ASP and academic engagement, 83-86; on ASP and cultural engagement, 81-83; on ASP and identity, 78-81; ASP as helping to reconnect, 40; External Medicine Wheel and, 138, 139; as involved in ASP, 28, 70-74; as mistrustful of the educational system, 17, 56, 101-2, 133; need for involvement in the educational system, 17, 26, 100, 101-2, 142, 158; as recognizing a shift in educational policy, 144; relationship between Aboriginal youth counsellors and, 56
Aboriginal community resources and ASP, 143, 144

Aboriginal cultures: as disconnected from mainstream education, 24; elders' role in, 159; Good Medicine in, x; mainstream schools' lack of understanding of, 17; need for inclusion in the educational system, 128; need for programs that honour, 18; significance of drum in, 151; sustaining, 154, 155. *See also* Aboriginal traditions, values, and beliefs; cultural interventions in ASP
Aboriginal epistemologies: incorporated into pedagogy at SHSS, 36, 38, 129 (*see also* pedagogical approaches, as adapted by mainstream teachers to suit Aboriginal learning needs); intergenerational teachings as inherent in, 142; as not represented in mainstream curricula, 3, 10, 13, 102; as positively influencing sense of identity, 14, 102; view of learning,

12; vs mainstream, 14. *See also* Aboriginal learning needs, preferences, and styles; epistemic conflicts

Aboriginal families, ASP, and cultural engagement, 39, 134, 154, 160

Aboriginal female students (case story interviewees): on ASP and power, 40-42; on ASP's elder, 135, 158; on ASP's impact on identity, 38-40; on ASP's impact on school culture, 35-38; background information about, 25; External Medicine Wheel and, 121, 128-30, 134, 135; Internal Medicine Wheel and, 151-53, 154, 155-56

Aboriginal friendship centres and ASP, 143

Aboriginal health centres and ASP, 143

Aboriginal history courses at SHSS, 86, 89, 131

Aboriginal learning needs, preferences, and styles: Aboriginal students on, 45-48; Aboriginal youth counsellors as communicating with school board about, 55; ASP as addressing, 83-84; ASP as encouraging greater consideration for, 145; characteristics of, 11-12, 21, 88, 110; as distinct from mainstream, 142; epistemic conflicts and, 52-53, 86; mainstream teachers and, 17, 18, 87, 111, 116-17 (*see also* pedagogical approaches); Native Room as suited to, 40, 43; as not represented in mainstream education, 4, 10, 13, 14; professional development programs as not addressing, 104, 106, 109, 147; recognized by OME as unique, 16; teacher-education programs as not addressing, 105. *See also* Aboriginal epistemologies; Aboriginal students, as critical thinkers

Aboriginal male students (case story interviewees): on ASP and relationships, 45-48; background information about, 25; External Medicine Wheel and, 123-24, 130-31; Internal Medicine Wheel and, 154-55, 155-56, 157; on learning preferences and student engagement, 44-45; on Native Room as inviting space, 42-44

Aboriginal parents and caregivers: on ASP and academic engagement, 83-86; on ASP and cultural engagement, 81-83; on ASP and identity, 78-81; External Medicine Wheel and, 132, 138; as involved in children's education, 28, 94, 99, 168-69; mainstream teachers' criticism of, 111, 116, 133; as marginalized within the educational landscape, 107; as mistrustful of the educational system, 107; need for involvement in the educational system, 17, 26, 142; as recognizing a shift in educational policy, 144. *See also* relationships

Aboriginal peoples: demographics of, 3, 24; Framework definition of, 4; Indigenous methodologies as rooted in, 15; not recognized as a founding nation, 11

Aboriginal public education, approach to, 4-5, 9

Aboriginal research, 14

Aboriginal societies, preservation of, 10. *See also* Aboriginal cultures

Aboriginal Student Program (ASP) at SHSS: Aboriginal youth counsellors' contributions to success of, 63, 64-65, 75-76; attendance in, 28, 97, 98, 167; as balancing Aboriginal knowledge with mainstream academic expectations, 102; central components of, 24; challenges of, 66-67, 90, 97, 100-1; as connecting Aboriginal students to SHSS, 45; as empowering Aboriginal students, 121, 127, 144; enrolment in, 28, 97-98, 167; as equitable and multicultural, 126-27; as facilitating cultural cohesion,

102; as focusing on the communal benefits of education, 96; funding issues with, 73-75, 76-77; as hybrid educational model, 142-46; mandates of, 52, 59, 60, 61, 66, 70-71, 145, 162; measuring the success of, 48-51, 75; need for Aboriginal community liaison in, 77-78; origins of, 20, 24, 63, 70; professional development offered by, 106, 108; program reports of, 29, 97, 100-3; as providing Aboriginal parents and caregivers with a voice, 80; recommendations for, 74-78, 101; retention rates of, 83; strengths of, 59; successes of, 22, 97, 100, 101, 103-4, 146, 158, 162; vision of, 122-23, 124-25, 126; as voluntary, not mandatory, for Aboriginal students, 42, 69, 81-82, 123, 132, 161; withdrawal rate of, 28, 99, 167. *See also* achievement, ASP as contributing to; case story; engagement, academic; engagement, cultural; identity, Aboriginal students'; interventions in ASP

Aboriginal Student Programs: as absent from elementary schools, 61-62; considerations surrounding, 98, 118, 130, 136; as creating space for Aboriginal initiatives, 139; as models of bicultural learning environments, 128; as offering hope of a better future, 163; at other schools, 19, 41, 46, 131, 157

Aboriginal student realities: ASP as sensitive to, 97, 126; cultural practices as addressing, 72; drum as symbol of, 139; examples of others understanding, 49, 52, 75-76, 86, 114, 138, 143; need for others to understand, 18, 53-54, 57, 58, 65, 67-69, 93-94

Aboriginal students: ASP as devoted to entire being of, 52, 99, 103; challenges of, 133; as critical thinkers, 44-45, 126, 135, 136, 137, 138, 139, 146, 155, 156 (*see also* critical thinking); increase in number of students self-identifying as, 98; influences on public school experiences of, 9-11; mainstream teachers' negative perceptions of, 112, 114, 116, 117, 118; and place in school culture, 5, 51-52, 122, 130. *See also* Aboriginal female students (case story interviewees); Aboriginal male students (case story interviewees); biculturalism; marginalization, of Aboriginal students; relationships

Aboriginal teachers, 75-76, 84

Aboriginal traditional knowledge: Aboriginal epistemologies and, 12; Aboriginal youth counsellors and, 25, 55; need for inclusion in mainstream curricula, 22, 162; as relevant and important to Aboriginal students, 155-56; self-determination as enabled by, 61; SHSS elder on the value of, 159

Aboriginal traditions, values, and beliefs: Aboriginal families' and community's lack of exposure to, 39, 81-82, 134, 154; ASP as rooted in, 71; as celebrated by mainstream teachers, 36, 129; as disconnected from mainstream educational experiences, 11; mainstream teachers' lack of knowledge about, 117, 147; need for inclusion in the educational system, 87-88; as positively influencing sense of identity, 14. *See also* Aboriginal cultures; cultural interventions in ASP; engagement, cultural

Aboriginal worldviews: Aboriginal youth counsellors as helping teachers understand, 145; classroom best practice for appreciating, 12-13; lack of understanding of, 17; need for inclusion in the educational system,

22, 127, 135; positive effect of including in pedagogy, 21
Aboriginal youth counsellors: as advocates, 40-41, 46, 56, 68, 86, 93, 121-22, 131, 143; on ASP as fostering identity, 59-62; as authority figures, 122; backgrounds of, 25; as conduits, 51, 57, 75, 94, 100; emotionally draining work of, 72, 75; External Medicine Wheel and, 132-33, 138; as fulfilling communal responsibilities, 61; as having carte blanche, 57; hiring of, 63, 73-74, 75; on the importance of relationships, 54-59; as large part of ASP's and Aboriginal students' success, 63, 64-65, 75-76, 92; as mediators, 41, 66, 76, 122, 145; as mentors, 66; on negotiating epistemic conflicts, 48-54; as partnering with mainstream teachers, 73, 93, 133, 145; praise for, 36, 37, 79, 85, 95, 113, 129-30, 132; as recruiters, 64; responsibilities of, 24, 76; as role models, 61, 62, 85; self-perception of, 51-52, 55, 62; various roles of, 58. *See also* relationships
accountability: mainstream teachers and, 85; school board vs Aboriginal youth counsellors' measures of, 48-51; school board vs school and program administrators' measures of, 75
achievement: ASP as contributing to, 44, 81, 97, 98-99, 103-4, 153; identity as fostering, 119; issues affecting, 17, 18-19; as OME challenge, 16; strategies for increasing, 140, 141-42, 150; trust as core of, 46, 130-31
achievement gap: as OME challenge, 16; reasons for, 13-14, 20, 145-46; statistics on, 10
action (component of External Medicine Wheel), 119, 120, 134-40, 158, 163
Aikenhead, G.S., 13

Alaska Native children, 4
American Indian children, 4
ancestors, 155
Andrea (parent): on ASP and academic engagement, 84, 85; on ASP and cultural engagement, 82; on ASP and identity, 80; background of, 26
Anishnawbe Nation, 151
Archibald, J., 12
assessment: of Aboriginal students, 104, 106-7, 108, 109; of ASP's success, 48-51, 75
assimilation: Aboriginal youth counsellors on, 54; in residential schools, 10, 150; at SHSS, 71
attendance, 111, 115-16
attendance records, ASP's, 28, 97, 98, 167

balance, 161, 163
Battiste, M., 10, 21, 127, 147
belonging: ASP as fostering a sense of, 37, 46, 79, 80, 95, 103, 131; community schools as fostering a sense of, 140; as power, 47
biases: as impediment to academic engagement, 53; importance of examining, 21, 118; teacher-education programs and, 104, 105-6, 108. *See also* critical thinking
biculturalism: Aboriginal Student Programs and, 128; ASP as enabling Aboriginal students to harness, 51-52, 102, 127-28, 132; mainstream teachers, identity, and, 112; and need for Aboriginal students to live in two worlds, 125, 155, 161; teacher-education programs and, 104, 105, 108. *See also* school culture
Big Drum, 151
Black Elk (elder), 148-49
Bob (teacher): background of, 25-26; on cultural interventions and Aboriginal student success, 90-92; on importance of relationships, 92-96; on navigating the educational environment,

86-87, 88-90; teaching style and philosophy of, 89-90
border crossers, 125-26, 136-37
Brayboy, M.J., 127
Brian (youth counsellor): on ASP as fostering identity, 59, 60-61; background of, 25; on the importance of relationships, 57; on negotiating epistemic conflicts, 48, 50, 51
Briggs, J., 5
British Columbia, 140
Brock University, 15-16

Canada as mosaic, 11
case story: approach to, 5, 15, 16; broader implications of, 97-98; goals of, 19, 21-22; impetus for, 19; interviewees for, 23, 25-27 (see also *names or titles of individual interviewees*); methodology of, 23, 25, 27-31; poignancy of individual stories in, 162; questions used in, 27 (*see also* faculty survey; student survey); reason for using pseudonyms in, 20; research team of, 15-16, 31. *See also* Aboriginal Student Program (ASP) at SHSS
Castagno, A.E., 127
Castellano, M.B., 20-21, 146
Catholic Aid Society, 58
ceremonies: case story as honouring, 30; as connected to learning, 12; as encouraging cultural engagement, 39, 139; food as important in, 157; spirituality and, 151-52. *See also* cultural interventions in ASP; engagement, cultural
Cherry (community member): on ASP and cultural engagement, 82-83; on ASP and identity, 79; background of, 26-27
Circle (spiritual tradition): case story as honouring, 27; meaning of, 148-49
clothing: distributed by ASP, 66, 157; as sustaining mainstream values, 58

cognitive dissonance, 111-12
colonialism: as affecting Aboriginal students' educational experiences, 3, 18-19; legacy of, 150, 154; as not critiqued in mainstream curricula, 11; as resulting in Aboriginal mistrust of the educational system, 107
combat metaphor, 50
community, ASP as fostering a sense of, 153, 154-55. *See also* Aboriginal community
community program coordinator (in community schools), 141
community program leader at SHSS: background of, 26, 62; on community and school engagement, 70-74; External Medicine Wheel and, 124, 132, 138; role of, 144; on strategic recommendations, 74-78; on success and relationships, 63-70
community schools, 139-41, 142-43
completion rates. *See* dropout rates, Aboriginal student
conceptual divides at SHSS, 109-12. *See also* epistemic conflicts
conflicts: Aboriginal youth counsellors as mediating, 41, 66, 76, 122; among Aboriginal students, 55; educational interventions as reducing, 169. *See also* epistemic conflicts; relationships
conscientization, theory of, 10
Constitution Act, 1982, 4
consultations, 139
Creator, 152, 153, 156-57
critical thinking: importance of, x, 21, 118, 125-26, 138, 147, 163-64; on research team, 31. *See also* Aboriginal students, as critical thinkers
cross-cultural relationships, 66, 70. *See also* relationships
cultural conflicts, 55. *See also* epistemic conflicts
cultural differences, 136-37

cultural discontinuity, 19
cultural dislocation, 21
cultural diversity, 11, 161
cultural identity. *See* identity, Aboriginal students'
cultural interventions in ASP, 29, 71, 81-82, 99, 152, 168-69; as fostering academic engagement, 143; as integral to Aboriginal student success, 90-92; mainstream teachers on, 113-14; roles in facilitating, 62, 72-73, 159. *See also* drum and drumming; engagement, cultural
cultural knowledge. *See* Aboriginal traditional knowledge
culturally responsive schooling, 139-40, 141-48; examples of, 125; mainstream teachers as practising, 73; as model for ASP, 65. *See also* Native Room at SHSS; pedagogical approaches
Cummins, J., 132
curricula. *See* mainstream curricula

dancing: as connected to learning, 12; as key element of Aboriginal identity, 151, 152
demographics of Aboriginal peoples, 3, 24
department chairpersons, 107
discourse styles, 14
diversity, cultural, 11, 161
dropout rates, Aboriginal student: from ASP, 99, 167; from school, 3, 11, 20, 24, 99, 142
drum and drumming: Aboriginal students and, 38, 40, 82, 100, 127, 130; Aboriginal students' identity and, 72, 82-83, 151-52; as connected to learning, 12; healing powers of, 71-72; importance of, 66, 91, 139, 159; mainstream teachers and, 38, 91, 113, 114, 115, 130; as part of mainstream school culture, 90-91; as re-engaging Aboriginal students academically, 50
Dryfoos, J., 139, 141

education: Aboriginal parents' awareness of value of, 80; Aboriginal peoples' view of, 158, 159; Bob and Paula's view of, 89; decreasing enrolment in Canadian public, 3; individual vs communal approach to, 95-96; proactive vs reactive approach to, 61-62
education policy, Ontario, 9, 162. *See also Ontario First Nation, Métis, and Inuit Educational Policy Framework* (Framework; 2007)
educational interventions in ASP, 28, 99-100, 168-69
educational reform, 13
educational spaces, 4, 139-40, 144. *See also* Native Room at SHSS
educational system, Aboriginal mistrust of, 17, 56, 101-2, 107, 133
educators, moral obligation of, 163. *See also* mainstream teachers
elder at SHSS, 159-62; Aboriginal students' praise for, 135, 158; background of, 26; importance of, 101, 102-3, 158; as link between different epistemologies, 145
elders: Aboriginal students' praise for, 39, 134; need for involvement in the educational system, 142, 147-48; prophecies of, 154; significance of, 12, 158-59; as supporting Aboriginal students, 72
elementary schools: absence of Aboriginal Student Programs in, 61-62; outreach and, 77, 102
emotional (component of Internal Medicine Wheel), 120, 149, 153-55, 158
engagement, academic: Aboriginal parents and community on, 83-86; Aboriginal youth counsellors as fostering, 37, 129; ASP as fostering,

Index 193

44-45, 50-51, 83-86, 99, 102, 103, 128, 129, 143, 153; community schools as fostering, 140; culturally responsive schooling as fostering, 141; few examples of successful, 19; identity as key to, 88; mainstream teachers' desire to strengthen, 115-17; oral traditions as fostering, 131; reasons for lack of, 20, 53-54, 110; as stemming from self-awareness of learning preferences, 136

engagement, cultural
- Aboriginal parents and community on, 81-83
- Aboriginal youth counsellors' experience of, 54
- ASP as fostering: in Aboriginal family members, 39, 134, 154, 160; in Aboriginal students, 38-39, 59-61, 81-83, 99, 100, 101, 114, 119, 134, 152. *See also* identity, Aboriginal students'

engagement with ASP by community and school, 70-74

enrolment: in ASP, 28, 97-98, 167; in Canadian public education, 3; in Ontario schools, 11

epistemic conflicts: Aboriginal parental involvement and, 94; Aboriginal youth counsellors on negotiating, 48-54; elders as easing, 161; between mainstream curricula and Aboriginal learning needs, 86-87; within mainstream learning environments, 41, 84, 122; professional development programs as not addressing, 106-7. *See also* conflicts

epistemic differences: need for mainstream teachers to understand, 94; as peacefully coexisting, 145; as used to extend learning, 136

epistemic preferences. *See* Aboriginal learning needs, preferences, and styles

epistemic space, 163

epistemologies, 14. *See also* Aboriginal epistemologies

Eurocentric curricula. *See* mainstream curricula

evaluation of Aboriginal students, 104, 106-7, 108, 109

evidence-based reform, 5

evidence-based research, 5

External Medicine Wheel, 119-21, 120(f), 149; action and, 119, 120, 134-40, 158, 163; as connected to Internal, 150, 158; knowledge and, 119-20, 134-40, 158, 163; relationships and, 119, 120, 128-33, 158, 163; vision and, 119, 121-28, 158, 163

faculty survey, 28(f), 104-18, 166, 171-76; few statistically significant differences in, 107-9, 175-76; implications of, 97, 108-9; objectives of, 29-30; qualitative responses to, 109-18

families and community schools, 140. *See also* Aboriginal families, ASP, and cultural engagement

feasts: as rekindling familial connections, 39, 134, 160; as return to school for Aboriginal community members, 102; as successful cultural intervention, 100, 101. *See also* cultural interventions in ASP

First Nations, 4

First Nations schools, 12

food and ceremonies, 157. *See also* nutritional interventions in ASP

formal education, 3. *See also* education

Freire, P., 10, 13, 138

friction. *See* conflicts; epistemic conflicts

funding and ASP, 73-75, 76-77

gender and relationships, 70

ghettos: Aboriginal peoples as living in, 53-54; ASP as not creating, 36, 92, 129, 132

Giroux, H.A., 124-26, 137
Good Medicine, x
Goulet, L., 101
Grandfather Drum, 151
grants for ASP, 74-75
guidance counsellors, 107

Harper, Stephen, 150
Hauser-Cram, P., 133
healing: drumming and, 71-72; as empowering Aboriginal peoples, 150; Trudeau's vision of, 157
health interventions in ASP. *See* nutritional interventions in ASP
heartbeat, drum and, 91, 151, 152, 159
hidden curriculum, 132
holistic education: ASP as, 52, 99, 103; Trudeau on, ix. *See also* External Medicine Wheel; Internal Medicine Wheel
home, 65, 69. *See also* Aboriginal student realities
hope, 124

identity, Aboriginal families', 39, 134
identity, Aboriginal students': Aboriginal community as fostering, 114, 158; Aboriginal epistemologies as positively influencing, 14, 102; Aboriginal parents and community on ASP and, 78-81; Aboriginal youth counsellors as fostering, 113; ASP as fostering, ix, 38-40, 59-62, 78-81, 98, 103, 104, 126, 127; ASP elder on, 160-61; as born from spirituality, 150-51, 161; as co-constructed, 136; critical thinking, learning preferences, and, 47, 119, 146; drumming as fostering, 72, 82-83, 151-52; as fostering academic achievement, 119; Framework on importance of, 17, 18; key elements of, 151-53; as key to academic engagement, 88; mainstream teachers and, 58, 112, 125,
130, 138; Medicine Wheels and, 120, 134-35, 149 (*see also* vision [component of External Medicine Wheel]); as not represented in mainstream curricula, 11; pedagogy and, 136; relationships and, 12, 58, 70, 130; wellness and, 157. *See also* Aboriginal students, as critical thinkers; engagement, cultural; relationships
identity, mainstream teachers', 136
identity, student, 10-11
In a Voice of Their Own: Urban Aboriginal Community Development (2006), 100
Indigenous knowledge: self-determination as linked to reclaiming, 127; sources of, 146. *See also* Aboriginal traditional knowledge
in-service initiatives. *See* professional development programs
intellect, 53. *See also* engagement, academic
intellectual (component of Internal Medicine Wheel), 120, 149, 155-56, 158. *See also* engagement, academic
intercultural relationships, 66, 70. *See also* relationships
Internal Medicine Wheel, 119-20, 120(f), 148; aspects of, 149; as connected to External, 150, 158; emotional and, 120, 149, 153-55, 158; intellectual and, 120, 149, 155-56, 158; physical and, 120, 149, 156-57, 158; spiritual and, 120, 149, 150-53, 158
interventions in ASP, 28-29, 99-100, 168-69; as culturally sensitive, 36, 44, 47, 56, 126, 128, 130; financial support for, 74; as fostering academic engagement, 129; as reconnecting Aboriginal students to school culture, 37
Inuit, 4

Index

James (community member), 26
Jane (community member): on ASP and academic engagement, 84, 85; on ASP and cultural engagement, 81, 82; on ASP and identity, 80-81; background of, 26
Jordan (youth counsellor): on ASP as fostering identity, 59, 60, 61-62; background of, 25, 50; on importance of relationships, 55, 56-57, 58-59; on negotiating epistemic conflicts, 48-54

Kanu, Y., 3
Katie (parent): on ASP and academic engagement, 83, 85; on ASP and cultural engagement, 82; on ASP and identity, 80; background of, 26
Kincheloe, J., 13
Knauer, K., 141
knowledge (component of External Medicine Wheel), 119-20, 134-40, 158, 163. *See also* Aboriginal traditional knowledge
knowledge, Indigenous: self-determination as linked to reclaiming, 127; sources of, 146. *See also* Aboriginal traditional knowledge
knowledge sharing, 67-68

language: Aboriginal youth counsellors and, 25; as fostering academic engagement, 50; identity and, 39-40, 135; learning and, 12; spirituality and, 153
learning: importance of recognizing different types of, 137; language and, 12
learning environments: Aboriginal students and mainstream, 96, 110, 130; ASP as fostering culturally responsive, 37-38, 128, 129; epistemic conflict within mainstream, 41, 84, 122; Paula and Bob on navigating, 86-90. *See also* culturally responsive schooling; mainstream classrooms; Native Room at SHSS
Linda (community member): on ASP and academic engagement, 83, 84, 85; on ASP and cultural engagement, 81, 82; on ASP and identity, 79, 80; background of, 26
Lomawaima, K.T., 142
lunches. *See* nutritional interventions in ASP

Macedo, D., 13
mainstream classrooms: Aboriginal students and, 111, 114; Aboriginal students on, 44-45; ASP as fostering culturally responsive, 38. *See also* learning environments; Native Room at SHSS; pedagogical approaches
mainstream concepts of teaching and learning: Aboriginal students as forced to comply with, 10; Paula and Bob as refusing to privilege, 88; as perpetuated by mainstream teachers' lack of self-examination, 106
mainstream curricula: as adapted by mainstream teachers to suit Aboriginal students, 87; epistemic conflict and, 86; inclusion of culturally relevant material in, 45; lack of Aboriginal content in, 11, 106, 110; need for Indigenization of, 5, 17, 22, 84, 116, 146-48, 162; as not engaging Aboriginal students, 14; as not representing Aboriginal epistemologies, 3, 10, 13, 162; as reason for Aboriginal dropout rate, 24. *See also* pedagogical approaches
mainstream educational practices: epistemic conflict and, 86; as promoting the knowledge paradigms of dominant groups, 3
mainstream epistemologies, 14

mainstream pedagogical approaches, 109, 111. *See also* pedagogical approaches

mainstream public schools: Aboriginal students as having difficulty with protocols in, 110-11; decreasing enrolment in, 3; as not addressing Aboriginal students' learning preferences, 142; as not understanding Aboriginal cultures, 17

mainstream teachers: Aboriginal parents' praise for, 84; accountability and, 85; cognitive dissonance and, 111-12; conflicts surrounding ASP and, 66-67, 95, 122, 123, 126; as lacking time to assist Aboriginal students, 75-76; as not understanding or meeting Aboriginal learning needs, 4, 13, 14, 132; as partnering with Aboriginal youth counsellors, 73, 93, 133, 145; as respecting Aboriginal epistemologies, 37-38; as supportive of ASP, 67. *See also* Bob (teacher); Native Room at SHSS; Paula (teacher); pedagogical approaches; relationships

Malott, C., 11, 13

Manitoba, 4, 140

marginalization: of Aboriginal parents, 107; of Aboriginal students, 13, 19, 36, 45, 52, 102, 112, 128, 163

marginalized populations, 140

Mark (youth counsellor): on ASP as fostering identity, 59-60; background of, 25; on importance of relationships, 56, 57, 59; on negotiating epistemic conflicts, 48-51, 52-53

Mary (caregiver): on ASP and academic engagement, 83; on ASP and cultural engagement, 81; on ASP and identity, 79; background of, 26

McCarty, T.L., 142

Medicine Wheel, 120(f), 127, 149. *See also* External Medicine Wheel; Internal Medicine Wheel

Melissa (community member): on ASP and cultural engagement, 81; background of, 26

Métis, 4, 24

Michell, H., 13

morality, 163

Mother Earth, 151, 152, 156

motivation. *See* engagement, academic

multiculturalism: ASP as, 126-27; as model for student identity, 10-11; at SHSS, 66, 71; teacher-education programs, Aboriginal learning needs, and, 105

multi-epistemic traditions, 105

Native language courses, 153

Native Room at SHSS: Aboriginal students' praise for, 37, 42-44, 82, 123-24, 153; as culturally sensitive learning environment, 36, 43-44, 45, 82, 103, 135-36; as fostering relationships, 47, 131; location in school, 92, 157; mainstream teachers' criticism of, 41, 43, 93, 95, 110, 112-13, 114-15, 122, 123, 126; mainstream teachers' praise for, 112, 114-15; purpose of, 42; as respite from mainstream classrooms, 40, 43, 91, 121; as space of educational and cultural support, 24, 37, 123-24; as symbol of Aboriginal community's presence, 143-44

Native Studies courses at SHSS: Aboriginal students on, 45, 83; in arts, 83, 86, 88-89; background on, 26; in history, 86, 89, 131; as key element of identity, 151, 153

Nieto, S., 132

non-Aboriginal community and ASP, 74

non-Aboriginal students. *See* relationships, Aboriginal and non-Aboriginal students

nutritional interventions in ASP, 28, 74, 75, 99, 156-57, 168-69

Ogbu, B., 101
Oglala Sioux Nation, 148
Ontario: Aboriginal student trends in, 52; colonialism in education in, 3; education policy in, 9, 162; multiculturalism in teacher-education programs in, 105
Ontario First Nation, Métis, and Inuit Educational Policy Framework (Framework; 2007): Aboriginal learning needs and, 9, 107; ASP as fulfilling mandate of, 139; as background to case story, 16-19; definition of Aboriginal peoples, 4; limitations of, 87; and silencing of Aboriginal knowledge, 147
Ontario Ministry of Education: as drawing attention to achievement gap, 13; two challenges faced by, 16
Ontario schools, enrolment in, 11
Ontario's New Approach to Aboriginal Affairs (2005), 16
oral traditions: as connected to learning, 12; epistemic conflict and, 86; as not reflected in mainstream classrooms, 14; as re-engaging Aboriginal students academically, 131

parental interventions in ASP, 28, 99, 168-69. *See also* Aboriginal parents and caregivers
Paula (teacher): Aboriginal students' praise for, 36, 129; background of, 25-26; on cultural interventions and Aboriginal student success, 90-92; on importance of relationships, 92-96; on navigating the educational environment, 86-90; teaching style and philosophy of, 88-89, 90
pedagogical approaches: Aboriginal students as not responding to mainstream, 44; as adapted by mainstream teachers to suit Aboriginal learning needs, 36, 45, 87, 89-90, 91, 124-25, 129, 130, 137; ASP as remote from mainstream, 97; epistemic conflict and, 86; Eurocentric vs cultural-historical, 21; as identity based, 136; mainstream, 109, 111; as means of rethinking relationships, 125-26; need to reflect Aboriginal learning needs, 17; as not adapted by mainstream teachers to suit Aboriginal learning needs, 106-7, 108, 109-10, 125, 147; politics and, 137; professional development programs and, 104, 106, 109, 118. *See also* mainstream curricula
Phillips, S.M., 140
physical (component of Internal Medicine Wheel), 120, 149, 156-57, 158
play as element of learning, 88
politics: pedagogy and, 137; as permeating public classrooms, 163
poverty: Aboriginal students as living in, 58, 65-66, 69; as impediment to academic engagement, 53-54
power: as belonging, 47; educational reform as manifestation of privileged, 13; as manifested in schools, 136, 163; need for mainstream teachers to reflect on effect of, 138
power relations and ASP, 40-42, 122
praxis, 138
pre-service professional development. *See* teacher-education programs
principal at SHSS: Aboriginal parents' and community's praise for, 85; background of, 26, 62; on community and school engagement, 71-74; External Medicine Wheel and, 124, 126-27, 139; managerial style of, 73, 76; on strategic recommendations, 74-77; on success and relationships, 64, 65-66, 68, 69-70; as supportive of ASP, 57, 63, 67, 144
principals, 141

privilege: mainstream teachers' belief in Aboriginal students', 93; mainstream teachers see Native Room as, 115; need for educators to consider their own, 118

professional development programs: as distanced from classroom pedagogical practices, 118; mainstream teachers' recommendations for, 115-17; as not preparing teachers to work with Aboriginal students, 104, 106-7, 108-9, 147; recommendations for, 147

Program of Choice, ASP as, 64, 98

program reports, ASP's, 29, 97, 100-3

Pruyn, M., 11

pseudonyms in case story, 20

public education. *See* education

race and relationships, 70

racism: as alienating Aboriginal learners, 142; schooling practices as perpetuating, 132

recommendations: for ASP, 74-78, 101; for professional development programs, 115-17, 147; for teacher-education programs, 147

reform, evidence-based, 5

regalia, 152

relationships: Aboriginal and non-Aboriginal students, 36, 37, 43, 47, 124, 131; Aboriginal parents and mainstream teachers and administrators, 105, 107, 108, 133; Aboriginal students and mainstream teachers, 41, 46-47, 52-53, 58, 66, 93, 121-22, 130, 133, 137 (*see also* Native Room at SHSS: mainstream teachers' criticism of); Aboriginal students and youth counsellors, 46-47, 49, 55, 59, 64-65, 68, 130-31; Aboriginal youth counsellors and Aboriginal community, 56; Aboriginal youth counsellors and mainstream teachers, 37, 57; Aboriginal youth counsellors and school administration, 57; Aboriginal youth counsellors on importance of, 54-59; among Aboriginal students, 55, 79, 95, 134-35; among research participants, ix; ASP as helping foster, 45-48; as central to Aboriginal epistemologies, 12; community schools as fostering, 140-41; as component of External Medicine Wheel, 119, 120, 128-33, 158, 163; importance of establishing collaborative, 124; Paula and Bob on importance of, 92-96; pedagogy as means of rethinking, 125-26; school and ASP administrators on importance of, 63-70

"re-search," 14, 30

research, evidence-based, 5

research study. *See* case story

reserves: Aboriginal students' transitioning to SHSS from, 52; as ghettos, 53-54

residential schools: assimilation in, 10, 150; legacy of, 56, 69, 107, 140, 143

respect: importance of, ix, 55, 59; ways of creating, 161

responsibility, 68-69, 154. *See also* self-determination

retention rates, ASP's, 83

Richardson, G., 21

role modelling, importance of, 116-17

Sarah (community member): on ASP and academic engagement, 83, 84-85; on ASP and identity, 78-79, 80; background of, 26

school and ASP administrators at SHSS: background of, 62; on community and school engagement, 70-74; on strategic recommendations, 74-78; on success and relationships, 63-70. *See also* relationships

Index

school board: as demanding quantifiable evidence of ASP's success, 48, 50; as supportive of ASP, 63, 67, 70
school closures, 3
school communities, 163-64
school culture: Aboriginal parents on ASP and, 132; Aboriginal students' place in, 5, 51-52, 122, 130; ASP's impact on, 20, 35-38, 46, 127, 129; ASP's position within, 66; importance of providing a secure space within, 128; Native Room's position within, 92
school records, SHSS's, 98-100, 167
school retention. *See* dropout rates, Aboriginal student
school system. *See* educational system, Aboriginal mistrust of
schooling. *See* culturally responsive schooling; education
self-determination: ASP as fostering, 59, 60-61, 62, 104, 158; External Medicine Wheel and, 120, 127
self-esteem, 79
self-image. *See* identity
sense of self. *See* identity
shepherd metaphor, 90
Silver, J., 100
Sirin, S.R., 133
Sitpek, D., 133
Slavin, R.E., 5
smudging, 71
Soaring Heights Secondary School (SHSS): Aboriginal students, catchment area, and, 64; Aboriginal students as choosing to attend, 134, 154; assimilation at, 71; background of, 16, 24; as engaged with ASP, 70-74; environment and relationships in, 47; intake procedure at, 98-99; multiculturalism at, 66, 71; as responsive to the needs of Aboriginal students, 19; socio-economic realities of, 65-66, 94; as typical Ontario school, 20. *See also* Aboriginal Student Program (ASP) at SHSS; case story
social action, need for, 163
social support interventions in ASP, 28, 99-100, 168-69
spaces, educational, 4, 139-40, 144. *See also* Native Room at SHSS
special education teachers, 107
Spencer, M.B., 133
Spirit, Trudeau on, ix, x
spiritual (component of Internal Medicine Wheel), 120, 149, 150-53, 158
spiritual traditions, 27
standardized curricula. *See* mainstream curricula
standardized tests, 13
State of Aboriginal Learning in Canada, The (2009), 11
statistics: faculty survey, 171-76; program interventions, 168; school records, 167; student survey, 170
stereotypes, 160
storytelling: as connected to learning, 12, 142; as largely absent from mainstream curricula, 14
strategic recommendations for ASP, 74-78
student retention, 70. *See also* dropout rates, Aboriginal student
student survey, 28(f), 29, 30, 103-4, 165, 170
success, Aboriginal student, 90-92. *See also* achievement; engagement, academic
success, ASP's: measuring, 48-51, 75; school and program administrators on, 63-70
Susan (parent): on ASP and academic engagement, 84, 85; on ASP and cultural engagement, 81, 82; on ASP and identity, 79, 80-81; background of, 27
Sutton, V. (source of Black Elk quotation), 148-49

Talbot, A., 140-41
talent show, 37, 72, 90-91, 114, 151
teacher-education programs: lack of Aboriginal content in, 4; as not preparing teachers to examine their own biases, 104, 105-6, 108; as not preparing teachers to work with Aboriginal students, 104, 105, 108; recommendations for, 147; students in, 105-6
teachers, Aboriginal, 75-76, 84
teachers, mainstream. *See* mainstream teachers
teaching: benefits of two-way approach to, 21; differing definitions of, 89. *See also* pedagogical approaches
Tecumseh Centre for Aboriginal Research and Education (Brock University), 15-16
tension. *See* conflicts; epistemic conflicts
Tharp, R.G., 3-4
traditional knowledge. *See* Aboriginal traditional knowledge
Trudeau, Lyn: on elders, 158-59, 161; foreword by, ix-x; on Medicine Wheels, 120, 148-57
trust: as core of academic achievement, 46, 130-31; importance of, 59, 155
Tyler, K.M., 19

United States as melting pot, 11

vice-principal at SHSS: background of, 26, 62; on strategic recommendations, 74; on success and relationships, 70; as working with Aboriginal youth counsellors, 68
vision (component of External Medicine Wheel), 119, 121-28, 158, 163
volunteer interventions in ASP, 28, 99, 168-69

Walk-In Closet, 66
wellness, 157-58
Western-based curricula. *See* mainstream curricula
Wilson, A., 127
Wind (spirit), ix, x
withdrawal rate, ASP's, 28, 99, 167. *See also* dropout rates, Aboriginal student
written texts: epistemic conflict and, 86-87; as prioritized in mainstream educational practices, 14

Youngblood Henderson, H.J., 147
youth counsellors. *See* Aboriginal youth counsellors

Printed and bound in Canada by Friesens

Set in Segoe and Warnock by Artegraphica Design Co. Ltd.

Copy editor: Joanne Richardson

Proofreader: Dallas Harrison

Indexer: Marnie Lamb

CPSIA information can be obtained at www.ICGtesting.com
Printed in the USA
LVOW041606110712

289682LV00005B/25/P

9 781609 287078